MEDIEVAL FUTURES

ATTITUDES TO THE FUTURE IN THE MIDDLE AGES

EDITED BY

J. A. BURROW and IAN P. WEI

THE BOYDELL PRESS

First published 2000
The Boydell Press, Woodbridge

ISBN 0 85115 779 3

The Boydell Press is an imprint of Boydell & Brewer Ltd
PO Box 9, Woodbridge, Suffolk IP12 3DF, UK
and of Boydell & Brewer Inc.
PO Box 41026, Rochester, NY 14604–4126, USA
website: http://www.boydell.co.uk

A catalogue record for this title is available
from the British Library

Library of Congress Cataloging-in-Publication Data

Medieval futures : attitudes to the future in the Middle Ages / edited by
J.A. Burrow and Ian P. Wei.
    p.   cm.
    Includes bibliographical references and index.
    ISBN 0–85115–779–3 (hb : alk. paper)
    1. Forecasting – History – To 1500.   2. Future in popular culture –
Europe – History – To 1500.   3. Civilization, Medieval.   I. Burrow,
J. A. (John Anthony)   II. Wei, Ian P.
CB158.M39 2000
303.49 – dc21   00–020945

This publication is printed on acid-free paper

Printed in Great Britain by
St Edmundsbury Press Ltd, Bury St Edmunds, Suffolk

MEDIEVAL FUTURES

ATTITUDES TO THE FUTURE IN THE MIDDLE AGES

Medieval Futures explores the rich variety of ways in which medieval people imagined the future, from the prophetic anticipation of the end of the world to the mundane expectation that the world would continue indefinitely, permitting ordinary human plans and provisions. The articles explore the ways in which the future was represented to serve the present, methods used to predict the future, and strategies adopted to plan and provide for it. Different conceptions of the future are shown to relate to different social groups and the emergence of new mentalities, suggesting that changing conceptions of the future were related to general shifts in medieval culture.

J. A. BURROW is Professor Emeritus, University of Bristol; IAN P. WEI is Senior Lecturer in History, and Director of the Centre for Medieval Studies, University of Bristol.

Contents

Preface

In August 1997, a conference entitled 'Medieval Futures' was held by the Centre for Medieval Studies at the University of Bristol. The present volume contains a selection of the papers delivered on that occasion, together with one new contribution. The conference was organized by Dr Brendan Smith and Professor John Burrow, assisted by Mr George Ferzoco and Dr Rhiannon Purdie. It was most generously funded by the university's Read-Tuckwell Bequest, and we are extremely grateful to the Read-Tuckwell Committee for their support. We are also grateful to the Arts Faculty Research Fund for a grant towards the translation of Professor Schmitt's paper.

Contributors

Professor Piero Boitani
Professor of Comparative Literature, University of Rome 'La Sapienza'

Dr Paul Brand
Senior Research Fellow of All Souls College, Oxford

Professor Elizabeth A. R. Brown
Professor of History *Emerita*, City University of New York

Dr Marcus Bull
Senior Lecturer in History, University of Bristol

Professor John Burrow
Emeritus Professor and Senior Research Fellow, University of Bristol

Dr Rhiannon Purdie
British Academy Research Fellow, University of St Andrews

Professor Phyllis B. Roberts
Professor of History *Emerita*, City University of New York

Professor Jean-Claude Schmitt
Directeur d'Etudes, Ecole des Hautes Etudes en Sciences Sociales, Paris

Mr Ian P. Wei
Senior Lecturer in History, and Director of the Centre for Medieval Studies, University of Bristol

Introduction

Most work on medieval attitudes to the future has concerned the eschatological, the millennial and the prophetic. It has resulted in many excellent studies which examine the lives and writings of people who warned of the coming of Antichrist, heralded the end of the world and the Last Judgement, or believed that they could see the working out of an all-embracing divine plan in human history.[1] It takes but a moment's reflection, however, to realise that this was only part of the way in which medieval people approached the future: in much more mundane ways they tried to predict, plan and provide for their futures. The contributors to this volume therefore share the common aim of bringing to the fore a fuller range of medieval beliefs and attitudes pertaining to the future. In particular, they seek to understand the relationships between these various beliefs and attitudes. This is an especially important task because, outside the work of a few brilliant scholars, prophetic and eschatological beliefs have often been treated as if they were too bizarre to be considered at the same time as other aspects of medieval culture. Thus, to give just one example, despite the universally acknowledged excellence of books about Joachim of Fiore by Marjorie Reeves and Bernard McGinn, books which place Joachim at the heart of intellectual and spiritual development in Western Europe, very few intellectual histories of the period give Joachim and his followers more than a passing mention.

The first section of the book is entitled 'Thinking about the Future', and the papers examine explicit references to and discussions of the future. Jean-

---

1   The bibliography is vast, but notable contributions include: *The Apocalypse in the Middle Ages*, ed. Richard K. Emmerson and Bernard McGinn (Ithaca, NY: Cornell University Press, 1992); Norman Cohn, *The Pursuit of the Millennium*, rev. edn (London: Temple Smith, 1970); Richard Kenneth Emmerson, *Antichrist in the Middle Ages: A Study of Medieval Apocalypticism, Art, and Literature* (Seattle: University of Washington Press, 1981); Richard Landes, *Relics, Apocalypse and the Deceits of History: Ademar of Chabannes, 989–1034* (Cambridge, MA: Harvard University Press, 1995); Robert E. Lerner, *The Powers of Prophecy: The Cedar of Lebanon Vision from the Mongol Onslaught to the Dawn of the Enlightenment* (Berkeley: University of California Press, 1983); Bernard McGinn, *Visions of the End: Apocalyptic Traditions in the Middle Ages* (New York: Columbia University Press, 1979); Bernard McGinn, *The Calabrian Abbot: Joachim of Fiore in the History of Western Thought* (New York: Macmillan, 1985); *Prophecy and Millenarianism: Essays in Honour of Marjorie Reeves*, ed. Ann Williams (Harlow: Longman, 1980); Marjorie Reeves, *The Influence of Prophecy in the Later Middle Ages* (Oxford: Clarendon Press, 1969); Marjorie Reeves, *Joachim of Fiore and the Prophetic Future: A Medieval Study in Historical Thinking*, rev. edn (Stroud: Sutton, 1976); *The Use and Abuse of Eschatology in the Middle Ages*, ed. Werner Verbeke, Daniel Verhelst and Andries Welkenhuysen (Leuven: Leuven University Press, 1988).

Claude Schmitt offers a broad overview of attitudes to the future, highlighting the significance of many issues addressed in subsequent papers. He discusses the way in which different beliefs about the future were reflected in the structure of language and the development of vocabulary, the different senses of the future which were expressed in charters and commercial contracts, and the variety of techniques which were used to foretell and control the future. Some of these techniques were condemned by ecclesiastical authorities, and Schmitt outlines the strategies which churchmen adopted in order to cultivate the eschatological and prophetic aspects of their faith, while rejecting 'false prophets'. Ian Wei focuses on the way in which different notions of the future were theorised by thirteenth-century masters of theology at the University of Paris. He examines their discussions of the means by which material provision could be made for the future, their insistence that certain types of prediction had to be made in order to solve moral problems in the present, their analysis of different types of foreknowledge, and their involvement in handling actual claims to prophecy. John Burrow looks at treatments of the virtue of prudence by Thomas Aquinas and by Middle English writers. He stresses their view that prudence could be exercised in a great range of human activities, and that it held out the double promise of future success in this world and future happiness in the next.

The second section, entitled 'Prophesying Futures', concerns different treatments of prophecy. Piero Boitani explores Dante's fusion of pagan and Christian traditions, and the way in which he linked fame and prophecy to invent a new future for poetry. Phyllis Roberts analyses the use of prophecies relating to Thomas Becket in a series of different political contexts: to boost his cult in the decades after 1170; to bolster royal authority in the fourteenth and fifteenth centuries; and to attack royal power in the sixteenth century.

The third and final section is entitled 'Providing for Futures'. Dealing with a range of social contexts, the papers look at the ways in which medieval people tried to dictate what would happen in the future, and at the problems which they encountered. Elizabeth Brown analyses the attempts made by early fourteenth-century French kings to control what would happen after they died, especially their efforts to ensure the future prosperity of their queens and chief ministers. Knowing that their successors would cite the inalienability of the royal patrimony in order to annul earlier donations, the kings adopted rhetorical and political strategies which were intended to protect these donations, ultimately enhancing the concept of royal authority. Marcus Bull uses primary sources associated with crusading to understand the way in which the aristocracy in eleventh- and twelfth-century France conceived of and prepared for the future. His analysis of imagery relating to family and property reveals the means by which they hoped to secure their future wealth and their spiritual welfare. Paul Brand considers how attempts to control the future were treated in English common law. While grants and judgements purporting to convey rights to a particular individual and his heir 'in perpetuity' often failed, he shows how from 1200 the common law began to give greater weight to future expectations and made it easier for grantors to control the future of entailed property. Finally Rhiannon Purdie looks at the playing of dice-games. She explains the rules which were to be followed by those who surrendered their futures to chance, the methods of cheating adopted by those who preferred illicit control of their futures, and the nature of the criticism which moralists directed at this popular activity.

There are, however, a number of important issues and questions which are addressed by papers in each section of the book. Many of the papers make it clear that medieval people frequently sought to represent the future in ways which would permit them to achieve something in the present. The point is most emphatically made by Phyllis Roberts in her analysis of prophecies associated with Thomas Becket from 1170 to the mid-sixteenth century. She demonstrates that prophetic texts were written and changed, and new prophecies came to the fore, as different groups pursued changing religious and political ends. When sixteenth-century prophecies turned Becket into a symbol of opposition to the crown, the Tudors recognised the political power of prophecy, countering first with their own prophecies, and then by using the law to undermine Becket's status as a saint, and to prevent the laity from dealing in political prophecies. Other papers also bring out the importance of understanding representations of the future in terms of the present needs of the people who produced them. Ian Wei, for example, discusses the theologians' view that certain types of prediction were necessary to solve moral difficulties in the present, and John Burrow points to the widely held perception that the virtue of prudence could usefully inform a multitude of human activities. Explaining the Church's efforts to control prophecy, and linking the development of new conceptions of the future to the emergence of secular political ideologies in the sixteenth century, Jean-Claude Schmitt makes the general point, implicit in most of the papers, that 'the future is a matter of power'.

Power was derived at least partly from the ability to predict the future, and many papers illustrate the numerous methods which were employed to achieve various kinds of foreknowledge. Some methods depended on the observation of phenomena in the present. Thus Jean-Claude Schmitt discusses the use of signs, wonders and dreams, noting that it was the need for interpretation which introduced issues of power and authority. A similar point is made by Ian Wei: Parisian theologians wanted predictions to be made by assessing current psychological condition and character, but the laity were expected to defer to confessors and ecclesiastical courts in making these predictions. Other methods of prediction relied on interpretation of the past. Piero Boitani, for example, demonstrates that Dante's vision of the future was partly shaped by classical traditions, and that his eschatological expectations were based on 'his theological view of history'. As John Burrow points out, Prudence was often represented as a figure with three eyes, and while the third eye looked to the future, the first was turned to the past. That prophecy often depended on the authority and tradition associated with particular texts is also apparent from the random opening of sacred books described by Jean-Claude Schmitt and Rhiannon Purdie, and the use of political prophecies examined by Phyllis Roberts.

Whatever the means by which predictions of the future were made, they were rarely accepted in a passive manner. On the contrary, foreknowledge was valued chiefly because it informed action, very often action intended to shape or alter the future in some way. In this sense prediction was just one of many strategies which medieval people adopted in order to control, plan and prepare for the future. Jean-Claude Schmitt points out that these strategies ranged from moral reform to the use of invocations and ritual gestures. Piero Boitani explains Dante's belief that poetry creates memory in the future. Methods of controlling the future are analysed most thoroughly, however, by the papers in the third section of the book. As Marcus Bull indicates, the aristocracy of eleventh- and twelfth-century France expected future success to result from a range of strategies which reflected their notions of family, property and spiritual welfare. Paul Brand reveals that it was increasingly possible after 1200 to use English common law to control future ownership of certain kinds of property, and to protect certain future rights. As Elizabeth Brown demonstrates, French kings combined political manoeuvres with legal rhetoric in their efforts to secure the future wealth of their queens and ministers. Rhiannon Purdie describes the techniques by which it was possible to cheat in dice-games.

The methods by which people endeavoured to predict and control the future depended largely on their conception of the future. The diversity of these methods can therefore be explained by the rich variety of ways in which medieval people thought about the future. The future was often conceived in prophetic and eschatological terms, with knowledge based on what was believed to be divine revelation, either experienced directly and very personally, or perceived through study of an all-embracing divine plan in human history. The future was also understood in purely human terms which allowed people to make mundane predictions, plans and provisions for their futures on the assumption that time would always be the same and would stretch on indefinitely. Apparently contradictory ways of thinking could co-exist within society, and sometimes within individuals who both believed that the world was going to end, and planned as if it would not. Many of the papers offer an understanding of how these different ways of thinking were combined by medieval people. Sometimes people proceeded without reflection or any great awareness of the complexity of their thought processes. This must have been the case, for example, with the charters discussed by Jean-Claude Schmitt. He demonstrates how several different conceptions of the future could be contained within a single charter granting land: a personal future which ended with the donor's death, an indefinite human future which continued through the generations, a cyclical future in which the same rituals would be enacted every year, and an eschatological future in which the donor hoped to enjoy salvation. Similarly, the French aristocracy of the eleventh and twelfth centuries did not stop to question the way in which they acquired property and pursued the interests of their families within a purely human future, while seeking spiritual happiness within another life altogether. As Marcus Bull explains, these different senses of the future were inextricably linked because piety was expressed in the context of the family and by giving property. Moreover, while the French kings examined by Elizabeth Brown were extremely deliberate in their actions, they probably did not pause to reflect on the way in which their actions related to several different senses of the future: their efforts to protect the interests of their wives and ministers made sense within a human and relatively short-term future; their readiness to annul their predecessors' donations in the interests of 'a crown which never dies' indicated a sense of human time which would never end; and their efforts to secure salvation by making pious donations related to a sense of the eschatological. But if many medieval people were barely conscious of the ways in which they combined different senses of the future, some performed these mental operations very knowingly. As Ian Wei demonstrates, Parisian masters of theology took great care in distinguishing between natural knowledge of a future which could be envisaged stretching on endlessly, and prophetic knowledge which was divinely revealed. They understood the relationship between these very different types of knowledge in terms of hierarchy: natural knowledge of the future could be used to perform many vital tasks in this life, because prophetic knowledge would always take precedence at the appropriate moments. John Burrow shows that Thomas Aquinas and many Middle English writers deemed prudence to look forward both to short- and middle-term futures in this life, and to judgement after death. Dante also conceived of the future in several ways, as Piero Boitani explains: his notion of fame supposed a human future; his expectation that the world would shortly end and his interest in bodily resurrection reflected a Christian eschatology; he also portrayed the blessed sharing God's eternal vision in which all time-bound events were simultaneously apparent. Part of Dante's achievement, however, was to cross the boundaries between these conceptions of the future. The individual's strongest earthly love would be resurrected with the body, thus colouring his or her eternal future. Fame, especially that of the poet, would persist in hell and heaven. Poetry was to contain a spark of eternal glory which would give it the power to create memory in a purely human future. Medieval scholars and writers thus displayed considerable sensitivity to the ways in which different senses of the future were combined by their contemporaries, and fully exploited the creative possibilities which these combinations opened up.

A number of papers in this book also seek to relate different conceptions of the future to different social groups and the emergence of new mentalities.

Attention is repeatedly drawn to the significance of the developing merchant class and the growing money-based economy. As Jean-Claude Schmitt explains, commercial contracts drawn up in towns differed from charters granting land in an agrarian milieu, because merchants and bankers measured and sold the future. Marcus Bull contrasts the values of the merchants with those of the aristocracy in the eleventh and twelfth centuries. According to churchmen, the characteristic vice of lords and knights was pride, which was at least partly a judgement upon their taste for display, consumption and giving in the present. Merchants, however, were criticised for avarice, a vice which they exhibited in saving, planning and speculating for a future with which they were sinfully preoccupied. Ian Wei argues that when thirteenth-century theologians separated natural knowledge of the future and prophetic knowledge, placing them at different levels in a hierarchy of truth, they discovered a legitimate way for churchmen to accept the values to which historians have given the label 'merchant time'. It is clear that conceptions of the future changed in the medieval period, and that these changes must be related to general shifts in medieval culture.

I

THINKING ABOUT THE FUTURE

Appropriating the Future

JEAN-CLAUDE SCHMITT*

HISTORIANS have strange relationships with the future. Sometimes they are tempted to endow their discipline with a prophetic function, as if they have only to project the changes of the past, which they know and understand, into the future in order to predict what will take place and thus steer future actions.[1] But history never repeats itself, and if thinking about the way past societies functioned helps us to understand our own, it does not provide us with certain knowledge of what is to come. Sometimes, on the other hand, historians turn away from the future and even from the present, claiming that the past alone is their area of expertise, as if our interpretation of the past could somehow be separated from all that we are today, from what we know, and also from what we hope for the future. More seriously still, they sometimes forget that we ourselves are the future of the past societies that, as historians, we study. It is usually the *gesta* of these societies that we study, that is to say the deeds they have done in what was their present. For some time now we have also been giving close consideration to their *memoria* – the way these societies reconstructed their own past and the 'sites of remembrance' (*lieux de mémoire*) that they chose as catalysts to the memory of that past. But we should also give some thought to their *futura* – the way these past societies projected themselves into their future, the future that we, at least in part, constitute. Our view of the past must take into account the idea that we are 'the future of the past' – 'die vergangene Zukunft', to use Reinhard Koselleck's phrase – the future of ancient societies, bearing in mind all the while that the future of which our present represents the partial realisation is only one of the futures that were then possible:[2] history is not a forward march along a

---

* Translated from the French by Peregrine Rand.
[1]   See in this connection Marc Bloch's well-known critique of the notion that history provides the means to guide actions, *Apologie pour l'histoire ou métier d'historien*, 5th edn (Paris: Armand Colin, 1964).
[2]   Reinhard Koselleck, *Vergangene Zukunft: zur Semantik geschichtlicher Zeiten* (Frankfurt a.M.: Suhrkamp, 1979), English translation *Futures Past: on the Semantics of Historical Time*, trans. Keith Tribe (Cambridge, MA: MIT Press, 1985). The idea is also mentioned by Marc

single, straight track, a continuous and necessary thread that we have simply to unwind from the past to our present and then into a future that is certain and knowable. On the contrary, it is a succession of possible choices, of futures that are all available at any given moment, of which only a few are realised and which we cannot know in advance.

Whether it is past societies' *memoria* or, on the other hand, their represen-tations of the future, their *futura*, that we study, it is always their present that we are examining as historians. It is to enable themselves to function in the present, and to resolve present conflicts, that societies exercise their memory and reconstruct their past. Similarly, when they project themselves into imagined futures – in the words of their prophets, utopian thinkers, or science-fiction writers – they are in fact speaking of themselves in their present, of their aspirations, hopes, fears, and present contradictions. St Augustine himself astutely noted this fact: there seem to be three time periods, the past (*praeteritum*), which depends on memory (*memoria*), the present (*praesens*), which may be observed (*contuitus*), and the future (*futurum*), which is the object of our expectations (*expectatio*). In reality there is only the present, because the past no longer exists and the future does not exist yet. Of the past and the future only the *images* exist, and these only in the present, in our minds. The future, like the past, is but an 'extension' of our minds.[3]

Augustine's remarks on the individual consciousness are equally true of the societies studied by the historian: societies' imagined futures, like their collective memories, raise the question of how those societies functioned in their present. This question must therefore be understood in a general sense, in all its breadth: the conception a society has of the future is not to be dis-cerned only in the grand prophetic, eschatological or utopian systems it has constructed. We ourselves, in the twentieth century, have had, or still have, many ways of appropriating the future other than the grand ideologies of modernity (which are, moreover, now obsolete).[4] Expectation, hope, plan-ning, speculation, competition, lotteries, credit, life expectancy – all these

Bloch: see Ulrich Rauff, *Ein Historiker im 20. Jahrhundert: Marc Bloch* (Frankfurt a.M.: Fischer, 1995), p. 92.

[3] Augustine, *Confessions*, ed. Lucas Verheijen, Corpus Christianorum, Series Latina, 27 (Turnhout: Brepols, 1981), book XI, XVIII, 24, p. 206: 'Futura ergo nondum sunt, et si nondum sunt, non sunt, et si non sunt, uideri omnino non possunt; sed praedici possunt ex praesentibus, quae iam sunt et uidentur.' Ibid., book XI, XX, 26, pp. 206–7: 'Quod autem nunc liquet et claret, nec futura sunt nec praeterita, nec proprie dicitur: tempora sunt tria, praeteritum, praesens et futurum, sed fortasse proprie diceretur: tempora sunt tria, praesens de praeteritis, praesens de praesentibus, praesens de futuris. Sunt enim haec in anima tria quaedam et alibi ea non uideo, praesens de praeteritis memoria, praesens de praesentibus contuitus, praesens de futuris expectatio.'

[4] For a radically different view, see the recent essay by Georges Minois, *Histoire de l'avenir: des prophéties à la prospective* (Paris: Fayard, 1996).

things concern the future on a more modest scale, on the individual level as well as on that of the group. The question of the future is raised, without our even noticing, whenever, in the course of our most ordinary sentences, we use the future tense.

1. Speaking in the Future

Our most common experience of the future is surely that of language. But even this is a complex matter, because there is not just one future tense, but several, or, rather, several grammatical *modalities* that express the future. And I believe this to be true of at least all the Indo-European languages, ancient and modern, we speak as well as of medieval Latin. But having said this, the way in which these modes of expression were used in different historical periods and in different languages, both scholarly and vernacular, must still be examined. There is the *future tense*, which clearly designates an action to come. There is also the *future perfect*, which delimits a past within the future, designating an action that is future in relation to us, but past in relation to a more distant future ('quand j'aurai labouré, je sèmerai'). Other verbal forms, while not strictly speaking future tenses, have a dimension of futurity: the *present participle* designates an action that is taking place, whose completion can only be foreseen; in Latin, the *gerundive* indicates the necessity of an action that must be accomplished but that is not yet realized; the *conditional* designates the possibility of what may happen in the future if a certain condition is fulfilled. The foregoing simple remarks are enough to show how language, even before any actual representation of the past, present or future, is a fundamental means of approaching the social usages of time, in their most spontaneous and largely unconscious expression: I can say what I am going to do tomorrow or in a week without constructing a theory of the future, of probability, of risk, or of providence.

Not only do we speak *in* the future, we also speak *of* the future; we name it. As I have already said, Augustine distinguished three time periods (reducible in fact to just the present) that are related to three modes of apprehension: the *praeteritum*, which is accessible to the *memoria*; the *praesens*, which depends on the *contuitus* (the scrutiny of present things); and the *futurum*, which is anticipated by the *expectatio*, expectation. In medieval Latin, 'future' is usually a plural noun: *futura*. Perhaps we should see in this plural a recognition of the future's complexity: thanks to religious belief the eschatological frame may be known, but the precise times at which things will happen – we know neither when we are going to die nor when the world is going to end – and the form they will take remain mysterious. Equally noteworthy is the noun, also in the plural, that designates the end of time: *novissima*. The 'newest' things are also the most distant in time. This probably relates to the idea that the end of history has always been written in the divine plan, that there will be nothing 'new' at the end of time under the gaze of God. In this sense, *novissima* expresses very well the duality of the Christian representation of historical time, which is both linear (from the Creation to the end of the world) and cyclical, since it is profoundly religious and connected to myth, insofar as it is created and regulated by the transcendent will of God.[5]

The romance languages follow Latin usage. The *Roman de la Rose* uses the noun *futur* several times, while Brunetto Latini lists 'cil trois tens, ce est li presens, li preterites et cil qui est a venir'.[6] The periphrasis 'cil qui est a venir' is interesting, as it shows no knowledge of the noun *avenir*, which would seem to be more recent. We might thus venture so far as to posit two historically opposed concepts of the future. The older of the two is represented by the word *futur*: the future, the *futura*, cannot be fully known, but it is located within a framework of understanding, foresight and action that is fixed, above all in the case of the eschatological time of religion or the cyclical time of ritual and the liturgy.[7] To this we might oppose the modern notion of 'time-to-come' (*avenir*), which designates a future that is open, completely unforeseeable, and irreversible, a time without God, the product of the 'disenchantment of the world'. It is in this division between the *futura* and the *avenir* that the transition from the Middle Ages to the Renaissance, from religious thought to modern rationality, is played out.

2. The Uses of the Future

We must first of all consider how the most ordinary, concrete actions are pregnant with futurity, and in which mental schemes – which conceptions of time, which expectations, which ideas of what is possible – the actions and decisions of men in the Middle Ages are, consciously or otherwise, rooted.

A first vantage point is provided by the formulae used in charters, even if these do shed light primarily on the modes of thought of clerics, of the literate people who composed them: charters of donations – for instance the dona-

---

[5]   On the cyclical conception of time in religious thought, such as in the liturgy, see the classic study by Henri Hubert, 'Etude sommaire de la représentation du temps dans la religion et la magie', in Henri Hubert and Marcel Mauss, *Mélanges d'histoire des religions* (Paris: Alcan, 1909), pp. 189–229. On the competing conceptions of time in the Middle Ages, see A. J. Gourevitch, *Les Catégories de la culture médiévale* (Paris: Gallimard, 1983), English translation A. J. Gurevich, *Categories of Medieval Culture*, trans. G. L. Campbell (London: Routledge, 1985).

[6]   Cf. Tobler-Lommatsch, *Altfranzösisches Wörterbuch*, s.v. *futur*.

[7]   For an example of ritual, cyclical time that guarantees the circulation of brides and dowries in a way that can be foreseen within a traditional rural community over the course of a limited number of generations, see Pierre Lamaison, 'Les stratégies matrimoniales dans un système complexe de parenté: Ribennes en Gévaudan (1650–1830)', *Annales E.S.C.*, 4 (1979), 721–43 (p. 728).

tion of land to a monastic community – were usually composed by the recipient, often a monastic community, and not by the donor, the lay *illiteratus* who, in return for his pious acts of generosity, would ask for prayers to be said for the salvation of his soul. But the fact that these formulae are so repetitive, and found in such numbers, would certainly suggest that they bear witness to concepts that were widely held.[8] The introductory formula, which scarcely changes from one document to another, is eloquent: 'Let it be known by all men, present and future'; 'Ego Johannes, tam presentibus quam futuris, in perpetuum dedi et concessi'; 'tam futuris quam presentibus in Christo fidelibus'; 'omnibus hanc paginam inspecturis'; 'omnibus ad quos iste littere pervenerint', and so on. The donor can also undertake in precise clauses to maintain the land he is giving until his death, 'quod ut ratum et firmum permaneat, presentem paginam sigilli mei munimine roboravi'. In all these formulae, it is human time and the time of history that is being referred to: a time that is limited by the length of a single life or, beyond, by the future generations of descendants, but within a framework of perpetual succession. At the same time, however, another future is brought into view when the donor invokes divine mercy and hopes for forgiveness for his sins: 'pro remedio anime mee et uxoris mee et pro animabus fratrum et sororum et omnium antecessorum quam successorum meorum'. Here it is no longer a question of the succession of generations in historical time, but of the eschatological future of salvation for the donor and his family.

The particular concept of the future that is given prominence depends on the type of deed: the granting of a piece of land to a family stipulates that it will be held 'from one generation to the next', but only on the condition that a certain number of obligations be fulfilled – that every year at the stipulated time a rent (*cens*) be paid that recognises the *seigneur*'s ultimate proprietorship, that the *censive* be neither sold nor partially ceded, and that the *seigneur*'s juridical rights be respected. In this case, the annual payment of a rent introduces another form of projection into the future: a cyclical, ritualised future, punctuated at regular intervals by the return of the same. This is especially true for one peasant, who is obliged to pay a given sum every year on seven different occasions: Easter, haymaking, harvest time, grape harvest time, Christmas, Shrovetide, and Mid-Lent!

Several different conceptions of the future are thus linked in these types of

---

8 For the sake of convenience, reference will be made to the acts reproduced and commented on in Georges Duby, *L'Economie rurale et la vie des campagnes dans l'Occident médiéval*, 2 vols (Paris: Aubier, 1962), II, 79 ff, esp. no. 79 (from the *Recueil des chartes de Cluny*, IV, 3302, dated 1049–1109), no. 82 (act of the abbey of Chaalis, in 1172), no. 84 (*Cartulaire de Saint-Vincent de Mâcon*), and no. 86 (*Recueil des pancartes de l'abbaye de la Ferté-sur-Grosne, c. 1160*). Other examples are from B. Pipon, *Le Chartrier de l'Abbaye aux Bois (1202–1341)*, Mémoires et Documents de l'Ecole des Chartes, 46 (Paris: Ecole des Chartes, 1996), and J. Cosse-Durlin, *Cartulaire de Saint-Nicaise de Reims* (Paris: Editions du CNRS, 1991), p. 27. There are many other examples.

documents concerning land-tenure from the central Middle Ages: the personal future of the donor, foreseeable only for the length of his life and limited by his death; sometimes, in the same frame, a future conceived of in terms of the recurrent cycle of the years, of ritual dates, of permanent dues; then the future of a longer history that will supposedly unfold 'in perpetuity', marked by the different generations of the donor's descendants; and, finally, the eschatological future that tips the time of men over into the eternity of God: beyond the time of bodies opens out the future of souls.

At least some of these conceptions of the future are characteristic only of the agrarian milieu dealt with in these deeds and of the particular type of action represented by these donations of land. For from this period onwards, in urban environments, commercial and financial activity introduces different concepts and uses of the future, as is testified by a Genoese contract of exchange stipulating that a non-specified sum in Genoese *sous* will be repaid twelve days later in Bruges at the rate of 30 *sous* for one florin.[9] The contract records a promise, that is to say an engagement concerning future time. The time is carefully measured – twelve days – and this near future is used to serve a disguised interest, a *usura*. In fact the normal rate of repayment at the time was 25 *sous* for a florin: so the twelve-day loan costs 5 *sous*. From this moment, then, the future also has a price.

3. Knowing and Influencing the Future

The desire to know the future in advance is undoubtedly common to all human societies. Being concerned about tomorrow, wishing to know whether it is a good moment to undertake an action, worrying about the time of one's death – these are found at all times and in all places.[10] But the means used to satisfy this desire vary from culture to culture, according to the belief systems and the forms of rationality that characterise them. For example, divination by the book can be seen to have an important role in societies in which the written word has widespread uses and enjoys a privileged ideological status.[11] Similarly, the objects that provide a focal point for a culture's preoccupation with the future can change, sometimes within that same culture's own history: in the course of the central Middle Ages, for instance, fear of one's own death was accompanied by a concern to know in advance the fate of one's soul at the individual judgement that would immediately follow death. Whence the new questions asked of the future. How long will the soul's suffering in Purgatory last? How can one shorten this post-death future that men

---

9 *Sources d'histoire médiévale (IXe–milieu du XIVe siècle)*, ed. G. Brunel and E. Lalou (Paris: Larousse, 1992), p. 471.
10 See for example Cicero, *De Divinatione*.
11 Jean-Pierre Vernant and others, *Divination et rationalité* (Paris: Seuil, 1974).

try to limit so as to hasten the soul's access to eternal bliss? The belief in Purgatory undeniably effected a profound change in the medieval West's representations of the future.[12]

In the culture of the Middle Ages the observation of signs, marvels, and *mirabilia* was also used to predict the future. For example, in the *Vita Maioli Abbatis* by Odilo of Cluny, the sudden appearance of a wolf that a knight manages to kill is interpreted as a sign of an imminent Saracen incursion.[13] It was also a wolf, according to Raoul Glaber, that one day entered the church in Orleans and, seizing the bell-rope, rang the bell. The inhabitants were terrified by the incident, and rightly so: the next year the town was ravaged by fire. 'Nobody was in any doubt', comments the chronicler, 'that the event had been preceded by a presage (*portentum*).'[14] It is a sudden disturbance in the ordinary train of events – the appearance of a comet, a solar eclipse, the birth of a monstrous calf, the unexpected collapse of a bridge, a vision of a crucifix that bleeds, weeps, or turns its face away, or the fact of dropping the Eucharistic species during the celebration of Mass (an event witnessed by John of Salisbury[15]) – that functions as a sign of future occurrences. It is usually interpreted unfavourably, as an ill omen announcing a catastrophe, an invasion, or the death of the sovereign. According to the Chronicle of Waltham (end of the twelfth century), the miraculous crucifix kept in the abbey bowed its head sadly when King Harold, the evening before his defeat at Hastings at the hands of William the Conqueror, came to prostrate himself before it: this was interpreted as a 'presage of future things' and as a 'bad omen'.[16]

The interpretation of dreams was another privileged area for the prediction of the future. The relinquishing of all conscious will during sleep, the flow of dream images that break the laws of ordinary perception, and the

---

12 In addition to the classic study by Jacques Le Goff, *La Naissance du purgatoire* (Paris: Gallimard, 1981), see the same author's article 'Les limbes', *Nouvelle revue de psychanalyse*, 34 (1986), 151–73.

13 Odilo of Cluny, *De Vita Beati Maioli Abbatis*, *Patrologia Latina*, 142, cols 943–62 (cols 959–62).

14 Rodulfus Glaber, *The Five Books of the Histories*, ed. and trans. John France, Oxford Medieval Texts (Oxford: Clarendon Press, 1989), book 2, V, 8, pp. 66–7.

15 John of Salisbury, *Memoirs of the Papal Court*, ed. and trans. Marjorie Chibnall (London: Nelson, 1956), p. 11: during a papal Mass, the blood fell on the carpet. The piece of carpet was carefully cut out and kept as a relic. It was immediately believed that the incident presaged a 'great danger', a belief that was not unjustified ('certe non fefellit opinio'), since that same year (1147–48) the crusade undertaken by Conrad, King of the Romans, and King Louis VII of France was defeated by the Saracens.

16 *The Waltham Chronicle: An Account of the Discovery of Our Holy Cross at Montacute and its Conveyance to Waltham*, ed. and trans. L. Watkiss and M. Chibnall (Oxford: Clarendon Press, 1994), pp. 46–7: 'Contigit autem interea miserabile dictu et a seculis incredibile. Nam imago crucifixi que prius erecta ad superiora respeciebat, cum se rex humiliaret in terram, demisit vultum, quasi tristis. *Signum quidem prescium futurorum!* [. . .] Visio autem *hoc infausto auspicio*, multo dolore correpti' (my italics).

apparent temporary dissociation of the sleeping body and the wakeful soul all support the idea that dreams provide direct and privileged access to knowledge of the future. But even here the dream-narrative slips into conventional narrative forms, as for example in the well-known hagiographic model of the pregnant mother's dream that is interpreted *a posteriori* as the prophetic announcement of the birth of the saint (the examples of Saint Bernard and Saint Dominic are well known). This narrative model can already be found at the end of the eleventh century, in the *Vita* of Saint Thierry: while his mother was pregnant with him, she one night saw herself in a dream wearing priest's clothes and celebrating Mass. Aware of the transgression that this represented for a woman and afraid of having had an 'empty' dream, inspired by the Devil, she turned to an old holy woman, who reassured her by revealing that the vision was 'true', that is to say of divine origin, and that it would be 'realized' by the birth of a son who would become a priest and would achieve sainthood.[17]

These few examples, chosen from the many that are available, show the extent of the gap that exists between the presage and the future event. The first announces the second, but only to those who can decipher the signs, for the presage does not depict the event to come in a clear, unequivocal way. Between them opens up a space for the interpretation of the 'signs', which is a matter of power and authority: in a context other than hagiography, it is easy to imagine that the dream of a woman dressed as a priest would have seemed to be of diabolical origin and that the woman would have been suspected of heresy.

The Church and the clergy have always been suspicious of soothsayers and especially of the *vetulae*, who claimed to be able to tell fortunes and interpret dreams. The list of illicit forms of divination, compiled by Saint Augustine (*De doctrina christiana*), taken up again by Isidore of Seville and Hincmar of Reims, and transmitted in the *Decretum* of Gratian and the *Policraticus* of John of Salisbury, was a key component of the catalogue of 'superstitions' condemned by the Church.[18] When we are dealing with these categories and their names, we should take into account the fact that the learned terminology that had been inherited from antiquity did not have much connection with reality: who were the medieval equivalents of, for instance, the *magi*, the *nigromantici*, the *hydromantii*, the *incantatores*, the *haruspices*, the *genethliaci* or the *mathematici*? The numerous miniatures illustrating Causa XXVI of the

---

17 M. Lauwers, 'L'institution et le genre: à propos de l'accès des femmes au sacré dans l'Occident médiéval', *Clio: Histoire, Femmes et Sociétés*, 2 (1995), 279–317 (p. 281).

18 John of Salisbury, *Policraticus*, ed. K. S. B. Keats-Rohan, Corpus Christianorum, Continuatio Mediaevalis, 118 (Turnhout: Brepols, 1993), book I, chapter 12. In book II, chapter 28, he recounts how, having been sent to receive instruction from a priest, he discovered that the priest in question practised magic and persuaded his pupils to look into a crystal ball with him.

second part of the *Decretum* of Gratian, 'Quidam sacerdos sortilegus esse et divinus convincitur apud episcopum', depict a whole range of divination techniques – divination by cards, by observing the flight and song of birds, by lines on the hand, by the stars, and so on.[19] This torrent of terms, as well as the variety of images, represented first and foremost the clergy's attempt to circumscribe the many forms taken by divination, since they could not control it, and to suppress the sacrilegious desire to examine the *occulta Dei* when ecclesiastical authority would have itself be the only legitimate interpreter.[20]

The same tension can be seen in the use of the 'Apostles' lots' or the 'Saints' lots' for divination. Since the high Middle Ages the clergy had railed continuously against 'superstitious' uses of the Psalter, the Gospels, or the Acts of the Apostles: these would be opened at random and the first verse that the eye lighted upon would be interpreted as an expression of divine approval of a choice, or a favourable presage for an action about to be undertaken. In about 1200 Alan of Lille can still write as follows:

> One must not dip randomly into tables or manuscripts in order to find out about the future; let no man be so audacious as to dip randomly into the Gospels or the Psalter or into anything else, or attempt any kind of divination in any matter whatsoever. If he does this, he must undergo penance at the discretion of the priest.[21]

In fact, the principal users of the 'Apostles' lots' were the priests themselves. The choice of many of the bishops of the high Middle Ages was supposedly confirmed, if not actually decided, by this method. Such was the case of, among others, Saint Martin of Tours, according to the narration of his election provided by Sulpicius Severus. In the case of this legitimate use of divination, the result of the 'Apostles' lots' was not supposed to be due to chance but was thought to be the manifestation of divine will: men could then act in the certain knowledge that they were in the right.

They were in fact attempting to know the future so as to be able to adapt their actions to it or even to act on it, to transform it. Providence had not fixed the course of things once and for all: man was still free to better himself, to do penance, to convert so as to change the miserable future that was promised him and prepare a better future for himself, both in this world and, above all, in the next. In Christian thought, man does not blindly submit to fate, *fatum*, as he does in Greek tragedy. He has the capacity to act on his destiny

---

[19] Anthony Melnikas, *The Corpus of the Miniatures in the Manuscripts of Decretum Gratiani*, 3 vols, Studia Gratiana, 16–18 (Rome: Studia Gratiana, 1975), II, causa XXVI, pp. 833–62.

[20] Jean-Claude Schmitt, 'Les «superstitions»', in *Histoire de la France religieuse*, ed. Jacques Le Goff and René Rémond, 4 vols (Paris: Seuil, 1988–92), I (1988), 419–551 (pp. 482–95).

[21] Ibid., p. 486.

and to transform his future, without this detracting in any way from the omnipotence and omniscience of God. The usefulness of dreams, visions, and prophecies is precisely to make him aware of what awaits him if he does not take a hand in his own fate: he must remember that it is never too late to do good. An example of a prophecy rendered obsolete by the action of men that attracted a great deal of commentary in the Middle Ages is provided by the Book of Jonah. The prophet Jonah receives Yahweh's orders to announce to the Ninevites that their city will be destroyed if they do not convert. As they do in fact convert, they have a very narrow escape, much to the irritation of the prophet, who, after leaving Nineveh, takes shelter in the shade of a gourd 'till he might see what would become of the city'. A miniature in an English Psalter dating from the beginning of the thirteenth century depicts Jonah's surprise as he discovers that his prophecy is not coming true.[22] But since Augustine (*City of God*, XXI, 24), exegetical commentaries on the Book of Jonah have insisted on the realisation of God's will, in spite of appearances: the 'wicked Nineveh' that was contained in the hardened hearts of the Ninevites was indeed destroyed as had been predicted, since the inhabitants had converted. Jonah was wrong only to expect Nineveh's material destruction. It is a deft solution, maintaining as it does both the omnipotence of God and man's free will.

There were yet more ways of influencing the future: all religious, liturgical and magical practices use symbolic means – invocations, ritual gestures, handling of objects – to affect the course of coming events, to act upon the future in one way or another. Either benevolently, as in the case of litanies calling upon saints to produce rain and bring good harvests, for example; or malevolently, as in the case of the curses that, at the end of charters, promise those who fail to act in accordance with their measures the unenviable fate of 'Dathan and Abiram'.[23]

Finally, there were also methods of acting on the future that purported to be scientific in the Middle Ages. Fourteenth-century popes surrounded themselves with doctors, such as Arnold of Villanova, whose task was to discover the elixir that would, by restoring the equilibrium of the humours of a body

---

[22] Munich, Bayerische Staatsbibliothek, CLM 835, fol. 111v. The full-page illustration is divided into six scenes. The two of the upper register depict the adventure of the whale, while the four others show the prophecy at Nineveh and its consequences: in the centre on the left, Jonah waits, asleep beneath the gourd; on the right, he prophesies the city's ruin ('Jonas hominibus Ninive subversionem civitatis predixit'). Below, the inhabitants of Nineveh, dressed in sackcloth and fasting, beg for divine mercy. On the right they give thanks to God against the background of an ideal, redeemed city that evokes the Heavenly Jerusalem.

[23] Lester K. Little, *Benedictine Maledictions: Liturgical Cursing in Romanesque France* (Ithaca: Cornell University Press, 1993).

that was weakened by age, guarantee them a 'prolonged life'.[24] The desire for eternal life is another aspect of the future.

4. The Prophet and the Priest

The future is a matter of power: the oracle who is capable of predicting the future by correctly interpreting signs, by holding the key to dreams, by confirming his gift of prophecy can gain access to royal courts, has the ear of the pope, and puts men on their guard against the dangers that threaten them. This power is, by its very nature, supernatural, since the future, as Saint Augustine points out, is not yet here. Knowing what does not yet exist partakes of the miraculous, it comes down to encroaching on God's territory. It is not at all surprising, therefore, that the Church, constantly repeating that time belongs to God alone, has always fought those 'superstitious' people who claimed to be able to predict the future.

This tension was particularly acute as an eschatological and prophetic dimension is essential to Christianity: John the Baptist, the Precursor, announces the coming of the Messiah, affirming the imminent realisation of the Old Testament prophecies. For his disciples, Jesus realizes the prophecy of Isaiah 62. 11: 'Tell ye the daughter of Sion, Behold, thy King cometh unto thee, meek, and sitting upon an ass, and a colt the foal of an ass' (Matthew 21. 5). They bring him a she-ass and an ass as he has ordered so that he might make his entry into Jerusalem in the way expected of the Messiah. In his very words, Jesus prophesies, though he unveils only a part of the mystery as he does so: 'Verily I say unto you, that this generation shall not pass, till all these things be done. Heaven and earth shall pass away: but my words shall not pass away. But of that day and that hour knoweth no man, no, not the angels which are in heaven, neither the Son, but the Father' (Mark 13. 30–32). From the very outset the essential question of the absolute future is raised, the question of the *futura*, of the Last Judgement, whose exact time even the Son and, after him, the Church do not know. They are thus placed in stark contrast to those who claim to predict it. The preacher Etienne de Bourbon attacks soothsayers as follows: 'seducunt homines . . . isti qui *divinos* se dicunt, cum *nil sciant de futuris*'.[25]

The peculiarity of the future conceived by Christianity and the Church is that its form is already known, while the precise time at which things will happen is not. The Apocalypse of St John, its countless commentaries, and

---

24 Agostino Paravicini Baglani, *Il corpo del papa*, Biblioteca di cultura storica, 204 (Turin: Einaudi, 1994).

25 Etienne de Bourbon, *Anecdotes historiques, légendes et apologues, tirés du recueil inédit d'Etienne de Bourbon, dominican du XIIIe siècle*, ed. A. Lecoy de la Marche (Paris: Renouard, 1877), p. 315, no. 357.

the iconography of tympana and manuscripts (commentaries on the Apocalypse by Beatus of Liébana, the apocalyptic visions in the *Scivias* of Hildegard of Bingen) have ensured that a precise knowledge of everything that will happen at the end of time is widespread; only the time at which things will happen is unknown. Confronted by this situation, the strategy adopted by the Church seems to have been threefold:

1. Firstly, it consisted in enclosing, as far as possible, prophetic charisma within strict limits by taking upon itself the task, not of prophesying, but of *teaching* the *futura* through preaching and through images: in its teachings concerning the future it had to stress the inexorable ageing of the world and hence the urgency, for everyone, of preparing oneself for the Day of Judgement.

2. Secondly, it consisted in reserving for its saints a well-defined and controlled sphere of limited prophetic ability that referred only to a near future and not to the end of time: the saint can predict the hour of his or her own death, like Christina of Markyate, who, when still a little girl, sees herself lying on her death bed, 'as if the future were already present' (*Denique prescripsit secum in animo, quasi jam fuisset quod futuram erat, se mortuam exponi*); but she takes care to say that no-one knows where their soul will go once it has been freed from the lifeless body (*exanimi cadavere, locum exalati spiritus non licere prenosci*).[26]

The saints' gift of prophecy has only a limited sphere of application: writing of Saint Cuthbert, Bede, his hagiographer, says that he '*in spiritu prophetaverit*', but that consisted only of predicting the death of Boisil and the end of a storm, of announcing that an eagle would feed him on his travels or that the devil was going to unleash a 'fantastic fire'.[27]

To this pole of legitimate but limited prophecy located at the heart of the ecclesiastical institution and represented by sainthood, the Church opposes those whom it names the 'false prophets'. They abound, for example, in the *Historia Francorum* of Gregory of Tours, which relates how a certain man from the Berry region, who had been driven mad by a swarm of flies, had been prophesying for two years in Arles, accompanied by a woman who called herself Marie. He attacked the bishop of Le Puy, who had him put to death. The bishop of Tours goes on to comment on the event: 'And so fell and died the Christ which should be called Anti-Christ.'[28] The sin of the 'false prophets' is twofold: on the one hand their prophetic ambition is greater than that of the saints themselves, for they have no hesitation in announcing the end of the world; on the other hand, and above all, they are prophesying on the

---

[26] C. H. Talbot, *The Life of Christina of Markyate: A Twelfth-Century Recluse*, 2nd edn (Oxford: Clarendon Press, 1987), pp. 38–9.

[27] Bede, *Vita sancti Cuthberti*, *Patrologia Latina*, 94, cols 735–90 (chaps VIII, XI, XII, XIII).

[28] *Historia Francorum*, *Patrologia Latina*, 71, cols 159–572 (book X, chap. XXV).

edge of the ecclesiastical system and even against the authority and institution of the Church.

But it is important to note that many prophetic figures, particularly female ones, which, while they were not rejected by ecclesiastical authority, were ambivalent in its eyes, slip in between these 'false prophets' and the saints. The best known of these is Hildegard of Bingen, whose moral authority, even in her own lifetime, was great: her visionary and theological commentaries, which stemmed from the Apocalypse, had the ear of both Saint Bernard and the pope. It must, however, be said that it was a long time before she was beatified.

3. Finally, the Church has always striven to restrain any literal millenarianism that, deriving its authority from Old Testament prophecies and especially from the Apocalypse, threatens to call for the immediate subversion of the social order, as if it were up to men to hasten the course of history. The interpretation proposed in Augustine's *City of God*, highly influential throughout the entire Middle Ages, was more nuanced: the ancient prophecies, articulated as the *shadows* of realities to come, are true because they have been verified by the coming of the Messiah and because they continue to be verified by the development of the Church.[29] They therefore guarantee that the *futura* truly will be brought about, but without allowing us to predict the exact moment and without giving credence to the calculations of those who work out the time elapsed between the Ascension and the Second Coming of Christ to be 400, 500, or 1000 years.[30] And, most importantly, without obliging us to interpret ancient prophecies either literally, at face value – for example the figure of a thousand years at the end of which the Beast is to be released is a perfect number, not a precise measure – or, on the other hand, in an exclusively spiritual way. The truth of the prophecies thus represents a happy medium, so to speak, and derives from allegorical and moral readings.[31] This standpoint was also adopted by iconography related to traditional biblical exegesis: the Munich *Codex aureus*, for example, which dates from the second half of the ninth century, depicts Christ in majesty with a cruciform halo, seated in a mandorla – which indicates that this is Christ the Judge of the Second Coming – framed by a lozenge whose four corners are in the form of circles occupied by four Old Testament prophets.[32] These four figures alternate, on the edge of the page, with the four Evangelists, who occupy its corners. The continuity of the Old Testament prophecies and the Gospels in

---

[29] Augustine, *City of God*, book XVIII, and the short treatise *De fide rerum quae non videntur*, chaps 8, 11. For the successors to Augustine, see especially Julian of Toledo, *Prognosticon Futuri Saeculi*, *Patrologia Latina*, 96, cols 453–524.

[30] Augustine, *City of God*, book XVIII, chap. LIII and book XX, chap. VII.

[31] Ibid., book XVIII, chap. III.

[32] Munich, Bayerische Staatsbibliothek, CLM 14000, fol. 6v (ninth century). The gold lettering at the top of the picture reads 'Ordine quadrato variis depicta figuris / agmine sanctorum gaudia magna vident'.

the eschatological prediction of Christ's return at the end of time is thus strikingly staged by the page layout. At the beginning of the thirteenth century, the *Bibles moralisées* take up the same fundamentally Augustinian conception of a New Testament reprise of the Old Testament prophecies that predicted not only the coming of the Messiah but also the present glory of the Church, all from the viewpoint of an eschatological future: for example, the young David appeasing King Saul 'signifies' Christ's redemption of man on the cross and his preparation of their final salvation.[33]

It is certain, however, that Augustinian prudence has not always been heeded. Recently Richard Landes has spoken of an explosion of millenarian speculation around the year 1000: this is to be seen in the work of Ademar of Chabannes, from Aquitaine, as well as in that of Raoul Glaber, from Burgundy, and many others.[34] None of these authors was a heretic. Nor was Joachim of Fiore, who later gave the precise date (1260) of the fall of the New Babylon and the coming of the realm of the Spirit. But the spiritualisation of the future could always be resorted to by the Church hierarchy and the magisterium, whenever millenarianism took the intolerable form of a movement capable of subverting the ecclesiastical order: such was the case when the Spirituals, with Gerardo di Borgo San Donnino, Gerardo Segarelli and then Fra Dolcino, taking their inspiration from Joachimist thought, launched a direct attack on the papacy.[35]

The Christian framework of conceptions of the future explains why, throughout the Middle Ages, the end of time appears to be an ultimate projection of its origin. Christian time does of course take place within history, but a holy history, which, like myth, finally has to fold back on itself and disappear in the eternity of God from which it came. But if this religious conception of the future long pervaded Western culture, we can also see what kind of break occurred in the modern era. The new form of the future in the sixteenth century is the utopia, in the sense defined and first named by Thomas More. It breaks with eschatology, with millenarianism and even with the myths of the inversion of the socio-religious order of the Middle Ages, such as that of the land of Cockaigne.[36] In fact it partakes of a conception of time whose

---

33 Vienna, Österreichschische Nationalbibliothek, MS 2554, fol. 38 (French *Bible moralisée*, beginning of thirteenth century).

34 Richard Landes, *Relics, Apocalypse and the Deceits of History: Ademar of Chabannes, 989–1034* (Cambridge, MA: Harvard University Press, 1995).

35 *La Fin des temps: terreurs et prophéties au moyen âge*, ed. and trans. Claude Carozzi and Huguette Taviani-Carozzi (Paris: Stock, 1982). Also Norman Cohn, *The Pursuit of the Millennium*, rev. edn (London, Temple Smith, 1970).

36 Arturo Graf, *Miti, Leggende et Superstizioni del Medio Evo*, 2 vols (Turin: Loescher, 1892–93), 229–38: 'Il paese di Cuccagna e paradisi artificiali'. See also Frantisek Graus, 'Social Utopias in the Middle Ages', *Past and Present*, 38 (1967), 3–19, which distinguishes the land of Cockaigne from concepts based on the classical notion of the Golden Age.

every feature is changing at about the same period, as Krystof Pomian has shown: a time that is henceforth considered absolutely irreversible; a time that, if not demythified, has at least been dehumanised in both its origins (with the Big Bang) and its possible end; an everyday time that is measured exactly by the clock and by the individual's watch; a time of which lived experience lengthens as life-expectancy increases; a conception of time that no longer privileges either the origin (Genesis) or the *futura* that correspond to it, but instead the time-to-come (*avenir*): a time-to-come whose end is defined only by human progress, by the desire for profit, the search for productive investments, for credit – in a word by Max Weber's Protestant Ethic[37] – and by secular political ideologies whose power can no longer be justified by either the past or the eschatological future.[38]

[37] See also Marc Bloch's judicious comments in *Histoire et Historiens*, ed. Etienne Bloch (Paris: Armand Colin, 1995), pp. 36–7: 'Our "capitalist" economy works in a constant state of precariousness; it is living on expectation. This is what we mean when we say that it is living on credit.'
[38] Krystof Pomian, *L'Ordre du temps* (Paris: Gallimard, 1984).

Predicting the Future to Judge the Present: Paris Theologians and Attitudes to the Future

IAN P. WEI

THE masters of theology at the University of Paris in the thirteenth century considered themselves to be at the summit of a hierarchy of learning, a position which gave them responsibility for the moral welfare of Christian society as a whole.[1] They were therefore obliged to consider the practical moral problems which Christians faced. Using their discussions of these problems, it is possible to address a number of questions about their attitudes to the future. First, did they discuss provision and planning for the future? If so, how did they envisage this future? Could predictions be made and, if so, what kind? Second, did their approach to problems in their present involve any element of prediction? If so, what kind? And how were predictions to be made? The analysis of practical moral issues was, however, only part of the task which masters of theology set themselves. They were equally concerned to achieve a theoretical understanding of knowledge and the process of knowing. It is therefore possible to ask how they regarded prediction in theory. It will become clear that they envisaged some forms of prediction which were entirely distinct from what they called prophecy, so it will be

A version of this paper was read to the Denys Hay Seminar at the University of Edinburgh. I am very grateful to my good friends and former colleagues at Edinburgh for their astute comments. I would particularly like to thank Dr Gary Dickson for his generous and extremely helpful advice.

[1] See Astrik L. Gabriel, 'The Ideal Master of the Mediaeval University', *The Catholic Historical Review*, 60 (1974), 1–40; R. Guelluy, 'La Place des théologiens dans l'église et la société médiévales', in *Miscellanea Historica in honorem Alberti de Meyer*, 2 vols (Leuven: University of Leuven, 1946), I, 571–89; Gabriel Le Bras, 'Velut splendor firmamenti: le docteur dans le droit de l'église médiévale', in *Mélanges offerts à Etienne Gilson* (Toronto: Pontifical Institute of Mediaeval Studies, 1959), pp. 373–88; J. Leclercq, 'L'Idéal du théologien au moyen âge: textes inédits', *Revue des Sciences Réligieuses*, 21 (1947), 121–48; Ian P. Wei, 'The Self-Image of the Masters of Theology at the University of Paris in the Late Thirteenth and Early Fourteenth Centuries', *Journal of Ecclesiastical History*, 46 (1995), 398–431.

necessary also to consider theoretical treatments of prophetic knowledge. The masters were not, however, merely observers of and commentators on the world around them. On the contrary, they exercised an authority which gave them roles to play outside the university.[2] Briefly, therefore, their handling of prophecy as a problem in the present will also be examined.

Finally, this analysis of the work of the masters of theology will permit some broader reflections on some of the major themes addressed by this book. First, the masters acknowledged the power of prophecy, while also envisaging people making mundane predictions, plans and provisions for the future, without reference to any divine inspiration. How then did the masters view the relationship between these different ways of thinking and knowing? Second, while some historians have looked at attitudes to time which were articulated explicitly by medieval people, others have drawn attention to implicit views of time, identifying attitudes and approaches which medieval people did not consciously express and for which they had no name. Thus Le Goff and Gurevich, for example, have pointed to 'the absence of a unified concept of time' in the Middle Ages, stressing rather a 'plurality of times'.[3] Crucially they have contrasted 'church time' and 'merchant time': 'church time' shaped by theology, linked to the process of salvation, sitting easily with agrarian rhythms, and of long standing in medieval society; 'merchant time' linked to credit and profit-making, requiring exact measurement, and emerging in a new urban environment.[4] In consciously articulating ideas about the future, did the masters of theology express these implicit attitudes, and did they reflect the mental shifts involved in the emergence of new mentalities?

1. Provision and Planning for the Future

Provision and planning for the future were of frequent concern to the masters of theology at Paris. To give just one example, they conducted a long-running debate about life annuities and perpetual annuities, which they called life rents (*redditus ad vitam*) and eternal rents (*redditus perpetui*). The fundamental issue was financial provision for the future. The buyer of a life rent gave a lump sum of money to the seller in return for annual rent payments for the rest of the buyer's life. In the case of an eternal rent the seller made annual

---

2   See Ian P. Wei, 'The Masters of Theology at the University of Paris in the Late Thirteenth and Early Fourteenth Centuries: An Authority Beyond the Schools', *Bulletin of the John Rylands University Library of Manchester*, 75 (1993), 37–63.

3   A. J. Gurevich, *Categories of Medieval Culture*, trans. G. L. Campbell (London: Routledge, 1985), pp. 143–4. Here Gurevich expresses his agreement with Jacques Le Goff: see note 4 below.

4   Gurevich, pp. 141–51; Jacques Le Goff, 'Merchant's Time and Church's Time in the Middle Ages', in his *Time, Work, and Culture in the Middle Ages*, trans. Arthur Goldhammer (Chicago: University of Chicago Press, 1980), pp. 29–42.

payments to the buyer and his heirs in perpetuity. Sometimes the buyer was the weaker party and purchased a life rent from some corporate body in order to secure a regular income. On other occasions, however, the seller was the weaker party and entered the contract because of an urgent need for ready money. The debate concerned whether or not this kind of contract was licit, and it was chiefly played out in the course of quodlibetal disputations held between the mid-1260s and 1290.

That the propriety of life and eternal rents should have been discussed in quodlibetal disputations, or quodlibets, suggests that the debate mattered beyond the university.[5] Quodlibetal disputations could only be held by regent masters at or close to Christmas and Easter. Masters were not, however, obliged to hold quodlibets and very few ever held them twice a year. Each quodlibet consisted of two distinct sessions. The first session was the *disputatio*. The audience was extremely varied and could include men who were not members of the university: it was a solemn and public occasion. The audience had a crucial role to play, because it dictated the subject matter of the disputation. Questions could be asked by anyone, *a quolibet*, and they could be about anything, *de quolibet*; hence the name. At the first session these questions would be discussed and the presiding master might or might not say very much. But at the second session, the *determinatio*, which was held within a few days, only the master spoke. He gave a definitive *solutio* or *determinatio* to each question raised at the first session. These questions necessarily reflected the interests and preoccupations of the audience. They ranged from abstract questions of philosophy and theology to questions which looked beyond the schools, referring to contemporary events and dealing with political and social issues at all levels of society. Furthermore, quodlibetal questions were collected in manuscripts intended for use outside the university. There are also references to masters putting their determinations in writing and under seal, although no quodlibetal question is known to survive in this form. Quodlibetal questions were also included in *summae* and manuals designed to assist confessors. Quodlibets therefore reflected both a magisterial response to

---

5 On quodlibetal disputations, see Leonard E. Boyle, 'The Quodlibets of St. Thomas and Pastoral Care', *The Thomist*, 38 (1974), 232–56; Palémon Glorieux, *La Littérature quodlibétique de 1260 à 1320*, 2 vols (Paris: Vrin, 1925 and 1935); Palémon Glorieux, 'L'Enseignement au moyen âge: techniques et méthodes en usage à la faculté de théologie de Paris au xiiie siècle', *Archives d'histoire doctrinale et littéraire du moyen âge*, 35 (1968), 65–186 (pp. 128–34); Wei, 'The Masters of Theology', 39–44; John F. Wippel, 'The Quodlibetal Question as a Distinctive Literary Genre', in *Les Genres littéraires dans les sources théologiques et philosophiques médiévales: definition, critique et exploitation. Actes du colloque international de Louvain-la-Neuve 25–27 mai 1981* (Louvain-la Neuve, 1982), pp. 67–84; John F. Wippel, 'Quodlibetal Questions, Chiefly in Theology Faculties', in *Les Questions disputées et les questions quodlibétiques dans les facultés de théologie, de droit et de médecine*, Typologie des sources du moyen âge occidental, 44–45 (Turnhout: Brepols, 1985), pp. 151–222.

the concerns of a wider clerical audience and the first step in a process of transmission beyond the schools.

The debate about life and eternal rents saw Henry of Ghent take a lonely stand against a host of other masters. Henry maintained that such contracts were illicit according to their form, which meant that they were wrong in every case. The other masters argued that they were legitimate in form, so that whether or not a particular contract was acceptable depended on circumstances. Both sides elaborated a range of extremely complex arguments, but the main outlines of the debate were straightforward.

Henry of Ghent condemned life and eternal rent contracts as usurious. In 1276 he was asked whether it was licit to buy life rents.[6] He pointed out that if someone gave a sum of money in return for an annual payment for the rest of his life, after a certain number of years he would have recovered his principal and received an additional sum. According to Henry, however, it would be more pious to give the same original sum and to receive it back all at once after the same period of time with the same additional sum, and yet that would be a case of manifest usury. To purchase a life rent in the hope of receiving something beyond the principal if one lived long enough was therefore even more clearly usurious. Henry stressed that what the buyer of the life rent eventually received was irrelevant; usury lay simply in the hope of receiving more than the principal. The form of the life rent contract was therefore flawed.

In the following year, 1277, Henry was brought back to the topic of life rents when he was asked whether it was licit to sell them.[7] Clearly there had been criticism of his earlier treatment of the issue and he was very much on the defensive. He called on God to witness that he had simply spoken the truth as he saw it, and not out of favour or hatred for anyone. His view of the truth had not changed, but if the Church took a different line, he would obey in this as in all matters. He was, however, a little more certain of his ground than before since 'great men' had indicated their agreement with him. Furthermore, one of these eminent supporters even claimed to have seen two papal bulls condemning the purchase of life rents and ordering restitution of anything received beyond the principal from them. Turning to the new question, Henry observed that in a life rent contract the seller intended to repay

6 Quodlibet I.39: 'Utrum liceat emere redditus ad vitam'. *Henrici de Gandavo Quodlibet I*, ed. R. Macken, Henrici de Gandavo Opera Omnia, 5 (Leuven: Leuven University Press, 1979), pp. 209–18. See also Odd Langholm, *Economics in the Medieval Schools: Wealth, Exchange, Value, Money and Usury according to the Paris Theological Tradition, 1200–1350*, Studien und Texte zur Geistesgeschichte des Mittelalters, 29 (Leiden: Brill, 1992), pp. 266, 272, 273, 298; Fabiano Veraja, *Le origini della controversia teologica sul contratto di censo nel XIII secolo*, Storia ed economia, 7 (Rome: Edizione di Storia e Letteratura, 1960), pp. 55–62.
7 Quodlibet II.15: 'Utrum licitum sit vendere redditus ad vitam'. *Henrici de Gandavo Quodlibet II*, ed. R. Wielockx, Henrici de Gandavo Opera Omnia, 6 (Leuven: Leuven University Press, 1983), pp. 96–101. See also Langholm, p. 273; Veraja, pp. 62–9.

less than he had received from the buyer, hoping that the buyer would live for a shorter time to make this possible. This was usury and the contract was therefore illicit for the seller in exactly the same way as it was illicit for the buyer. While later admitting a restricted number of highly complex situations in which life and eternal rents might be legitimate, Henry maintained his basic position in the face of considerable opposition.[8]

Numerous other masters were asked similar questions and they insisted that life and eternal rents were licit in the right circumstances. They defended this view by arguing that the rents constituted sales. They were therefore perfectly licit provided that there was justice in exchange, in other words provided there was equality in the deal. Thus in the academic year 1277–78 Matthew of Aquasparta argued that life rents were licit if everything possible had been done to establish equality in exchange, which meant giving due consideration to age, health, and infirmity.[9] This was not a certain equality, but a probable one, based on reasonable expectation in particular cases. In 1284–85 Gervase of Mont-Saint-Eloi noted that the buyer of a life rent must not proceed if he estimated that he would probably receive substantially more than he paid out; this would be to do serious harm to his neighbour.[10] Furthermore, an impoverished seller must not be forced by necessity to sell at a loss by a buyer prosperous enough to make him the loan which he really needed. In 1285 Richard of Middleton maintained that life rents were licit when there was equality between buyer and seller as required by natural law, when due weight had been given to the buyer's age, health, risk to his life and other circumstances, when the price had been considered, and when it was not easy to tell who had the better deal.[11] If the buyer then died before recovering the principal, the seller was not obliged to restore any of the price. If the buyer lived long enough to receive more than he paid, he was not obliged to

---

[8] Quodlibet VIII.24: 'Utrum liceat emere redditus perpetuos'. Henry of Ghent, *Aurea Quodlibeta*, 2 vols (Venice, 1613), II, 46v–47r. Quodlibet XII.21: 'Utrum licet alicui dare ecclesiae cuiquam certam summam pecuniae ad emendum terras ad opus illius ecclesiae, ut detur ei certa summa pecuniae ad vitam suam'. Henry of Ghent, *Quodlibet XII, quaestiones 1–30*, ed. J. Decorte, Henrici de Gandavo Opera Omnia, 16 (Leuven: Leuven University Press, 1987), pp. 109–15. See also Langholm, pp. 271, 274–5, 298, 339, 340; Veraja, pp. 106–11, 125–31. Langholm, however, exaggerates the extent to which Henry had accepted the position adopted by Gervase of Mont-Saint-Eloi and Richard of Middleton.

[9] Quodlibet I.9: 'Utrum liceat emere redditus, uel pensiones ad uitam, utpote si liceat dare centum libras et, omnibus diebus uite sue, quolibet anno recipere centum solidos, uel determinatas mensuras bladi et uini'. Ed. Veraja, pp. 201–3. See also Veraja, pp. 69–73; Langholm, pp. 325–7.

[10] Quodlibet III, question 25 in the surviving sequence of his quodlibetal questions: 'Querebatur de emptione et venditione reddituum ad vitam'. Ed. Veraja, pp. 203–4. See also Langholm, pp. 287–8; Veraja, pp. 101–6.

[11] Quodlibet II.23 (II.22 in Glorieux, *La Littérature quodlibétique*, I, 269): 'Utrum liceat emere, vel vendere redditus ad vitam'. *Quolibeta doctoris eximii Ricardi de Mediavilla ordinis minorum* (Brescia, 1591), pp. 65–71. See also Langholm, pp. 330–41; Veraja, pp. 111–23.

restore anything. But if the buyer clearly had the better of the deal and had paid too little, the contract was illicit and he was bound either to make up the just price or return what he had received beyond the principal. If, on the other hand, the seller clearly enjoyed the better deal, having received too high a price, the contract was again illicit and he was obliged to return what he had received beyond the just price or leave whatever had been bought with the buyer's heir until he had recovered the principal. Richard then applied exactly the same argument to explain why it was licit to buy eternal rents. He recognised concern that, when rents were purchased in perpetuity, an equal exchange was impossible because the buyer or his heirs must inevitably receive more than they originally paid. He pointed out, however, that according to natural law one loved a thing more for oneself than for one's son, and more for one's son than for one's grandson, and so on. The price should be determined with this in mind, up to an agreed point. In 1288 Godfrey of Fontaines considered how a fitting equivalence could be established in the purchase of a life or eternal rent.[12] His approach was somewhat different. It could not be a matter of precise equality because eternal rent payments stretched into infinity and because it was uncertain for how long life rent payments would have to be paid. Nor was it a question of analysing particular cases. Rather it was a question of the prices which buyers and sellers collectively were prepared to accept. In other words, the just price was a common estimate established in the marketplace. A range of masters thus countered Henry of Ghent's arguments by asserting that life and eternal rent contracts were sales and therefore legitimate provided a fair exchange took place.

There was, however, an obvious objection. It could be argued that life and eternal rents involved the sale of money, and that this was improper because money was meant to be a medium of exchange. A number of masters therefore justified life and eternal rents by redefining what was sold. According to Gervase of Mont-Saint-Eloi in 1284–85, a life rent did not mean that the buyer received more than he had given because he received something indeterminate, or rather the 'right to receive a rent for the rest of his life' whose value was therefore indeterminate.[13] Similarly in 1285 Richard of Middleton explained that what the buyer bought was not actually money, but the right to receive a certain sum of money annually for life.[14] In 1288 Godfrey of Fontaines also demonstrated that a life rent contract was a legitimate sales contract because a life rent was a right to receive money: it was something

12 Quodlibet V.14: 'Utrum licitum sit emere redditus ad vitam et recipere de redditibus emptis ultra sortem'. *Les Quodlibet cinq, six et sept de Godefroid de Fontaines*, ed. M. de Wulf and J. Hoffmans, Les Philosophes Belges, 3 (Louvain: Institut Supérieur de Philosophie de l'Université, 1914), pp. 63–9. See also Langholm, pp. 293–4; Veraja, pp. 131–43.
13 Quodlibet III, question 25. Ed. Veraja, pp. 203–4. See also Veraja, pp. 101–6; Langholm, pp. 287–8.
14 Quodlibet II.23. *Quolibeta doctoris eximii Ricardi de Mediavilla*, pp. 65–71. See also Langholm, pp. 330–41; Veraja, pp. 111–23.

incorporeal, distinct from the corporeal thing itself.[15] Although money itself could not properly be sold, the right to receive it could.

This debate about life and eternal rents reveals several aspects of the masters' attitudes to the future. It is immediately obvious that the masters discussed provision for the future. More importantly, when they did so, they envisaged a future which stretched on endlessly. One master imagined generation succeeding generation; another conceived of payments stretching into infinity. There were no references here to the end of the world. But while this future apparently went on forever, it was measurable along the way; indeed it had to be measured out if fair deals were to be struck. Furthermore, for most masters, making licit provision in this kind of future required an element of prediction. For when they required circumstances to be assessed, they really meant future circumstances. How long was an individual likely to live, bearing in mind age and health? What risks did his lifestyle entail? The masters were not calling for certain predictions, but they expected predictions of the probable. Finally, this debate also reveals something about how the Church coped with urban financial practices and what historians have called 'merchant time'. It is important to note whose financial futures were being secured by life and eternal rents. According to the disputations, churchmen bought life rents, churches sold them, and churchmen advised others to buy them, especially poor scholars and beguines. In other words, the masters were not commenting on merchant practice at some distance from their clerical world. The clerical world was already thoroughly implicated in a type of financial provision which turned on time measured out in money. One master even defended the selling of time. Giles of Rome noted that some people condemned usury on the grounds that it involved the sale of time which belonged to everyone.[16] They claimed that when someone lent ten units of some currency in return for twelve units after a year, the lender sold a period of one year. Giles dismissed this as a reason for condemning usury, arguing that time could be sold in other situations without sin, for example if someone gave ten horses to another person on the understanding that twelve would be returned in a year. The masters were thus legitimating something which had taken place: the Church's adoption of what we might call 'merchant time'. Moreover, it was in 'merchant time' that churchmen could see the future and predict the probable.

---

[15] Quodlibet V.14. *Les Quodlibet cinq, six et sept de Godefroid de Fontaines*, pp. 63–9. See also Langholm, pp. 293–4; Veraja, pp. 131–43.

[16] Quodlibet V.24: 'Utrum liceat emere redditus ad vitam'. *B. Aegidii Columnae Romani Quodlibeta* (Louvain, 1646; repr. Frankfurt am Main: Minerva G.M.B.H., 1966), pp. 336–9. See also Langholm, pp. 386–9; Veraja, pp. 143–5. Although he did not entirely agree with Henry of Ghent, Giles of Rome was the only master to offer him partial support in his condemnation of life rents.

2. Predicting the Future to Solve Present Problems

Perhaps it is unsurprising that the masters should have considered it necessary to make some sort of prediction when providing for the future. They attached just as much importance to prediction, however, when they tackled problems which were clearly located in the present. This is apparent in their treatment of many issues, but the key points can be made by examining two quodlibetal questions concerning restitution.

In 1281–82 Henry of Ghent was invited to consider the case of someone who held property which ought to be restored to its rightful owner. Was the holder obliged to make restitution at once?[17] Considered as a matter of principle, immediate restitution was obviously required. In particular cases, however, matters were much more complicated because the circumstances of both the holder and the rightful owner had to be considered. Taking these into account, Henry made a series of distinctions. He began by considering the circumstances of the rightful owner. If an immediate return would be harmful to him, restitution should be delayed. For example, a sword should not be returned to its owner if he were in a state of fury.[18] If, on the other hand, immediate restitution would not be harmful to the owner, either the holder was in possession of the property against the owner's will or the owner had given his consent. In the latter case, immediate restitution was unnecessary, provided the owner's consent was genuinely free. If, however, the owner had not consented to the present arrangement, the holder's circumstances came into play. From this point of view, the holder's intentions were especially important. If he did not intend to make restitution wholly or in part at some time, his intention must change immediately and he must return the property at once. But if he meant to return the property wholly or in part at some time, everything depended on his reasons for delaying. If he was waiting for a better opportunity to make restitution, delay was acceptable as long as he was genuinely ready to make restitution. Henry expanded on this point by giving examples. If the owner knew nothing about the debt and the holder could not himself make restitution at that time without causing scandal or disgrace, he could licitly await a convenient time when he could make restitution secretly through another person or when he could himself make restitution without his delay being perceived. If the holder knew that restitution

---

17 Quodlibet VI.24: 'Utrum qui habet penes se quod restituendum est alteri, teneatur ipsum statim restituere'. *Henrici de Gandavo Quodlibet VI*, ed. G. A. Wilson, Henrici de Gandavo Opera Omnia, 10 (Leuven: Leuven University Press, 1987), pp. 222–7.

18 This was an example frequently cited by Parisian masters of theology, and drawn from Cicero, *De Officiis*, III.25. See Cicero, *De Officiis*, with translation by Walter Miller, The Loeb Classical Library (London: Heinemann, 1913; repr. 1968), pp. 370–1.

would at this time provoke an excessively hostile reaction from the owner, he could properly await a moment when the owner would be calmer. In both cases, however, a holder who was at fault in retaining possession for too long might have to pay compensation. If, however, the holder was not waiting for a better opportunity to make restitution, the relative need of the holder and the rightful owner had to be assessed. If the holder did not have great need of all or part of what he owed, immediate restitution was necessary. On the other hand, if he did have such a need, the owner's circumstances were again relevant. If the owner's need of the property was just as great, it should be returned at once. But if the owner was not in great need, the holder could delay restitution of all or part of the property, provided that his need was so great that had the rightful owner been aware of it, and had he followed right reason and been moved by brotherly love, he would have been obliged to consent. It was not, however, for the holder to assess his own need. This was a matter for ecclesiastical judges, either in court or in confession. In court the judge must ensure that someone who was entirely ready to make restitution did not suffer extreme need, and this judgement must be made according to the status and condition of each individual. Similarly the confessor could permit a delay by not insisting on immediate restitution. More specifically, he could advise the holder that he was not bound to make restitution in his current situation, but that he must be spiritually prepared to make restitution if his situation improved or the owner's declined. It had to be stressed that he was not in a secure position lest he become too bold and confident in retaining the property.

Prediction comes into Henry's analysis at two points. First, the holder should not make immediate restitution if he can predict that the owner would react in such a way as to cause harm. Second, the holder should not make immediate restitution if he can predict that scandal would result, meaning that others would somehow be led into sin. These were 'what if' predictions. Looking at potential courses of action, it was necessary to be able to predict what would happen in each case. But how were these predictions to be made? Henry indicated two practical steps. First, the future could be predicted by assessing current psychological state. This made it possible to anticipate reactions. So if one judged a man to be in a state of fury, one did not give him back his sword because the consequences were all too predictable. Indeed the furious sword-owner whose sword was in another's hands crops up in many questions to indicate the kind of judgement which was required. Second, individuals were not to make predictions on their own. Henry clearly expected confessors to play an important role in making 'what if' predictions.

Another question about restitution was put to Guy of Cluny in 1302–03. A woman possessed money from usury and married a man who believed that her money had been licitly acquired. After they had been married for some time, was the wife obliged to reveal the truth to her husband, and was he obliged to believe her?[19] The point of the last part of the question was presumably that he would have to make restitution if he believed her. According to Guy, if the woman possessed patrimonial goods, she was bound to make restitution, as was her husband in so far as he was aware of the facts. If, however, she did not have goods of this kind, everything depended on the nature of her relationship with her husband and in particular on the extent to which she was dominated by him. If she was not dominated, she perhaps had powers of administration under her husband and could gradually make restitution by giving alms. If, however, she was dominated by her husband and had no administrative authority, because he employed a seneschal and furthermore he was very careful with her goods, she must consider whether her husband was an adulterer. If he was, she could leave him and make restitution from her property. If he was not, she had to consider her husband's character. If he was a good and God-fearing man, she must reveal the truth to him and he was bound to make restitution. If he was a hard, greedy man and revelation would achieve nothing, she should keep silent and lament, resolving to make restitution willingly if she could find a way. This left the last part of the question. If the woman made such a revelation, was her husband obliged to believe her? Guy argued that he must believe her if he considered her to be a good woman, but not if he felt she was bad, hostile to her husband, and careless with household goods. In this case prediction was based not on an assessment of psychological state, but on judgement of character. By assessing her husband's character, the wife could predict his reaction to revelation of the truth about her money, and then she could decide what to do in the present. To sum up the masters' approach, solving problems in the present required predictions of the future. They were 'what if' predictions which were to be made by assessing present psychological condition and character, and with the help of confessors.

3. Predicting the Future in Theory

The importance which the masters attached to prediction as a technique for solving practical moral problems was perhaps one of the reasons why they also treated knowledge of the future in a systematic and theoretical way. The work of Thomas Aquinas may be taken as an example. His ideas about pru-

---

19 Quodlibet II.5: 'Contrahit ista cum aliquo et habet de usura usque ad centum libras. Bene, iste maritus ignorat et credit quod omnia ista sint bene acquisita. Modo est questio: cum ista fuerit cum viro suo per aliqua tempora, utrum teneatur sibi istud revelare, vel quomodo poterit istud revelare; et si dicat ista marito, utrum teneatur maritus sibi credere'. Paris, Bibliothèque nationale, fonds latin, 15850, fol. 41ra–rb. See Palémon Glorieux, 'Notices sur quelques théologiens de Paris de la fin du XIIIe siècle', *Archives d'histoire doctrinale et littéraire du moyen âge*, 3 (1928), 201–38 (pp. 204–9, 215–17).

dence and foresight are explored elsewhere in this book by John Burrow, and it is another aspect of Aquinas' analysis of knowledge of the future which will be considered here. His basic position was very clear. He stated it on several occasions and used it consistently to analyse various aspects of knowledge of the future.

Aquinas argued that future things could be known in two ways: in themselves and in their causes.[20] Only God could know future things in themselves:

> In themselves things that are future can be known only by God. To him they are present even while, in the course of events, they remain future, in so far as his eternal vision looks simultaneously on the whole course of time. . . .[21]

In their causes, however, future things could be known by human beings. More specifically, there were three types of cause and three corresponding states of knowledge. First, there were causes which necessarily and always produced their effects. This meant that if a man knew such causes, he could foreknow and foretell their future effects with certainty. As Aquinas put it, 'future things which come necessarily from their causes can be known with certainty'.[22] Aquinas explained that it was in this manner that astrologers could predict future eclipses[23] or that the sun would rise tomorrow.[24] Second, there were causes which, although they did not produce their effects of necessity and always, almost invariably did so. Their future effects could therefore be foretold, not with certainty, but in the knowledge that they were highly likely. As Aquinas explained, 'Other things, that come from their causes in most cases, are not foreknowable with certainty but with a measure of probability. . . .'[25] Thus astrologers could examine the stars and then forecast rain or drought,[26] while doctors could predict future health or death.[27] Third, there were causes which could not be relied upon to produce particular effects at all. Their effects had to be deemed 'casual and chance events'[28] and they could not be foreknown at all.

Aquinas used this core analysis to sort out what was licit and what was illicit in attempts to know the future. To claim to foreknow future things in

---

[20] *Summa Theologiae* [henceforth ST], 1a.57.3; St Thomas Aquinas, *Summa Theologiae*, ed. Thomas Gilby and T. C. O'Brien, 60 vols (London: Blackfriars, 1964–1973), IX, 130–5. [Henceforth volume and page numbers will refer to this edition and translation.] ST, 1a.86.4; XII, 98–103. ST, 2a2ae.95.1; XL, 36–41.

[21] ST, 1a.86.4; XII, 101.

[22] ST, 1a.57.3; IX, 133.

[23] ST, 1a.86.4; XII, 100–1. ST, 2a2ae.95.1; XL, 38–9.

[24] ST, 1a.57.3; IX, 133.

[25] ST, 1a.57.3; IX, 133.

[26] ST, 2a2ae.95.1; XL, 38–9.

[27] ST, 1a.57.3; IX, 133. 2a2ae.95.1; XL, 38–9.

[28] ST, 1a.57.3; IX, 133.

themselves, except by God's revelation, was to usurp what belonged to God, and to sin.[29] This kind of divination involved the activity of demons 'either because they are expressly invoked to disclose the future or they invade these futile searchings into the future in order to entangle men's minds with vain conceits'.[30] But if a sequence of cause and effect could be identified, and if the type of relationship existing between the two were known, predictions were licit. Aquinas analysed various types of prediction in these terms, including, for example, divination by the stars, divination by dreams, divination by auguries and omens, and divination by casting lots.[31]

To pursue just one example, in the *Summa Theologiae* Aquinas considered the question, 'is divination by the stars unlawful?'[32] He began by remarking that:

> demonic powers thrust themselves into men's useless and futile quest for knowledge of the future so that our souls may become mazed in vanity and falsehood. For this is what happens to us if we try to learn from the stars future events which they cannot tell us. Consequently, we should consider what information about the future can be gained from observing stars and planets. It is evident that events which follow necessary physical laws can be foreknown by their means, for example, astronomers predict future eclipses.[33]

He then dismissed the view that stars signified rather than caused future events. The corporeal world had to be understood in terms of causes and effects, and stars could not possibly be the effects of events which were to happen in the future. He went on to note 'two kinds of effects which are not caused by celestial bodies': first, 'all those which happen by accident both in the world of nature and in human affairs', and second, 'acts of man's freedom' involving 'his faculty of will and reason'.[34] Man's reason and will were not corporeal, and since no corporeal being could make an impression on an incorporeal being, heavenly bodies could not make a direct impression on man's mind or free will. Aquinas added just one qualification: the stars could dispose a man to one action rather than another because they made an impression on the human body and thus on the senses and the bodily organs which influenced human acts. Free will and reason could always override this, but most men followed corporeal passions, so that astrologers were often correct in their predictions. Aquinas' main point, however, was clear:

> if anyone attempts from the stars to foretell future contingent or chance events, or to know with certitude the future activities of men, he is acting

29 ST, 2a2ae.95.1; XL, 38–9.
30 ST, 2a2ae.95.2; XL, 43.
31 ST, 2a2ae.95.5–8; XL, 50–69.
32 ST, 2a2ae.95.5; XL, 50–5.
33 ST, 2a2ae.95.5; XL, 51–3.
34 ST, 2a2ae.95.5; XL, 53.

under a false and groundless presupposition, and opening himself to the intrusion of diabolic powers. Consequently, this kind of fortune-telling is superstitious and wrong. But if someone uses astronomic observation to forecast future events which are actually determined by physical laws, for instance, drought and rainfall, and so forth, then this is neither superstitious nor sinful.[35]

For masters like Thomas Aquinas there was evidently a licit way to know the future which had nothing to do with divine revelation and prophecy. This knowledge depended on understanding sequences of cause and effect. It was natural knowledge that could be divided up into areas of specialisation and taught. The examples given by Aquinas are significant: legitimate predictions could be made by astrologers and doctors. This was a kind of knowledge where specialisation counted and predictions were made by experts. The masters were great believers in experts and in areas of professional specialisation.[36] Confessors were experts: experts in judging the psychological state and character of their flock, and so in making the relevant predictions.[37] The masters themselves were experts: experts in the study of knowledge and the process of knowing, men who did not necessarily make predictions themselves, but who set out when the relevant experts should make predictions in every area of life. This was part of their role at the summit of a hierarchy of learning.[38]

4. Prophecy in Theory

It would, however, be entirely incorrect to suppose that the masters ignored prophetic knowledge or lacked interest in the eschatological. On the contrary, they were much concerned with prophecy and matters such as the Last Judgement.[39] Indeed Thomas Aquinas devoted more of the *Summa Theologiae*

---

[35] ST, 2a2ae.95.5; XL, 55.

[36] For the growing tendency of learned churchmen to classify people in terms of professions, see Peter Biller, 'Confession in the Middle Ages: Introduction', in *Handling Sin: Confession in the Middle Ages*, ed. Peter Biller and A. J. Minnis, York Studies in Medieval Theology, 2 (York: York Medieval Press, 1998), pp. 3–33 (pp. 16–18); Jacques Le Goff, 'Trades and Professions as represented in Medieval Confessors' Manuals', in his *Time, Work, and Culture in the Middle Ages*, pp. 107–21; Pierre Michaud-Quantin, 'Les Categories sociales dans le vocabulaire des canonistes et moralistes au XIIIe siècle', in his *Etudes sur le vocabulaire philosophique du moyen âge* (Rome: Edizioni dell'Ateneo, 1970), pp. 163–86 (pp. 180–5).

[37] Biller, p. 10, describes 'hearing confession', along with preaching, as 'the professional activity of the vast majority of the friars'. Le Goff, p. 118, refers to the authors of confessors' manuals as 'specialists in matters of professional conscience'.

[38] See note 1.

[39] For their discussions of prophecy, see Bert Roest, 'Divination, Visions and Prophecy according to Albert the Great', in *Media Latinitas: A Collection of Essays to Mark the Occasion*

to prophecy than to the natural type of prediction which has just been considered.[40] He consistently defined prophecy as knowledge revealed by God and beyond natural human capacity. As he explained, 'Those truths which surpass all human knowledge and which are revealed from God cannot find confirmation in that human reasoning which they transcend, but only in the working of divine power.'[41] Prophetic knowledge did not, however, only concern the future:

> prophetic knowledge is brought about by a divine light which makes possible the knowledge of all realities, whether they be human or divine, spiritual or corporeal. And so prophetic revelation extends to all such realities.[42]

On the other hand, prophecy was especially about the future:

> Yet we should consider that because prophecy relates to what is far from our range of knowledge, then the more a reality is distant from human knowledge, the more properly will that reality belong to prophecy.
>
> There are three degrees of remoteness from human knowing. The first covers what is hidden from this or that individual, whether in sense or intellect, yet is not hidden from men in general; just as a man knows by his senses what is adjacent to him in place while another person, with the same senses, fails to know because he is not adjacent. Thus . . . the thoughts of one person's heart can be manifested prophetically to another. In this way too the knowledge which one has by demonstration can be revealed to us in prophecy.
>
> The second degree comprises those truths which universally surpass the knowledge of all men, not because they are intrinsically unknowable, but because of a defect in human knowledge. An example of this is the mystery of the Trinity . . .
>
> Third, and most remote of all, is that which surpasses the knowledge of all men, because the truths concerned are not knowable; such are future contingents whose truth is not determined.
>
> Now because what is universal and self-caused surpasses what is particular and caused by another, so the revelation of future events most properly belongs to prophecy.[43]

---

of the Retirement of L. J. Engels, ed. R. I. A. Nip and others, Instrumenta Patristica, 28 (Turnhout: Brepols, 1996), pp. 323–8; Jean-Pierre Torrell, *Théorie de la prophétie et philosophie de la connaissance aux environs de 1230: la contribution d'Hugues de Saint-Cher*, Spicilegium Sacrum Lovaniense, études et documents, 40 (Louvain: Spicilegium Sacrum Lovaniense, 1977); Jean-Pierre Torrell, *Recherches sur la théorie de la prophétie au moyen âge XIIe–XIVe siècles: études et textes*, Dokimion, 13 (Fribourg: Editions Universitaires Fribourg Suisse, 1992).

[40] See especially ST, 2a2ae.171–4; XLV, 4–93.
[41] ST, 2a2ae.171.1; XLV, 7.
[42] ST, 2a2ae.171.3; XLV, 15.
[43] ST, 2a2ae.171.4; XLV, 15–17; I have slightly adjusted the translation.

According to Aquinas, prophetic knowledge was therefore completely different from natural knowledge of the future in its origins, and other differences followed. Aquinas drew the contrast explicitly. Natural knowledge of the future was naturally acquired, only covered effects within the range of human experience, and could be subject to error. Prophecy derived from divine revelation, could relate to any event whatever, and was infallible.[44] Moreover, prophecy also differed from natural knowledge of the future in its social implications. God could give prophetic knowledge to anyone, without regard for their intellectual ability and education.[45] In the *Summa Theologiae* Aquinas asked 'does prophecy call for natural dispositions?'[46] He concluded emphatically that it did not:

> We need to reflect that God who is universal cause in the order of action does not antecedently require, in corporeal effects, either matter or any material pre-disposition. God can immediately cause to be, all at once, matter, disposition and form. So too in spiritual effects God requires no pre-existing disposition, but can, all at once, bring about the spiritual effect, with a suitable disposition of the sort which would be demanded in the order of nature. Furthermore God could by creation, all at once, produce the subject himself, so that the soul in this person would be disposed towards prophecy in its creation and be given a prophet's grace.[47]

As Aquinas viewed it, prophetic knowledge therefore cut across, indeed demolished, the hierarchy of learning which the masters valued so much, not least because they considered themselves to be at its summit. Prophecy was not a kind of knowledge where there could be specialisation, professional training, or experts.

5. Prophecy as a Problem in the Present

In theory, therefore, prophecy posed a difficult problem for the masters of theology, and a degree of ambivalence might be supposed on their part. Yet prophecy could not be, and was not, a purely theoretical matter for them. Prophecy was an issue in their present and the masters had responsibilities to fulfil. Events surrounding the visit of Arnold of Villanova to Paris in 1300 illustrate the point.

---

44 ST, 2a2ae.172.1; XLV, 31: 'Knowledge from divine revelation can relate to any event whatever and is infallible: by contrast, naturally acquired knowledge only covers effects within the range of human experience. Supernatural prophecy possesses immutable truth: natural prophecy can be subject to error'.
45 See J. M. Cocking, *Imagination: A Study in the History of Ideas* (London: Routledge, 1991), p. 155.
46 ST, 2a2ae.172.3; XLV, 34–9.
47 ST, 2a2ae.172.3; XLV, 37.

Arnold of Villanova was a physician who practised at the royal court of Aragon in the 1280s, and taught at Montpellier in the 1290s.[48] After 1300 he was physician to popes Boniface VIII, Benedict XI, and Clement V. While pursuing his medical career, Arnold also wrote works of prophecy based on scriptural interpretation. One of his works was a treatise on the time of the coming of Antichrist, *De tempore adventus Antichristi*.[49] In it he foretold that Antichrist would appear in a holy place, between 1376 and 1378. In July 1300 James II of Aragon sent Arnold to Paris to carry out diplomatic negotiations with the king of France. There Arnold set about publicising and disseminating his treatise on the coming of Antichrist, a work which he had begun in the late 1280s and finished by 1297. Several masters of theology denounced him because of his treatise, accusing him of error, impiety and blasphemy. This led to his arrest and an appearance before the bishop of Paris and all the masters of theology. His treatise was condemned and he was compelled to renounce it. Arnold claimed, however, that he had been treated improperly, and he appealed to the pope. His appeal was dated 12 October 1300 and the witnesses included Peter of Auvergne, a master of theology in Paris. Arnold's battles continued after he left Paris, but this brief account of his Parisian sojourn illustrates the way in which the masters of theology were involved in dealing with prophecies about the coming of Antichrist.

Peter of Auvergne was pressed on this matter. When he held a quodlibetal disputation at Christmas 1300, he was asked a series of questions about the coming of Antichrist.[50] The first question, 'whether Antichrist is to come soon', led him to criticise Arnold's treatise directly.[51] Most tellingly, however, someone asked: 'whether it is expedient to know the exact time of Antichrist's coming'.[52] Peter began his response by discussing what it was to be

---

[48] For accounts of Arnold's life and of events in Paris in 1300, see Clifford R. Backman, 'The Reception of Arnau de Vilanova's Religious Ideas', in *Christendom and its Discontents*, ed. Scott L. Waugh and Peter D. Diehl (Cambridge: Cambridge University Press, 1996), pp. 112–31; B. Hauréau, 'Arnauld de Villeneuve', *Histoire littéraire de la France*, 28 (1881), 26–126; Harold Lee, Marjorie Reeves and Giulio Silano, *Western Mediterranean Prophecy: The School of Joachim of Fiore and the Fourteenth-Century 'Breviloquium'* (Toronto: Pontifical Institute of Mediaeval Studies, 1989), pp. 27–46; Gordon Leff, *Heresy in the Later Middle Ages: The Relation of Heterodoxy to Dissent c.1250–c.1450*, 2 vols (Manchester: Manchester University Press, 1967), I, 176–85; Joseph Ziegler, *Medicine and Religion c.1300: The Case of Arnau de Vilanova* (Oxford: Clarendon Press, 1998), pp. 21–34.

[49] Ed. Josep Perarnau, 'El text primitiu del De mysterio cymbalorum ecclesiae d'Arnau de Vilanova', *Arxiu de Textos Catalans Antics*, 7/8 (1988–1989), 7–169 (pp. 134–69).

[50] Quodlibet V.15–17. Ed. Josep Perarnau, 'Guiu Terrena Critica Arnau de Vilanova: Edició de la «Quaestio utrum per notitiam sacrae scripturae possit determinate sciri tempus antichristi»', *Arxiu de Textos Catalans Antics*, 7/8 (1988–1989), 171–222 (pp. 213–18). See Glorieux, *La Littérature quodlibétique*, I, 262.

[51] Quodlibet V.15: 'Utrum antichristus sit venturus in brevi'. Ed. Perarnau, 'Guiu Terrena', pp. 213–14.

[52] Quodlibet V.16: 'Utrum expediens sit homini scire tempus determinatum adventus antichristi'. Ed. Perarnau, 'Guiu Terrena', pp. 214–16. This is an edition of Vat. lat. 932, fols

expedient. Some things were expedient straightforwardly, while others were only expedient in certain circumstances or to certain people. Then he tackled the question which he had been asked. Knowing exactly when Antichrist would appear was not straightforwardly expedient to the faithful, because they might be driven to inordinate fear and end up believing false prophets as if they were messengers sent by Christ to tell them about the end of the world. On the other hand, knowing the time of Antichrist's arrival was expedient in certain circumstances and to certain people. Such foreknowledge would certainly be useful to someone who had the disposition to prepare himself to reject Antichrist's doctrine and to resist constantly Antichrist's persecutions so that he did not abandon divine law because of them. Useful, but not straightforwardly so: that perhaps sums up the masters' position in the face of prophetic knowledge.

6. Conclusions

There can be no doubt that the masters discussed provision for the future. In so doing, they envisaged a future which stretched on without end, which could be measured out, and within which probable predictions could be made. Problems located entirely in the present also required predictions. They were 'what if' predictions based on assessment of psychological condition and character, and they were to be made with the help of a confessor. None of this knowledge of the future was divinely revealed: it was not prophecy. Masters like Aquinas gave this knowledge a theoretical formulation as natural knowledge, based on understanding sequences of cause and effect. It was knowledge which could be taught, in which areas of specialisation could be defined, and which could be shared out amongst professional experts. Prophecy was presented as a totally different kind of knowledge. Its origins in divine revelation were different, and it was different in its social implications because it could be given to anyone, with no regard for professional expertise. But as an issue in the present, the masters still had to deal with claims to prophecy, and awkward problems ensued.

What does this reveal about the co-existence of prophetic views of the future with mundane predictions, plans and provisions? For the masters, the key was the drastic and radical separation of natural knowledge of the future from prophetic knowledge. This separation permitted masters to analyse provision for the future and to use forms of natural prediction to solve any moral problem. It allowed them to approach prediction in terms of professional specialisation and competence, and to deploy the expertise of the physician, the

---

160r–161v. My analysis, however, relies on Paris, Bibliothèque nationale, fonds latin, 14562, fols 73va–74ra, which differs at several points.

astrologer, and the confessor. This had to be done because it was so often necessary to predict the future to judge the present. It was permissible because
there was always the overriding power of prophetic knowledge which had su-
perior origins and was certain, thus taking precedence over merely probable
forms of knowledge, whatever their social embodiment.

As for the relationship between explicitly articulated beliefs and implicit
attitudes, the separation between natural foreknowledge and prophecy was
again crucial. This separation permitted the masters to embrace the values to
which historians have given the label 'merchant time'. As long as they were
dealing with natural knowledge of what would probably happen, the future
could be treated as endless, measurable, and even for sale. This was a valid
approach as long as it was realised that there was another form of knowing
which contained higher truths. Indeed it was perhaps helpful that not everyone knew prophetically. The masters thus engineered an immensely significant accommodation between what started out as two hugely different ways
of thinking, between the traditional values of 'church time' and the new
values of 'merchant time'. They were no longer in opposition, but slotted into
different positions in a hierarchy of truth. People lived with the probable, but
knew that others might have access to a different and certain truth to which
all would have to defer. In their treatment of the future it may be suggested
that the masters rationalised a way of thinking employed by many people in
medieval society from some point in the twelfth century onwards.

The Third Eye of Prudence

JOHN BURROW

THE title of this essay is suggested by a passage in Geoffrey Chaucer's poem *Troilus and Criseyde*. As a result of an exchange of prisoners, Criseyde has been transferred from Troy to the Greek camp. While still in Troy, she had promised her lover to return within ten days; but now she finds that the prospect frightens her, and she wishes that she had taken Troilus's advice and stolen away from Troy in his company. She realises that she made a bad decision:

> 'Prudence, allas, oon of thyne eyen thre
> Me lakked alwey, er that I come here!
> On tyme ypassed wel remembred me,
> And present tyme ek koud ich wel ise,
> But future tyme, er I was in the snare,
> Koude I nat sen; that causeth now my care.'[1]

Prudence here looks in three directions: towards past time through memory, towards present time, and, with her third eye, towards future time. It is this third eye which, Criseyde now thinks, failed her when she agreed to go along with the exchange of prisoners.

The strange image of a head with three eyes (or sometimes with three faces), looking away at right angles from each other, appears elsewhere among the emblems of prudence, both in literature and in the visual arts. Two examples will suffice here. In Canto XXIX of the *Purgatorio* Dante, having arrived in the earthly paradise, sees a divine pageant which includes the four cardinal virtues 'following the measure of one of them that had three eyes in her head':

---

[1] *Troilus and Criseyde*, V. 744–9, cited from *The Riverside Chaucer*, ed. L. D. Benson (Boston: Houghton Mifflin, 1987). The note to the passage gives references for sources and analogues.

Da la sinistra quattro facean festa,
in porpore vestita, dietro al modo
d'una di lor ch'avea tre occhi in testa.[2]

Thus Prudence leads the other three virtues – Temperance, Justice, and Fortitude – in their celebratory dance. Pictorial examples from the Middle Ages are not hard to find; but the most remarkable treatment of the subject is by Titian, in a painting known as 'An Allegory of Prudence', now in the National Gallery in London. This picture shows three human faces placed together above the faces of three animals. On the left, in shadow, is the face of an old man, above that of a wolf; in the middle, the faces of a man in his prime and a lion look straight out at the viewer; and on the right, the faces of a young man and a dog look away into the light. Distributed between them, above, is a Latin inscription: 'EX PRAETERITO' above the old face, 'PRAESENS PRUDENTER AGIT' above the mature face, and 'NI FUTURAM ACTIONEM DETURPET' above the young face on the right. The whole inscription, put together, means: 'Drawing on the past, the present acts prudently, lest it should make a mess of future action'. In a brilliant essay on Titian's painting, Erwin Panofsky explains the inscription as follows:

> We are given to understand [. . .] that the three faces, in addition to typifying three stages of human life (youth, maturity and old age), are meant to symbolize the three modes or forms of time in general; past, present, and future. And we are further asked to connect these three modes or forms of time with the idea of prudence or, more specifically, with the three psychological faculties in combined exercise of which this virtue consists: memory, which remembers, and learns from, the past: intelligence, which judges of, and acts in, the present: and foresight, which anticipates, and provides for or against, the future.[3]

---

2 'By the left wheel four other ladies made festival, clothed in purple, following the measure of one of them that had three eyes in her head': *Purgatorio*, XXIX. 130–2; *The Divine Comedy: Purgatorio*, ed. and trans. C. S. Singleton, 2 vols (Princeton: Princeton University Press, 1973). In the *Convivio*, Dante writes: 'Conviensi adunque essere prudente, cioè savio: e a ciò essere si richiede buona memoria de le vedute cose, buona conoscenza de le presenti e buona providenza de le future', ed. G. Busnelli and G. Vandelli (Florence: Felice Le Monnier, 1954), IV, xxvii. 5. L. J. Matthews cites from Matteo Frescobaldi, a minor follower of Dante: 'Prudenza fate che sia vostra guida, / Che con gli tre occhi tre tempi governa': Matthews, '*Troilus and Criseyde*, V 743–749: Another Possible Source', *Neuphilologische Mitteilungen*, 82 (1981), 211–13.
3 E. Panofsky, 'Titian's *Allegory of Prudence*: A Postscript', in his *Meaning in the Visual Arts* (London: Penguin, 1970), pp. 181–205 (p. 184). Plate 28 reproduces the Titian; and Panofsky refers to other representations of 'three-headed Prudence' on pp. 186–7, reproducing two in Plates 29 and 31. L. J. Matthews cites two pictorial examples from illustrated manuscripts of the *Purgatorio*, one of which has a gloss: 'guardare nel tempo avenire, administrare il presente [. . .] memorare il passato': 'Chaucer's Personification of Prudence in *Troilus* (V. 743–749): Sources in the Visual Arts and Manuscript Scholia', *English Language Notes*, 13 (1975–6), 249–55.

These examples are enough to suggest that the idea of 'looking to the future' carried, for the likes of Chaucer, Dante, and Titian, more moral and even spiritual significance than we would commonly attach to it today: it was a function of a cardinal virtue, of the third eye of prudence. For a more analytic account of the matter, one may turn to Thomas Aquinas, in his *Summa Theologiae*. Thomas devotes most of the *Secunda secundae* to the virtues, the three theological virtues followed by the four cardinal virtues. Like Dante, he places *prudentia* at the head of the latter, devoting to it ten *quaestiones*.[4] Among the authorities he cites are Christ's words to the apostles, 'Estote prudentes sicut serpentes' (Matthew 10. 16), and a passage from Cicero's *De Inventione*. This passage played an important part in forming later conceptions of prudence. In it, Cicero specified three 'parts' of prudence: *memoria*, *intellegentia*, and *providentia*, that is, memory, understanding, and foresight. He associates these with, respectively, past, present, and future time:

> Prudentia est rerum bonarum et malarum neutrarumque scientia. Partes eius: memoria, intellegentia, providentia. Memoria est per quam animus repetit illa quae fuerunt; intellegentia, per quam ea perspicit quae sunt; providentia, per quam futurum aliquid videtur ante quam factum est.[5]

Of these three 'parts', Aquinas explains, the principal one is *providentia* or foresight, since the main business of prudence is with the future: 'Prudentia praecipue est futurorum: praecipua enim pars eius est providentia futurorum'.[6] More precisely, its business is with 'future contingents'. For prudence is a practical virtue, concerned with those actions and events in the future which – unlike those from the past or present – could be otherwise, and so can be

---

[4] 2a2ae.47–56. Latin quotations and English translations are taken from St Thomas Aquinas, *Summa Theologiae*, ed. Thomas Gilby and T. C. O'Brien, 60 vols (London: Blackfriars, 1964–1973), XXXVI (1974).

[5] 'Wisdom is the knowledge of what is good, what is bad and what is neither good nor bad. Its parts are memory, intelligence, and foresight. Memory is the faculty by which the mind recalls what has happened. Intelligence is the faculty by which it ascertains what is. Foresight is the faculty by which it is seen that something is going to occur before it occurs': *De Inventione*, II, 53, ed. and trans. H. M. Hubbell, The Loeb Classical Library (London: Heinemann, 1949), p. 326. Another influential account, not cited by Aquinas, is in the *De formula honestae vitae* of Martin of Braga (commonly ascribed to Seneca): 'Si prudens est animus tuus, tribus temporibus dispensetur: praesentia ordina, futura praevide, praeterita recordare', in *Annaei Senecae Opera*, ed. F. Haase, 3 vols (Leipsig: Teubner, 1884–87), III, 470. Panofsky, p. 185, quotes a concise formulation from the *Repertorium morale* of Berchorius: prudence consists 'in praeteritorum recordatione, in praesentium ordinatione, in futurorum meditatione'.

[6] 'Now prudence has a special concern for the future, of which provision is a main part': 2a2ae.55.7. Cf. Dante, *Convivio*, III. i. 10: 'sì come dice Boezio, "non basta di guardare pur quello che è dinanzi a li occhi", cioè lo presente, e però n' è data la provedenza che riguarda oltre, a quello che può avvenire' (ed. cit., p. 261).

directed to a good end by human foresight, or, as we might prefer to say, planning.[7]

The cardinal virtues, including prudence, owe their formulation largely to classical writers such as Aristotle and Cicero; so we may now be inclined to think of them as secular or worldly qualities, in contrast to the specifically Christian, Pauline, set of faith, hope, and charity. Medieval writers, however, did not see it that way at all. Aquinas makes no such observation when, in the *Secunda secundae*, he passes smoothly from the three theological to the four cardinal virtues. As Rosemond Tuve amply demonstrated in her book *Allegorical Imagery*, Christian writers identified the cardinal four among those virtues inspired by no less than the Holy Ghost itself, according to the messianic prophecy of Isaiah: 'And the spirit of the Lord shall rest upon him: the spirit of wisdom and of understanding, the spirit of counsel and of fortitude, the spirit of knowledge and of godliness. And he shall be filled with the spirit of the fear of the Lord' (Isaiah 11. 2–3).[8] Hence, Aquinas devotes one *quaestio* in his discussion of prudence to the Holy Spirit's gift of 'counsel' or *consilium*, concluding that 'the gift of counsel complements prudence, as aiding it and bringing it to completion' (2a2ae.52). 'Counsel' plays a central role in the theory of prudence. The end or purpose of counsel, Aquinas says, is 'the discovery of what has to be done', either by private deliberation, or by consultation with others; and it is through the grace of the Holy Spirit helping and perfecting such activities that prudence can figure, not only as a very practical moral virtue, but also as a high spiritual gift.

Yet Aquinas was well aware that, in the real world, prudential foresight was not always 'perfected' by the Holy Spirit, and indeed that it could be turned to evil ends. He has an article (2a2ae.47.13) posing the question whether prudence is possible for sinners, in which he takes more general account of the actual varieties of *prudentia* among men. Here he distinguishes three types. One is *prudentia falsa*, not the real thing but deceitfully resembling it: 'Cum enim prudens sit qui bene disponit ea quae sunt agenda propter aliquem bonum finem, ille qui propter malum finem aliqua disponit congruentia illi fini habet falsam prudentiam'.[9] He gives the example of the 'prudent

---

7 2a2ae.49.6: 'Past events obtain a sort of necessity, for what has been done cannot be undone. The same applies to present events, precisely as present; for instance, Socrates is necessarily sitting while he is seated. Consequently only those future contingents which a man can shape to the purpose of human life are matters for prudence'.

8 R. Tuve, *Allegorical Imagery: Some Medieval Books and their Posterity* (Princeton: Princeton University Press, 1966), chap. 2. Cf. the Middle English *Book of Vices and Virtues*: 'Of þe four cardinal vertues speken moche þe olde philosofres, but þe Holy Gost yeveþ hem moche bettre and techeþ hem an hundred so wel', ed. W. N. Francis, Early English Text Society (EETS), 217 (1942), p. 122.

9 'While the prudent man is he who well adapts his actions to a right end, he who contrives fitting means to a wrong end has false prudence': 2a2ae.47.13. Aquinas quotes Romans 8. 6: 'Prudentia carnis mors est'.

robber', whose experience and expertise enable him to devise good ways of committing future crimes. The second type is *prudentia vera sed imperfecta*, true but imperfect prudence. Aquinas chiefly has in mind here all those 'particular affairs' where men exercise foresight in the course of some specialised activity: 'puta cum aliquis adinvenit vias accommodatas ad negotiandum vel ad navigandum, dicitur prudens negotiator vel nauta'.[10] This kind of expert planning, it should be noted, can properly be called prudent; but such prudence is imperfect because skilled businessmen or sailors may themselves be wicked. This cannot be the case, however, with *prudentia vera et perfecta*, true and perfect prudence: 'quae ad bonum finem totius vitae recte consiliatur, judicat et praecipit; et haec sola dicitur prudentia simpliciter; quae in peccatoribus esse non potest'.[11]

Having considered prudence thus in its application to the life of the individual, as the virtue 'with which a man rules himself', Aquinas turns (2a2ae.50) to the ruling of the many (*multitudo*) in the manifold affairs of social and political life. Here he distinguishes four walks of life where one may exercise that virtuous *providentia* which looks to and provides for the future, in the interests of others. These four 'species' of prudence he calls *regnativa*, *politica*, *oeconomica*, and *militaris*. The first of these is proper to kings and other rulers, exercising it for the benefit of their subjects. As Thomas Usk observed in his *Testament of Love*:

> What is worth thy body, but it be governed with thy soule? Right so litel or naught is worth erthely power, but if reignatif prudence in heedes governe the smale.[12]

Prudentia politica is required of the subjects themselves, in so far as they are concerned with the common good (2a2ae.50.2). This might now be called 'vision' in a politician. The third term, *oeconomica*, follows Aristotle in referring to the management of family and household welfare and finances (2a2ae.50.3). The only other form of association short of the whole political community that Aquinas recognises, for what we would now call planning purposes, is the army. Hence *prudentia militaris*: 'executio militiae pertinet ad

---

10 'When a man versed in the methods of commerce or navigation is called a prudent trader or sailor': 2a2ae.47.13.
11 'Which, with a view to the final good for the whole of human life, rightly deliberates, decides, and commands. This alone is prudence pure and simple, and in sinners it just cannot be': 2a2ae.47.13.
12 *Testament of Love*, book II, chap. ii, ed. W. W. Skeat, *Chaucerian and Other Pieces* (Oxford: Oxford University Press, 1897), p. 52. An anti-Yorkist text of 1459 speaks of 'the grete regitive prudennce and pollitique provisioun' of Henry VI: cited by *Middle English Dictionary* under *regitif* adj. In the heaven of prudence, Dante presents King Solomon as a supreme example of 'regal prudenza' (*Paradiso*, XIII. 104).

fortitudinem, sed directio ad prudentiam, et praecipue secundum quod est in duce exercitus.'[13]

So much for Aquinas. It is not my intention, of course, to suggest that people in the Middle Ages commonly thought about *providentia* in such precise scholastic terms. Apart from anything else, vernacular languages could only imperfectly match the stability and exactness of Thomas's Latin terminology. One may be surprised to discover, for instance, that the dictionaries give no datable example of the word 'future' in English before the 1380s, when Chaucer used it, in his translation of the *Consolatio* of Boethius and also in the passage from *Troilus* with which I began; and the term for many years thereafter achieved only a very restricted currency in English.[14] More common in Middle English are derivatives of the word *providentia* in its prudential sense 'foresight', either as 'purveiaunce' (the French form) or, later, as 'providence'.[15] From the fourteenth century, too, the word 'prudence' itself, along with the corresponding adjective and adverb, achieves currency as a familiar term in English.[16] I have selected a few examples here, mainly from fourteenth- and fifteenth-century English and Scots writers. These may serve to illustrate both the range of human activities for which prudence is required, and also the ability of medieval writers to see moral, even spiritual, issues in matters which to us may seem purely practical.

There are, to begin with, many examples of prudential language applied to particular arts and crafts in these texts. Thus Thomas Hoccleve advises a poet contemplating a new work to exercise 'forsighte' (*providentia*), like an architect planning a house:

> Who by prudence
> Rule him shal, no thyng shal out from him breke
> Hastily ne of rakil negligence.[17]

Again, John Lydgate praises the prudence of a Greek hero for taking up a well defensible position when attacked – a case of *prudentia militaris*:

---

13 'Actual fighting calls for courage, but its direction calls for prudence, especially that of the good generalship of the officer commanding': 2a2ae.50.4.

14 *MED*, under *futur(e* n. and *futur(e* adj. Seven of the eighteen quotations given come from Chaucer's translation of Boethius. The Old English words were 'toweardness' and 'toweard'.

15 *MED*, under *purveiaunce* n., sense 1, *providence* n., sense (b). 'Foresight' was the native equivalent: *MED*, under *for(e-sight*, citing *Cursor Mundi* 10012: 'four vertus principals . . . rightwisnes and meth, forsight and strenght'.

16 *MED*, under *prudence* n., *prudent* adj., *prudentli* adv.

17 *Dialogue with a Friend*, lines 653–5, ed. F. J. Furnivall, in Furnivall and I. Gollancz, *Hoccleve's Works: The Minor Poems*, revised by J. Mitchell and A. I. Doyle, EETS, e.s. 61, 73 (1892, 1925, in one volume 1970). The passage draws on the *Poetria nova* of Geoffrey of Vinsauf, lines 43–59, ed. E. Faral, *Les Arts poétiques du XIIe et du XIIIe siècles* (Paris: Champion, 1924), pp. 198–9: 'Opus totum prudens in pectoris arcem / Contrahe' (lines 58–9).

And on this hille / he fond a narow passage,
Which that he took / of ful high prudence.[18]

The strangest example of this kind is provided by William Langland. Towards the end of his *Piers Plowman*, Langland treats the four cardinal virtues as gifts granted to the early church by the Holy Spirit, the 'spirit of prudence' first among them. *Spiritus Prudencie* taught men, he says, to 'devyse wel the ende' and – most unexpectedly – to buy a ladle with a long handle before setting out to stir a cooking-pot and prevent it from boiling over:

And lerned men a ladel bugge with a long stele
That caste for to kepe a crokke, and save the fatte above.[19]

Langland's quirky mind provides an extreme instance of the mundane activities which were held to require prudential management; but the virtue is also required, of course, in matters of more consequence. It figures very large in books of advice for princes, as what Aquinas called *prudentia regnativa*. The *Regiment of Princes*, written by Thomas Hoccleve for Prince Hal shortly before he became Henry V, devotes one section to 'a kynges prudence' (lines 4747–858). Like Dante, Hoccleve speaks of Prudence as a damsel leading the other cardinal virtues; and she lights their way: 'Prudence gooth byfore, and yeveth light / Of counseil, what þo other thre do schal'.[20] He goes on to be more specific:

Prudence is vertu of entendement;
She makith man by resoun him governe.
Who-so þat list to be wys and prudent,
And þe light folwe wole of hir lanterne,
He moste caste his look in every herne
Of þynges past, and ben, & þat schul be:
The ende seeþ, and eek mesureth, sche.   (4761–7)

---

18 *Lydgate's Siege of Thebes*, ed. A. Erdmann, EETS, e.s. 108 (1911), lines 2198–9. A later passage concerning the old prophet Amphiorax displays the terms 'prudence', 'prudent', 'purveiaunce', 'providence', 'provide', and 'counsel' in a typical constellation (lines 2794–988). On the theme of prudence in the poem, see J. Simpson, ' "Dysemol daies and fatal houres": Lydgate's *Destruction of Thebes* and Chaucer's *Knight's Tale*', in *The Long Fifteenth Century: Essays for Douglas Gray*, ed. H. Cooper and S. Mapstone (Oxford: Clarendon Press, 1997), pp. 15–33.
19 Cited from A. V. C. Schmidt's edition of the B Text (London: Dent, 1995), Passus XIX, lines 281–2. On Langland's treatment of the cardinal virtues, see J. A. Burrow, *Langland's Fictions* (Oxford: Clarendon Press, 1993), pp. 68–70.
20 *Hoccleve's Works: The Regiment of Princes*, ed. F. J. Furnivall, EETS, e.s. 72 (1897), lines 4756–7. Prudence leads the other cardinal virtues and lights their way like a lamp (compare line 4764, cited below) in the *Moralium dogma philosophorum*, probably by William of Conches: 'Has omnes praecedit prudentia quasi lucerna, tanquam viam aliis monstrans', *Patrologia Latina*, 171, col. 1010.

In what follows, Hoccleve advises the prince to ensure his future success by winning the love of his subjects and not alienating them by financial mismanagement. He must live within his income, and reward his servants regularly. The advice is eminently practical, but it leads to a final promise: such a ruler, if he fears God, will not only prosper on earth, he will also 'in hevene regne in perpetuel glorie' (4858). Prudence could get the best of both futures, the here and the hereafter. Similar thoughts are expressed by Christine de Pizan in her treatise *Le Livre des trois vertus*, addressed about 1405 to Margaret of Burgundy, a young princess of the French royal house. The speaker is Prudence Mondaine (book I, chapters XI–XIX). She recommends the princess to cultivate the good will of others and to manage her household finances with care – mundane, sometimes even Machiavellian, advice, which nevertheless culminates with the promise of a reward in heaven, as well as success on earth:

> Et en ceste maniere, par les vii susdits enseignements de Prudence tenir avec les autres susdictes vertus [. . .] pourra la sage dame acquerir los, gloire, renommee, grant honneur en cest monde et a la parfin paradis, qui est promis aux biens vivans.[21]

A later fifteenth-century mirror for princes, the *Active Policy of a Prince* by George Ashby (d. 1475), takes its whole organisation from the prudential division of the *tria tempora*.[22] Writing for the benefit of Edward, young son of Henry VI, Ashby advises the Prince successively to learn from the past (lines 127–217), to conduct himself wisely in the present (218–372), and to look always to the future (373–883). This long last section on *tempus futurum* applies the doctrine of *providentia* to the life of a fifteenth-century ruler. A vivid passage on the need to foresee and guard against treachery, conspiracy, and rebellion (380–456) evokes the perilous times of the Wars of the Roses. Ashby then goes on to speak of the need to make provision for the future well-being of the household, the commons, the law, and the army, as well as the ruler's own offspring. The words 'prudence', 'provision', and 'provide' occur frequently throughout this section, especially 'provide' in the pregnant sense defined by the Oxford English Dictionary: 'To exercise foresight in taking due measures in view of a possible event'.[23] At the end of the poem, Ashby leaves Edward with four lines which summarise the whole doctrine:

> Thinges past, remembre & wele devide;
> Thinges present, considre & wele governe;

---

[21] *Le Livre des trois vertus*, ed. C. C. Willard and E. Hicks (Paris: Champion, 1989), book I, chap. XIX (p. 76).
[22] Ed. M. Bateson, in *George Ashby's Poems*, EETS, e.s. 76 (1899), pp. 12–41.
[23] 'Provide' occurs at lines 387, 464, 485, 499, 520; 'provision' at 380, 488, 492, 628; 'prudence' or 'prudent(ly)' at 442, 575, 628, 676, 830.

For thinges commyng, prudently provide;
Al thinges in his tyme peise & discerne. (912–15)

Leaving *prudentia regnativa*, let me turn to a more domestic example. The *Tale of Melibee* is the second of the two contributions made by Geoffrey Chaucer to the entertainment on the pilgrimage to Canterbury. Chaucer translated this from a French version of a popular thirteenth-century Latin treatise by Albertanus of Brescia, entitled *Liber consolationis et consilii*.[24] Its main subject, in fact, is counsel rather than consolation: the need for mature consideration and good advice before embarking on a course of action. The story, such as it is, concerns a man, Melibee, whose wife and daughter are assaulted and injured in his absence. The question then is whether Melibee should go on to avenge himself on his enemies. He takes a variety of advice, some good, some bad; but it is his wife herself whose good counsel leads eventually to a peaceable outcome. The wife's name is Prudence; and it is this name that provides, in fact, the key to the whole; for what the tale displays, in painfully slow motion, is an instance of prudential *providentia* or 'purveiaunce' in action, anticipating future events and looking for a good end:

Thanne dame Prudence, whan she saugh the goode wyl of hir housbonde, delibered and took avys in hirself, thinkinge how she myghte brynge this nede unto a good conclusioun and to a good ende.[25]

She is using her third eye. Modern readers of the *Canterbury Tales* find little to admire or enjoy in the *Melibee*, and some critics have even tried to save the tale by reading it as a comic parody. Yet the contemporary popularity of the Latin original and its many vernacular derivatives is not difficult to understand.[26] The modern word 'prudence' is a chilly term for a much shrunken

---

24 Chaucer's French source, *Le Livre de Mellibee et Prudence*, is edited by J. B. Severs in *Sources and Analogues of Chaucer's Canterbury Tales*, ed. W. F. Bryan and G. Dempster (London: Routledge and Kegan Paul, 1958), pp. 568–614. For the Latin original, see the edition by T. Sundby, *Albertano of Brescia's Liber Consilii et Consolationis*, Chaucer Society Publications, Second Series, 8 (1873). In four chapters of the Latin, omitted in the French and therefore by Chaucer, Prudence describes the nature, species, effects, and acquisition of the virtue for which she stands (chapters VI–IX), citing Cicero, 'Seneca', and other authorities.

25 *Canterbury Tales*, VII. 1726–7. On prudence in Chaucer generally, see J. D. Burnley, *Chaucer's Language and the Philosophers' Tradition* (Cambridge: Brewer, 1979), chap. 3, 'Practical Wisdom'.

26 There were at least four French versions, as well as others in Italian, German, and Dutch: *Sources and Analogues*, p. 560. Chaucer's version, apart from its currency in the *Canterbury Tales*, appears as a separate item in five other manuscripts, evidence of its popularity: J. M. Manly and E. Rickert, *The Text of the Canterbury Tales*, 8 vols (Chicago: Chicago University Press, 1940), II, 371. In the section on taking counsel, which follows that on prudence in the *Regiment of Princes*, Hoccleve no doubt had *Melibee* chiefly in mind when invoking Chaucer as an authority on the matter: ed. cit. 4978–5012.

concept, nor do we today speak much of 'foresight', let alone 'counsel'; but for Chaucer and his age such words represented a still rich and living complex of moral ideas.

A better illustration of this richness is provided by one of the poems in the collection of animal fables composed by the Scottish poet Robert Henryson some time in the second half of the fifteenth century: *The Preaching of the Swallow*. Here it is not an allegorical female but a bird who represents prudent foresight.[27] The story opens in the spring countryside. Seeing a fowler planting hemp and flax seeds, the wise swallow vainly urges the other birds to scrape them up and eat them, since the man intends the crop to supply thread for his nets and so ensnare them. Again in the summer, when the plants have grown, the swallow desperately repeats the same advice, but again to no effect. So, when winter comes round, the fowler is able to make his nets, capture the birds, and kill them. The swallow alone survives to point the moral:

> 'Lo,' quod scho, 'thus it happinnis mony syis
> On thame that will not tak counsall nor reid
> Off prudent men or clerkis that ar wyis.' (1882–4)

These lines concisely summarise what the swallow had previously urged on her feather-headed fellow birds, notably in her summertime preaching:

> 'For clerkis sayis it is nocht sufficient
> To considder that is befoir thyne ee;
> Bot prudence is ane inwart argument
> That garris ane man provyde befoir and se
> Quhat gude, quhat evill, is liklie for to be
> Off everilk thingis at the fynall end,
> And swa fra perrell ethar him defend.' (1755–61)

The essence of prudence, again, is *providentia*: to 'provyde befoir', looking to the future, to the 'fynall end'. *Respice finem*.[28]

There is more to Henryson's poem than this, however; for he sets the doctrine of *providentia*, as expounded by the swallow in the story, in a much broader philosophical and spiritual context. The story itself is preceded by a

---

[27] On the significance of the swallow, see *The Poems of Robert Henryson*, ed. D. Fox (Oxford: Clarendon Press, 1981), pp. 275–6. My quotations are taken from this edition. I earlier discussed the poem in 'Henryson: *The Preaching of the Swallow*', in Burrow, *Essays on Medieval Literature* (Oxford: Clarendon Press, 1984), pp. 148–60.

[28] Prudence is a common theme of proverbs, both Latin and vernacular. The swallow quotes a line from the *Disticha Catonis* at line 1754: 'Nam levius laedit quicquid praevidimus ante' ('For whatever we foresee in advance does us less harm'). The foolish lark counters with anti-prudential sayings at lines 1763–7. See the notes of Fox.

prologue of thirteen stanzas concerned with God and his creation. The first of these stanzas already introduces the poem's key word, speaking of the perfect prudence of God, with this explanation:

> For quhy to him all thing is ay present,
> Rycht as it is or ony tyme sall be,
> Befoir the sicht off his divinitie.   (1626–8)

Since God is outside time, as Boethius among others explains, the past, the present, and the future are all alike eternally present to him. Hence one cannot, in the case of God, speak of either memory or foresight, in the ordinary human senses. God's *providentia* or 'purveiaunce' is perfect and infallible, beyond all human capacity. However, the poem then moves on to the time-bound world which God has created, and the prologue ends with a description of the four seasons of the year. This description both serves to introduce a story which passes through the seasons, from spring to winter, and also establishes the conditions under which human *providentia* must operate. Human foresight is necessary, because we, unlike God, cannot simply see the future; but it is also possible, because that future partakes of the divinely created order and is therefore not simply random and unpredictable. There are some things, at least, that the third eye of human prudence can perceive.

The Preaching of the Swallow, like all Henryson's fables, ends with a *moralitas*, here allegorising the story. The fowler is Satan; the seeds he sows are wicked thoughts; the foolish birds are worldly sinners; and the swallow is a holy preacher. The effect of these allegorical equations is to shift the theme of the poem onto a higher, eschatological plane:

> Best is bewar in maist prosperitie;
> For in this warld thair is na thing lestand;
> Is na man wait how lang his stait will stand,
> His lyfe will lest, nor how that he sall end
> Efter his deith, nor quhidder he sall wend.   (1939–43)

'Best is bewar'. Prudence is a virtue concerned not only with this world but also with the next. The future to which it looks extends beyond the grave; and, as Hoccleve and Christine among others observed, it holds out the promise of paradise.

The medieval system of the virtues included two whose orientation was specifically towards the future: hope among the theological virtues, and prudence among the cardinals. The latter had an extraordinary range of application, commonly eliding distinctions such as we today would make between the practical and the moral or spiritual. The third eye of prudence looked forward, at its furthest range, to the last things, death and judgement; but it also made possible what would now be called middle- and short-term planning. Princes and heads of households, politicians and businessmen, soldiers and sailors, poets and cooks – all, in their different ways, depended upon *providentia* to make the best of their activities and affairs. By 'obtaining knowledge of the future from knowledge of things present or past', they might hope to direct events to a good end, both in this world and in the next.

II
PROPHESYING FUTURES

Those who will call this time ancient:
The Futures of Prophecy and Poetry
In memoriam Howard H. Schless

PIERO BOITANI

THOSE who will call this time ancient are . . . you and I. The phrase is used by Dante in a famous passage of the *Paradiso* to indicate his posterity. It is a beautiful phrase, *color che questo tempo chiameranno antico*, for it implies a keen sense of the future on Dante's part, and also gives the future a very peculiar connotation, that of an age which looks as it were mainly to the past, at Dante's own time, and considers it not just old, but ancient. With a single stroke, the line in fact creates the future and shapes it as our present contemplating the abyss of time, at the beginning of which lies the speaker's present becoming in his own vision and under our very eyes a remote antiquity. There is only one other example I know in literature ancient, medieval, modern, and post-modern, of a sight that can leap so far and 'contain' the future – God's promise to Abraham of a seed as countless as the stars in Genesis, initiating the whole history of Israel, Christianity, and Islam.

This is the kind of future I am going to look into in this paper: the future a poet invents at the end of an epoch which its future eventually called the Middle Ages. I shall speak of Dante because I think he sums up several medieval notions of the future while transcending them both culturally and philosophically, and because I hope that his *summa* might provide a starting-point for our debate. Let me begin, therefore, by examining the passage from which the momentous line of my title comes.[1] We are in the fifth heaven of Para-

---

1 The text of the *Commedia* I used here is *La Commedia secondo l'antica vulgata*, ed. G. Petrocchi (Florence: Le Lettere, 1994 reprint). The English translations are from Dante, *The Divine Comedy*, trans. C. H. Sisson (Manchester: Carcanet, 1980). On cantos XV–XVII of *Paradiso* (the central ones of the cantica) see A. Jacomuzzi, *L'imago al cerchio* (Milan: Silva, 1968), pp. 155–91; J. T. Schnapp, *The Transfiguration of History at the Center of Dante's 'Paradise'* (Princeton: Princeton University Press, 1986); F. Forti, 'Cacciaguida', in *Enciclopedia Dantesca*, I (Rome: Istituto della Enciclopedia Italiana, 1970), pp. 733–9; M. M. Chiarenza, 'Time and Eternity in the Myths of Paradiso XVII', in *Dante, Petrarch, Boccaccio: Studies in*

dise, that of Mars, and Dante, accompanied by Beatrice, is talking to his ancestor, the Crusader Cacciaguida. Cacciaguida has, in Canto XV of *Paradiso*, welcomed his descendant with a series of lofty greetings that indirectly present Dante as a new Aeneas and a new Messiah. Then, through Cantos XV–XVI, he has described at length the virtuous Florence of the good old days. Finally, in Canto XVII he has, at his great-grandchild's own request, disclosed to Dante his imminent future: his exile, his political isolation, his first asylum at the court of Cangrande della Scala. Cacciaguida ends this part of his speech with a solemn investiture. I do not want you to envy your enemies, he says, *poscia che s'infutura la tua vita / via più là che 'l punir di lor perfidie*, because your fame extends into the future much further than the punishment of their evil doings.

And here we are again. Using his ancestor's lips, Dante once more storms the future. *S'infutura la tua vita* is a typically Dantean coinage, which of course means that the poet's name will last far into the future, yet says this by employing not the word for a shadowy projection such as fame, but life itself, *vita*. Life, that is, as this man's unique entity of flesh, blood, brain, soul, and work in real time and against death – a life that survives dying even as it lives, a life that 'infutures itself', that, thrusting itself into the future, shapes what will be by what already is.

This may be enough for the man, but it certainly is not for the poet. Cacciaguida has been weaving the cloth Dante had held out in readiness for him, so Dante now wants more of the same and pretends to ask his ancestor for further advice. If time rides against him to give him the blow of exile, he had better arm himself against the possibility that through his poetry (*per miei carmi*) he lose not only his native town, Florence, but also other places, other cities that might welcome him. Down in Hell and then up through Purgatory and Paradise he has learnt things which, if he repeats them, will have a bitter taste for many people. On the other hand,

> e s'io al vero son timido amico,
> temo di perder viver tra coloro
> che questo tempo chiameranno antico.

> (And if I am a timid friend to truth,
> I fear to lose the life I may have among those
> Who will call the present time, ancient times).[2]

---

the Italian Trecento in Honor of C. S. *Singleton*, ed. A. S. Bernardo and A. L. Pellegrini (Binghamton, N.Y.: Medieval and Renaissance Texts and Studies 22, 1983), pp. 133–56; A. M. Chiavacci Leonardi, 'Paradiso XVII', in *Filologia e critica dantesca: Studi offerti a Aldo Vallone* (Florence: Olschki, 1989), pp. 309–27; C. Hardie, 'Cacciaguida's Prophecy in *Paradiso* XVII', *Traditio*, 19 (1963), 267–94.
2 *Paradiso* XVII, 118–20; see Aristotle, *Nicomachean Ethics* I, iv, and *Convivio* IV, viii, 15.

The alternative, then, is between the many who might taste the strong bitterness of his words now and those who will call this time ancient, between loss of place in the present and loss of life in the future, the only life Dante will actually call *viver*. The price to pay for this *viver* is telling the truth in his poetry, in his account of the other world. Knowing that the report of Dante's journey through the other world is in fact a fiction, we, who are those that call his time ancient, feel that the commitment of this poet to his truth is more than a mere rhetorical gesture. He creates his truth and makes us believe in it as *the* truth. He imagines posterity and creates us. It is at this point that he receives full prophetic investiture. In answering him, Cacciaguida invites Dante to make manifest all that he has seen, removing all falsehood and letting people scratch wherever they may itch, because his voice will ultimately be 'vital food', and his cry shall be like the wind that strikes the highest summits with greater force:

> Ché se la voce tua sarà molesta
> nel primo gusto, vital nodrimento
> lascerà poi, quando sarà digesta.
>   Questo tuo grido farà come vento,
> che le più alte cime più percuote;
> e ciò non fa d'onor poco argomento.

> (For if your words are objectionable
> At the first taste, they will yield nourishment
> Afterwards, once they have been digested.
> This cry of yours will do as the wind does,
> Strike hardest on the summits which are highest;
> And that is no small argument of honour).[3]

Voce, *grido*, and *vento*, the three words which in *Purgatorio* XI had been employed – as we shall soon see – to indicate the vanity of human fame, are used here with a precise biblical connotation: Dante's writing is like John the Baptist's voice crying in the desert (*questo tuo grido* is the *Commedia* itself!),[4] like the wind that always accompanies the utterances of God and his prophets, like the bread of life Jesus promises his followers. That, precisely, is the future – when, after the first, harsh taste, in that *poi* which unfolds time, the message will have been 'digested', producing nourishment and life for humankind and honour for the writer. Dante's poetry is *vita* and *veritas*. And *via* indeed. For the way, as Cacciaguida now adds, identifies with the journey through the other world, through 'these wheels, the mountain, and the woeful valley', and the manner in which, during this journey, only the souls 'known through fame' have been shown to the pilgrim – because the mind of

3 *Paradiso* XVII, 130–5; cp. Boethius, *De Consolatione* III, 1, 3, for the vital food.
4 See A. M. Chiavacci Leonardi's Introduction and commentary to *Paradiso* XVII in her edition of the *Paradiso* (Milan: Mondadori, 1997), pp. 473–4 and 492.

the listener will not find rest nor fix its 'faith' unless it finds 'examples' that are well known. Fame, in other words, is the *via* to *veritas* and *vita* inasmuch as it is the stone upon which faith can be built.

By linking fame, writing, truth, and prophecy, Dante invents for poetry a wholly new future. He does this in two original ways. First, he fuses two different traditions, the classical and the Biblical, the pagan and the Christian. Cacciaguida appears as both an Anchises and a divine Father, Dante the poet as both a Virgil and an Evangelist. Second, to us, for whom Dante's age is indeed ancient, the souls he meets in the other world are not *di fama note* in the way they were in the poet's own time: rather, they are known to us almost exclusively through the fame Dante has bestowed on them with his poem. Without *Inferno* V Francesca and Paolo, historical characters as much as they are, would have sunk into total oblivion. Poetry does not only create posterity, it also supplies them with the content of the future – with what becomes myth.

I shall go back to this theme presently. But first I would like to explore as it were the mechanism of the future in Dante's *Commedia*. How does Cacciaguida gain sight of Dante's coming exile and 'infuturing' life? The poem is full of prophecies *ex post*, of vaticinations regarding events that have already taken place at the time Dante wrote about them. These are, of course, part of the fictional fabric of this as of many other pieces of literature. But one of Dante's peculiarities as a writer is that of supplying explanations even when they seem superfluous and, in doing so, disclosing new perspectives. In *Paradiso* XVII we learn that Cacciaguida is able to discern both the near and the distant future with the same clarity that on earth applies to elementary propositions of geometry because he contemplates things contingent, before they exist in themselves, in the 'point to which all times are present'. The blessed have the privilege of fixing their eyes on God, in whose eternal sight contingency, deployed only in the material world, is 'wholly depicted'. There is, in other words, a theological and a metaphysical reason for Cacciaguida's view of the future. God, as Thomas Aquinas maintains, 'knows all contingent things not only in their causes, but also as each one of them is actually in itself (*est actu in se ipso*)'. He knows them not in succession, but simultaneously, because they are present in his eternity.[5] The blessed exploit precisely this divine time warp. There, Dante says, all that will exist already is. The future of prophecy, and of the poetry that presents itself as prophecy, is the eternal present of full being.

Nothing would appear more alien to a modern than this ontological root of the future. Modernity attempts to pierce through the darkness of would-be contingencies by observing natural and human phenomena, by counting on the development of technology, and by studying history – that is, by trying to

---

5   *Summa Theologiae* 1a.14.13, resp. See also Boethius, *De Consolatione* V, 4–6.

decipher the world of becoming, not that of being. True, our scientific and economic laws are often enough considered articles of faith, with disastrous consequences for our, and our children's, future. But the only way in which we can seriously imagine the future is by applying probability, if not mathematical certainty, to what exists, not to what is (though we frequently confuse the two or believe only in the former). Not so for Dante, nor I would hold for the Middle Ages in general. There certainly is a moment in medieval history when, as Jacques Le Goff told us over twenty years ago,[6] the time of the merchant takes shape next to that of the Church, and I have no doubt that, as the present volume itself indicates, the realities and necessities of building, administration, family succession, politics, and the law, did force human beings in Western Europe to think of the future in empirical terms. But experience is only the first step towards science, and in any case for a medieval Aristotelian the First Science is not physics but metaphysics.

Dante knows the new kind of time and of future, but decides to go beyond it. At the very beginning of his journey, when, just out of the dark wood, he tries to climb the *dilettoso colle* and is pushed back by the leopard, the lion, and the wolf, he feels like a merchant who, he says, buys goods and piles them up and then the time comes that makes him lose everything.[7] This is the time, so to speak, of capitalism – of investing, acquiring, stocking, losing. But immediately afterwards, when Virgil appears, Dante leaves the time of the merchant and enters a different temporal dimension, in which his pilgrimage will be one *all'etterno dal tempo*, from time to eternity.[8] Here again, the choice is for the future of being, not of existence. One of the most singular and significant punishments to which the damned in Dante's hell are subjected is not their being unable to see the future, but their being unable to see the present. Like longsighted people, they see things that are far in the future – Farinata says in *Inferno* X – because God's light still shines powerfully for them. But when these things come close or exist, when the future turns into the present, *tutto è vano / nostro intelletto*. And the supreme tragedy will occur when the future stops. Then, on Doomsday, the Epicureans, who believe that the soul dies with the body, will be buried forever in their infernal tombs with the bodies they will have taken back from the valley of Josaphat. Then, at the end of time, *tutta morta / fia nostra conoscenza*, all the knowledge of the damned shall be dead, *because* 'the door of the future will be locked'. There is a splendidly tragic paradox here, from which we – the modern Epicureans – might perhaps learn something. Human beings may preserve some kind of knowledge, may somehow survive, only if they can, however dimly, perceive the future. It is the greatest, albeit oblique, statement of the value of the future that the Middle Ages have left to us.

---

6 Jacques Le Goff, *Pour un autre moyen âge* (Paris: Gallimard, 1978).
7 *Inferno* I, 56.
8 See F. Masciandaro, *La problematica del tempo nella 'Commedia'* (Ravenna: Longo, 1976).

That this statement ought to be seen, as far as Dante is concerned, in what I would call a 'carnally metaphysical' perspective, is clear enough from the *Commedia*'s own inner future. The souls whom Dante meets during his journey are mere shadows or lights. But Dante firmly believes in the resurrection of the flesh, and this means that for him an extraordinary fullness of being is attached to the future. When, in *Inferno* VI, he asks Virgil whether the torments of the damned will increase, decrease or stay the same after the Last Judgment, Virgil replies with the logic of Aristotle's *Ethics*, according to which the more perfect a being is, the more is it capable of experiencing joy and pain. Although the damned will never reach absolute perfection, yet they will receive 'more being' once they pick up their bodies again, because the true being of a human is the complete union of flesh and spirit. Hence their torments will be greater after Doomsday than they are now. The same logic applies to the blessed, as no less a soul than Solomon explains in *Paradiso* XIV. Here, what strikes the reader is the triumph of the *flesh* that dominates the speaker's view of the future.[9] When – Solomon says – our flesh, then glorified and holy, is put on us once more, our persons will be in greater perfection as being complete at last, and therefore the light which is now given us by God will increase. Yet this is not all: the present effulgence of the blessed will in fact be far surpassed in brightness by the flesh which the earth now covers, like (here Dante borrows the image from Bonaventure,[10] but goes far beyond it) charcoal which gives out a flame and yet glows more brightly than the flame itself so that it keeps its outline and appearance:

> Ma sì come carbon che fiamma rende,
> e per vivo candor quella soverchia,
> sì che la sua parvenza si difende;
>   così questo folgor che già ne cerchia
> fia vinto in apparenza da la carne
> che tutto dì la terra ricoperchia.

> (But, like charcoal which gives out a flame
> And yet glows more brightly than the flame itself
> So that it keeps its outline and appearance,
> So the radiance which surrounds us now
> Will be outshone by the brilliance of the flesh
> Which now lies buried in the earth).[11]

---

9   See G. Muresu, 'La "gloria della carne": disfacimento e trasfigurazione (*Paradiso* XIV)', *Rassegna della letteratura italiana*, 91 (1987), 253–68; P. Dronke, '*Orizzonte che rischiari*: Notes towards the Interpretation of *Paradiso* XIV', now in his *The Medieval Poet and his World* (Rome: Edizioni di Storia e Letteratura, 1984), pp. 407–30.

10   *In IV Sententiarum . . . Libros*, d. 49, p. 2, a. 2, quoted by A. M. Chiavacci Leonardi in her commentary to the *Paradiso*, p. 397.

11   *Paradiso* XIV, 52–7.

The flesh is the charcoal, the concrete substance and the core of light. The future of ontology is paradoxically materialistic. There is no mere mysticism in this vision of the future, nor just a view by analogy as in Paul's famous 1 Corinthians 15 – no seed sown in death and quickened into grain, no difference between the glory of the bodies celestial and that of the bodies terrestrial, but rather the overwhelming brightness of the latter. Furthermore, when Solomon ends his speech, the spirits of the *sapientes* in the heaven of the Sun are so quick to say *Amen!* that 'truly', Dante writes, 'they showed desire for their dead bodies'. But this desire is not heavenly, it is rooted in completely earthly love, as Dante immediately specifies in a splendid aside:

> forse non pur per lor, ma per le mamme,
> per li padri e per li altri che fuor cari
> anzi che fosser sempiterne fiamme.

> (Perhaps not just for themselves, but for their mothers,
> For their fathers and others who were dear to them
> Before they turned into eternal flames).[12]

The glory of the resurrection of the flesh is subject to the laws of the flesh, in fact in a sense it appears to be but a projection of the flesh's own human attachments. Here the ultimate future, preached by centuries of Christian theology on the strength of Jesus' resurrection as recounted in the Gospels, is made to grow out of man's deepest feelings; it shines as the fulfilment of the most elemental present. This is neither the future of the prophet nor that of the poet, but the future, so to speak, of mummy and daddy.

Dante's final horizon is, then, the eternity of reunion, the future of the individual being rooted in his or her earthly past. But this will only come at the end of time. Before that moment there lies the future of history, the future humankind has to go through as such, as a social and political body. Here, what dominates Dante is anxiety, urgency, eschatological passion. Dante is perfectly capable of envisaging the immediate, material future. In *Purgatorio* XXIII, for instance, he has Forese Donati utter a marvellous prophecy of the kind we still used to get from Catholic priests in the 1950s and which you might hear today from Muslim fundamentalists. Already I can see a time ahead – Forese says – in which the impudent women of Florence will be preached against from the pulpit because they go about showing their breasts to the very nipples! But Dante does not seem to be interested, except as a conservative censor, in this Boccaccesque future of topless ladies. He believes, instead, that the time in which he lives belongs to the sixth and last age of the world, that the movement of the heavens will soon come to an end, and that Paradise itself already is almost full[13] – in short, he thinks that Doomsday is imminent.

12 *Paradiso* XIV, 64–6.
13 *Convivio* II, xiv, 13–14; *Paradiso* XXX, 131–2.

His view of the future is conditioned by this belief, which he shares with early Christians as well as with later Joachimite preachers and contemporary Spiritual Franciscans.[14] And it is here that his prophetic voice rings out most loudly and most dramatically. It would lie beside the scope of this paper to explore this very peculiar dimension of Dante's future. But we must not forget how important it is in his works and in the fabric itself of the *Commedia*. From the very beginning of the poem, in *Inferno* I, readers are faced with Virgil's dark prophecy about the *veltro*, the Hound that, born 'between *feltro* and *feltro*', will feed on neither land nor money, but on wisdom, love and virtue, and will pursue the whorish wolf of greed in every city, making her die with pain and driving her back to Hell, where she belongs. The same prophecy is hinted at in *Purgatorio* XX, and its thrust is then picked up again in *Purgatorio* XXXIII, where it is presented as the final part of the pageant which precedes, accompanies and follows Beatrice's appearance. Here, the Hound is replaced by an even more mysterious 515 who, Beatrice says, will be sent by God to kill the whore and the giant that have played such a prominent role in her procession.

What interests me here is not so much who the Hound and the 515 might be.[15] If one places these passages in the context of Dante's Letters, the *Monarchia*, and other references in the *Commedia* itself, it seems very likely that, by both the *veltro* and the Leader (515 translated into Roman numerals and then turned into an anagram yields *DVX*), the poet meant a Roman emperor, more specifically Henry VII, who should defeat the avarice of the Papacy (and of Paris and Florence) and bring order back to Italy and Europe. What seems to me essential to note is, rather, that this eschatological vision of the future – a future, I repeat, which Dante feels is very close – is founded on his theological view of history, that is, of the past (the 515 comes at the end of a procession which allegorically re-enacts the whole human history from the expectation of Christ's first coming in the Old and New Testament to the history of the Church from the Incarnation to 1300), and on his political convictions, that is, on his view of the present. In other words, Dante tries to foresee the future in a manner which is not substantially different from that of the modern political scientist. Where, on the other hand, his method is entirely different is in the language and the imagery of the projection. These are not mathematical, but classical, medieval, and above all biblical: Virgil's Fourth

---

14 See M. Reeves, *The Influence of Prophecy in the Later Middle Ages: A Study in Joachimism* (Oxford: Clarendon Press, 1969); Norman Cohn, *The Pursuit of the Millennium*, rev. edn (London: Temple Smith, 1970); C. T. Davis, 'Dante's Vision of History' and 'Poverty and Eschatology in the *Commedia*', in *Dante's Italy and Other Essays* (Philadelphia: University of Pennsylvania Press, 1984), pp. 23–70.

15 The literature is of course vast. The essential contributions, with those of C. T. Davis quoted above, are the following: C. T. Davis, 'Veltro', in *Enciclopedia Dantesca*, V, 908–12; R. E. Kaske, 'Dante's "DXV" and "Veltro" ', *Traditio*, 17 (1961), 185–254; J. Hein, *Enigmaticité et messianisme dans la 'Divine Comedie'* (Florence: Olschki, 1992).

Eclogue, the Sibylline oracles, the prophecies of the Tiburtine Sibyl, Adso, pseudo-Methodius, Jeremiah, Daniel, and in particular Revelation, with whose seven golden candelabra the procession of *Purgatorio* XXIX begins and on whose 666 the 515 of *Purgatorio* XXXIII is modelled.[16]

Yet it is precisely the language and the imagery that make the difference with the modern political scientist: Dante's is in no way a forecast, but a prophecy. There is no calculation of probabilities in his lines, but an obscure certainty, a passionate anxiety, an enigmatic fury and despair – in short, an apocalyptic frame of mind. And indeed, Beatrice's speech on the 515 ends with a prophetic investiture that anticipates Cacciaguida's:

> Tu nota; e sì come da me son porte,
> così queste parole segna a' vivi
> del viver ch'è un correre a la morte.

> (Take note: and as my words are carried from me,
> Make sure that they are delivered to the living
> Whose life is nothing but a race to death).[17]

The prophet and the poet are one and the same thing. Yet, significantly, the audience of both are not those who will call this time ancient, but all those who live in the present and whose contingent future is but a race to death.

It is the prospect of death that determines Dante's last idea of the future, the survival of fame and poetry. I have examined elsewhere the very ancient ideal of *fama* which, from *Gilgamesh* to classical literature, from the Bible through Christian writings, from epic to lyric and courtly poetry, from philosophy to theology, pervades the *imaginaire* of Western man.[18] Dante is heir to this tradition and at the same time an innovator. The roots of his thought about fame appear, in the first place, firmly classical. The incarnation itself of glory and poetic tradition is for him Virgil, 'famous sage' and 'honour and light of the other poets', as Dante calls him when he meets him in the dark wood, and 'glory of Latin . . . through whom our language showed all its

---

[16] See N. Mineo, *Profetismo e apocalittica in Dante* (Catania: Facoltà di Lettere, Università di Catania, 1968); P. Armour, 'L'"Apocalisse" nel canto XXIX del "Purgatorio" ', in *Dante e la Bibbia*, ed. G. Barblan (Florence: Olschki, 1986), pp. 145–9; D. Costa, *Irenic Apocalypse: Some Uses of Apocalyptic in Dante, Petrarch and Rabelais* (Saratoga: Anma Libri, 1981); R. B. Herzman, 'Dante and the Apocalypse', in *The Apocalypse in the Middle Ages*, ed. R. K. Emmerson and B. McGinn (Ithaca: Cornell University Press, 1992), pp. 398–413. For the final cantos of *Purgatorio*, see K. Foster, *God's Tree* (London: Blackfriars, 1957), pp. 33–49; P. Dronke, *Dante and Medieval Latin Traditions* (Cambridge: Cambridge University Press, 1986), pp. 55–81; P. Armour, *Dante's Griffin and the History of the World* (Oxford: Clarendon Press, 1989); J. A. Scott, *Dante's Purgatory* (Philadelphia: University of Pennsylvania Press, 1996).

[17] *Purgatorio* XXXIII, 52–4.

[18] *Chaucer and the Imaginary World of Fame* (Cambridge: Brewer, 1984).

power', as the troubadour Sordello proclaims in *Purgatorio* VII.[19] Beatrice herself, the lady who embodies Christian love, faith, and theology, acknowledges, with words inspired by the *Aeneid*, Virgil's fame, a survival across the abyss of time, from the past through the present and on to the future, until the end of the world:

> O anima cortese mantoana,
> di cui la fama ancor nel mondo dura,
> e durerà quanto 'l mondo lontana . . .
>
> (O courteous spirit of that Mantuan
> Whose fame endures still in the world, and will
> Endure as long as the world itself shall last).[20]

That for Dante the past of pagan culture survives in a very special future is witnessed by Limbo, the place where, forever desiring without any hope to see God, are confined Trojan and Roman legendary and historical characters, ancient and Arabic scientists and philosophers, and the great classical poets. All these, whom Dante himself calls 'spiriti magni', are characterized by magnanimity as conceived in Aristotle's *Ethics* and hence as having its essence in honour, the greatest of the external goods, the prize of virtue attributed to the gods themselves.[21] Dante, however, goes far beyond Aristotle and medieval theology. For him, that honour so typical of earthly life is also mirrored in the other world. The fame of these spirits, which still resounds on earth, acquires a special grace in heaven which – Virgil, who is one of them, explains – keeps them separate from the other inhabitants of Limbo and of Hell. In short, Greek *timē* cannot save, but is somehow stronger than an exclusively Christian horizon.

Virgil himself is after all a strong upholder of fame, an active ideologist of it. When he and Dante reach the steep stones of Malebolge, Dante, out of breath, sits down. Virgil immediately presses him to get up, because, he says, sitting on a cushion or staying in bed is not the way to fame, without which a man spends his whole life leaving such traces upon earth as smoke leaves in air, or foam in water.[22] The images used in these lines derive from a passage in the Book of Wisdom where the unjust are seen as pronouncing them 'in anguish of spirit' on Doomsday. 'Talia dixerunt in inferno hi qui peccaverunt', the Vulgate recites, 'because the hope of the ungodly is like a light hoarfrost driven away by a storm, like smoke dispersed before the wind', whereas the hope of the just is 'full of immortality'.[23] The point, here, is that Dante's Virgil replaces 'hope' by 'fame', thus making the pagan idea of the latter be

---

19 *Inferno* I, 82–4, 89; *Purgatorio* VII, 16–18.
20 *Inferno* II, 58–60.
21 *Inferno* IV, 73–151; see F. Forti, *Magnanimitade* (Bologna: Patron, 1977), pp. 9–48.
22 *Inferno* XXIV, 46–51.
23 Wisdom 5. 14–16.

supported by 'Solomon', and interpreting Wisdom itself the way in which Sapiential literature ought in fact to be read, i.e., as an eclectic encounter of Hebrew and Greek culture. In this original and very modern manner the roots of Dante's thought about fame go with Antiquity beyond Christianity and with the Bible beyond Antiquity.

At the same time, through Virgil's use of Wisdom, Dante explains why (with a few notable exceptions he disregards both as a character and as a poet) his damned obsessively long for fame – because, according to 'Solomon', those who have sinned and are in Hell feel the transience of life and renown as a bursting pain. Deprived of true immortality and condemned to eternal death, they hang on to the earthly 'vestige' that Dante can give them by recording their names. Brunetto Latini, who in his lifetime taught Dante 'how man makes himself eternal', recommends to his pupil his own work, the *Tresor*, in which, he says, he still lives, and tells him he cannot fail to reach a 'glorious port'. The tragic irony, of course, is that the eternity and the glory of which Brunetto and Dante speak are radically different things, the former's being earthly, the latter's heavenly.[24] Fame, in sum, is the only future of Hell, and the poet who chooses whether or not to remember any of the damned is the god of fame and of the future throughout the *Inferno*.

The perspective changes in Purgatory and Paradise, but not to the point of being completely overturned. A central Canto in the *Commedia* is *Purgatorio* XI,[25] where the proud are punished and where Dante, through the famous illuminator Oderisi da Gubbio, condemns vainglory, one of pride's daughters and the constant pagan and Christian counterpart to fame. Oderisi uses the biblical images of wind and grass as the symbols of fame's transience, but his apparently Boethian address contains qualifications worth noting. First, he speaks against the empty glory of human endeavours which, he says, remains green on top, as if it were a tree's foliage, for a very short time *se non è giunta da l'etati grosse*, unless it be followed by rough, barbarous ages. Thus, fame is a question of degree of civilisation: in an age of decadence, the glory of a past artist survives longer; in an age of splendour, it dies sooner. It is an idea of the future of culture that looks exactly opposite to ours.

Oderisi then applies his idea of vainglory to the present and the immediate future, where his own renown is already being overcome by that of another illuminator, Franco Bolognese. Finally, he turns to the history of painting and poetry, with Cimabue being supplanted by Giotto, 'so that the former's fame is dark', and with Guido Cavalcanti replacing Guido Guinizzelli in the 'gloria de la lingua', and both being about to be ousted by a third poet who clearly is Dante himself:

---

[24] *Inferno* XV, 119–20; 55–7.
[25] On which see A. Quaglio's commentary in D. Alighieri, *Commedia, Purgatorio*, ed. A. E. Quaglio and E. Pasquini (Milan: Garzanti, 1982), and A. M. Chiavacci Leonardi's Introduction and commentary in her edition of the *Purgatorio* (Milan: Mondadori, 1994).

> Credette Cimabue ne la pittura
> tener lo campo, e ora ha Giotto il grido,
> sì che la fama di colui è scura.
>   Così ha tolto l'uno a l'altro Guido
> la gloria de la lingua; e forse è nato
> chi l'uno e l'altro caccerà del nido.
>
> (Cimabue thought he held the field
> In painting, and now the cry is for Giotto,
> So that the other's fame is now obscured.
> So one Guido has taken from the other
> The glory of the language; and perhaps there is born
> One who may chase them both out of the nest).[26]

What Dante describes in these lines is not just the empty mechanism of earthly glory, but also no less than one of the two ways in which the arts establish their traditions and canons, in which, that is, they create their past and their future. And there is no doubt that for him this is a very modern, true *agon*, a Freudian-Oedipal, Bloomian struggle each artist engages in against his predecessor or father.[27] Cimabue thought he 'held the field' of battle, and now Giotto has the 'grido', that is, both the *rumor* or fame and the cry of victory. One Guido has wrestled from the other the glory of the new poetry, and the third contestant will, as the Italian very significantly has it, 'kick or chase them both out of their nests'. Constant warfare is the future of poetry.

Only at this point does Oderisi return to orthodox ideas of vainglory by inserting it within increasingly wider circles of images. Here is worldly fame, a breath of wind which moves from place to place, from man to man. Here is the fame of an old man, ready to part with his flesh, and that of a baby who dies before he can even say the first words: they are exactly the same. The time of man's life and death will make no difference to fame when a thousand years have passed. And compared to eternity a thousand years are shorter than the flickering of an eye compared to the movement of the slowest heaven, which turns around one degree every hundred years![28] There indeed is our future, the drying of grass into hay, the falling off of flowers, the vanity of vanities.

In the perspective of eternity, the future of fame is flattened out. As the time of words, it has no horizon of being, but peters out in the increasing entropy of becoming. But this does not mean that the transmission of culture and the struggle for the canon are any less urgent. Dante condemns vainglory whilst exalting himself and paradoxically saving the future of decadence.

---

26 *Purgatorio* XI, 94–9.
27 See H. Bloom, *Agon* (Oxford: Oxford University Press, 1982).
28 See *Purgatorio* XI, 100–8.

Nothing, of course, can ultimately preserve a name, but in history memory is saved by the poet's *Wille zur Macht* and by . . . the Dark Ages.

Nor is the future opened up by fame necessarily confined to Hell. In *Paradiso* VI, where the glory of the Roman Eagle is extolled, Justinian describes the good spirits who dwell in the heaven of Mercury as people who have acted 'in order to gain honour and fame'. In *Paradiso* IX Cunizza da Romano, in introducing the soul of Folco of Marseilles, praises his fame and the way by which 'man should make himself excel so that his first life may leave another one after it'. Fame, here a projection of virtue, produces *vita*, a future both on earth and in heaven.

But in *Purgatorio* and *Paradiso* it is poetry that discloses increasing future vistas. The name which lasts most and most honours a man – Statius proclaims in *Purgatorio* XXI – is that of the poet. And indeed Dante's and Virgil's encounter with the author of the *Thebaid* represents Dante's dramatic enactment of the second way in which poetic tradition, the school of poetry, is formed. There is no *agon* here, no Oedipal struggle against the father, but rather a mother-son relationship. The *Aeneid*, the 'divine flame that has kindled more than a thousand', was – Statius reveals – his *mamma* and *nutrice, poetando*. And Virgil's poetry acted as prophecy, too, as the seed of another culture: it was the Fourth Eclogue that showed Statius, he remarks in *Purgatorio* XXII, the way to true faith, turning him into a Christian. Poetry begets poetry; poetry foreshadows and generates the future. The feeling is so intense, and the two concepts are so powerfully dramatised that modern readers have the impression that no humanist, no Renaissance writer, no Romantic poet has ever come as close as Dante to the same faith in poetry as the mother itself of the future.

As the pilgrim ascends higher up into Paradise, poetry becomes increasingly important. Immediately after the meeting with Cacciaguida with which I started this paper, Dante invokes the Pegasean goddess, i.e., the poetic muse who, he writes, makes human minds glorious and long-lasting, while they in turn give, with her help, immortal life to cities and kingdoms.[29] Poetry is here once and for all consecrated as the double key to the future. Poetry perpetuates the name of its servants, who perpetuate through poetry the life of things, making human society survive as memory.

This conception, which is after all the classical one and which is based on the strength of the written word in a world dominated by orality, will remain central in post-medieval civilisation (and indeed become dominant with printing) down to the second industrial revolution, that is, to our own time of new oral media. In Dante, it acquires a particular connotation when he comes to write the *Paradiso*. Throughout the third cantica, he pursues even more keenly than in the preceding two his own personal glory as a poet. It is

---

[29] *Paradiso* XVIII, 82–7.

here that, aware of the 'aringo', the supreme *agon* he has entered, he proclaims his poem 'sacred'; and here that he firmly and openly voices his hope for the laurel crown and the conquest of the Golden Fleece.[30] Yet Dante knows only too well that the glory of Him who moves all is the only truly blinding one and that it is ultimately ineffable. His purpose in the *Paradiso* will then be – as it is clear from Canto I – that of 'revealing' at least the *shadow* of the blessed kingdom recorded in his memory.[31] In one of the final invocations of the *Paradiso* and of the whole poem, right in the middle of the divine vision, Dante picks up and intensifies the prayer of Canto I, addressing God himself. With infinite humility and impudent boldness he asks the supreme Light to lend his mind a little of the splendour with which it shone then and to make his tongue so powerful that he might leave at least a spark of the divine glory to posterity, for, he ambiguously adds, 'if something of it comes back to my mind and sounds a little in these verses of mine, your triumph will more easily be conceived':

> O somma luce che tanto ti levi
> da' concetti mortali, a la mia mente
> ripresta un poco di quel che parevi,
>
> e fa la lingua mia tanto possente,
> ch'una favilla sol de la tua gloria
> possa lasciare a la futura gente;
>
> ché, per tornare alquanto a mia memoria
> e per sonare un poco in questi versi,
> più si conceperà di tua vittoria.

> (O supreme light who rise far above
> Mortal notions, lend my memory
> A little of what then appeared to me,
> And give my tongue all the power it needs
> So that a single spark of your glory
> May be transmitted to people in the future;
> For, if something of it comes back to my mind
> And sounds a little in these verses of mine,
> Your triumph will more easily be conceived).[32]

Una favilla sol de la tua gloria / possa lasciare a la futura gente. That, for Dante, is the ultimate future of his poetry – becoming a spark of the divine glory for those who will call his time ancient.

It is a nice irony to note that Dante's ideas of the future soon became ancient indeed. His apocalyptic and political prophecies proved to be com-

---

30 *Paradiso* I, 16–33; XXV, 1–9.
31 I have dealt with this theme most recently in 'Dante's Sublime: Ancient, Medieval and Modern', *Poetica*, 47 (1997), 1–32.
32 *Paradiso* XXXIII, 67–75.

pletely wrong, the future of being progressively lost relevance, the concept of the poet as a prophet turned into an increasingly rhetorical stance. Yet a first paradox is that the spark of that glory still survives, perhaps because the ages which followed Dante's were, are, really dark. And the second is that the poetry of the *Commedia* proved prophetic indeed, not in the sense nor in the sections Dante anticipated, but in exactly opposite ways. Modern literature, opera, cinema – one is tempted to say, modern social custom – would be inconceivable without Paolo and above all Francesca, the two murdered adulterers condemned by Dante and saved by time. Modern civilisation is founded upon the impulses to explore and go beyond all limits for which his Ulysses was sunk by an alien God. Is it astonishing that the future should have turned out to be but a sanctification of Hell?

Prophecy, Hagiography and St Thomas of Canterbury

PHYLLIS B. ROBERTS

IN 1996, the *New York Times*, one of the major newspapers in the United States, celebrated its centennial. By the standards of more ancient civilisations and cultures, this anniversary may seem hardly worth noting, but given the demise of so many newspapers and magazines in the last half century and the reputation of the *Times* as the newspaper of record, the achievement of a one-hundredth birthday was worthy of celebration. In honour of the occasion, several special feature issues were given over to a review of the *Times's* coverage of the events of the last century. Most striking, however, was an issue that appeared in late September 1996 called 'Looking Forward, Looking Back' which afforded a variety of writers on everything from fashion, to leisure, to the culture wars, to philosophy and 'pop' psychology to speculate about the next hundred years of the twenty-first century.

More to the point as we consider here the meaning of 'Medieval Futures', i.e., what the concept of the future meant for an age long past, was the editorial comment that how we view the future very much depends upon our perceptions of the past and present. Writers, artists and, perhaps most of all, reformers of various types 'have long deployed visions of the future as parables, offering insight into their times . . . [using] *then* as a prism through which to cast light on *now*'.[1]

Any discussion, therefore, of 'Medieval Futures' must take into account the role of prophecy, part of the vocabulary of those who articulate a vision of the future. As prophecy has long embodied a critique of the present, it has had its own critics and sceptics, some who would see it as little more than fortune-telling or gazing into a crystal ball. Nevertheless, one cannot deny the power of prophecy as prediction, as evidenced in the long and venerable ancient traditions of astrology and of the interpretation of dreams. In the Bible, for example, did not Pharaoh believe in and act upon Joseph's proph-

---

[1] Jack Rosenthal, 'Looking Forward, Looking Back', *New York Times Magazine*, 29 September 1996, 45.

ecy of seven fat years followed by seven lean years? (Genesis 41. 25–57.) Did not Shakespeare's Macbeth believe and act upon the witches' prediction that he would become Thane of Cawdor and king thereafter? (*Macbeth*, I.3.) Examples such as these, from sources sacred and secular, are potent reminders of a belief in the power of prophecy to predict the future, and, furthermore, prompt action upon those prophecies. In the course of this essay, which concerns itself with the prophecies that relate to the medieval St Thomas of Canterbury, we shall be examining a body of material that is significant, but not for the accuracy of the prophecies or how well they 'turned out'. What is important about these Becket prophecies is that they were a mirror, as it were, reflecting the 'now' of the Middle Ages that people often believed in and frequently acted upon. As a way of viewing the future, prophecy can never escape its 'then' and 'now'.

Moreover, the history of prophecy has also long been grounded in particular historical circumstances and reflective of the values of the society. The prophets of ancient Israel, for example, calling upon the children of Abraham to remember the covenant with Yahweh, in books such as Jeremiah, Hosea, and the Minor Prophets, railed against the evils of corruption and its consequences, and warned that punishment would be meted out by the enemies of the Israelites who would become the instruments of the wrath of the Lord. The language of biblical prophecy also varied. It could be simple and direct or more figurative and ornate. Isaiah and Ezekiel offer examples of the use of allegory and parable in the prophetic tradition, while in the Apocalypse of St John the Divine, prophecy takes the form of a vision. From its very beginnings, Christianity had to deal with the greatest of prophecies, the expectation of a transformation of the world by Christ's second coming. The Church had to accommodate and/or fight against millennial and chiliastic beliefs that hoped for a deliverance from the evils of the world and its existing order.[2]

The classical world also had a long tradition of divination and prophecy embodied in such works as the Sibylline Books, which consisted chiefly of admonitions 'to adopt certain rituals to expiate some evil or to avert some threatened calamity',[3] and various other short collections of Greek Oracles, which were either clear and direct or evasive and deliberately enigmatic like the Oracle at Delphi. Prophecy must therefore be viewed in context. Its links with a particular present, biblical or classical, Jewish or Christian, offer a particular vision through which future events were often seen and interpreted.

---

[2] For a discussion of the biblical and classical sources of prophecy, see Rupert Taylor, *The Political Prophecy in England* (New York: Columbia University Press, 1911), pp. 27–38, and Jonathan K. Van Patten, 'Magic, Prophecy, and the Law of Treason in Reformation England', *The American Journal of Legal History*, 27 (1983), 1–31 (pp. 27–8). See also the essays in the recently published volume *Prophecy: The Power of Inspired Language in History 1300–2000*, ed. Bertrand Taithe and Tim Thornton (Stroud: Sutton, 1997).

[3] Taylor, p. 28.

Prophecies also collected around great persons, heroes, and in the Christian tradition, prophecy came to be linked with hagiography, which brings us, as we consider the meaning of 'Medieval Futures', to Chaucer's 'holy, blissful martyr' – St Thomas of Canterbury.

I shall be dealing with three major examples of Becket prophecies: first, those prophecies and legends that circulated after the martyrdom in 1170, which related to Becket himself and fashioned the hagiography and cult of Becket; second, Becket prophecies that came to be associated with the sanctification of the English monarchy and were used to legitimise the rule of fourteenth- and fifteenth-century kings; finally, in the sixteenth century, how prophecies involving Becket were linked to the anti-royal propaganda of the age and formed the background of Henry VIII's proclamation of 1538 which contained specific directives purging the name and image of Thomas Becket.

The details of Thomas Becket's life, his friendship with King Henry II and his elevation from royal chancellor to archbishop of Canterbury, have become familiar to a variety of audiences. The drama of Thomas's life and martyrdom at the hands of King Henry's knights in the Cathedral Church at Canterbury on 29 December 1170 has attracted the attention of scholars, historians and playwrights as well.[4] As David Knowles has observed, that Tuesday afternoon at Canterbury had remarkable coverage.[5] Nine of Becket's biographers describe the murder in detail; four were actually present. News of the murder in the cathedral at Canterbury spread rapidly, provoking a cry of horror throughout Christendom. Becket soon came to be seen as dying a martyr for the Church whose rights and freedoms were threatened by an evil king. The Church acted swiftly, and Thomas Becket was canonised on 21 February 1173, less than three years later. In July 1174, King Henry II did public penance at Canterbury. Pilgrimages to Canterbury began soon after the martyrdom and quickly attracted many illustrious visitors, including King Richard Lion Heart of England, King Louis VII of France, the archbishops of Cologne and Lyon, and Lothar of Segni, later to be Pope Innocent III, who visited Canterbury while still a young student in Paris. Finally, after many years of delay and frustrating negotiation, another controversial archbishop, Stephen Langton, presided over the translation of the relics of St Thomas the martyr to a new shrine at Canterbury on Tuesday 7 July 1220.

In the years following the martyrdom and the translation of the relics, the cult of St Thomas Becket spread rapidly across western Europe mixing fact,

---

[4] For accounts of Becket's life and the sequence of events leading up to his murder, see Frank Barlow, *Thomas Becket* (London: Weidenfeld and Nicolson, 1986); David Knowles, *Thomas Becket* (London: Adam & Charles Black, 1970); *Materials for the History of Thomas Becket, Archbishop of Canterbury*, ed. J. C. Robertson, Rolls Series, 6 vols (London, 1875–85); Phyllis B. Roberts, *Thomas Becket in the Medieval Latin Preaching Tradition: An Inventory of Sermons about St Thomas Becket c.1170–c.1400*, Instrumenta Patristica, 25 (The Hague: Martinus Nijhoff, 1992), pp. 9–12.

[5] Knowles, p. 140.

legend and prophecy. Among the earliest biographers, William fitzStephen, who wrote his *Life* between 1173 and 1175 and has been described as 'the best and most satisfying of all the biographers',[6] includes anecdotal material that illustrates how prophecies relating to Becket himself were woven into the developing legend of Becket:

> The Lord knew and predestined the blessed Thomas [to His service] before ever he issued from the womb and revealed to his mother what manner of man he would be. For during pregnancy she saw in a dream that she carried in her womb the whole church of Canterbury. As soon as the child saw the light of day, the midwife lifted him up in her arms saying, 'I have raised from the ground a future archbishop'.[7]

Stories such as these became the common currency of preachers, who played a not inconsiderable role in the diffusion of the cult of the martyred archbishop. Extant sermons preached on the occasion of the two feastdays, 29 December, the date of his death, and 7 July, the date of the translation of the relics, illustrate how the mix of the Becket of history, legend and prophecy was understood by the preachers of the Church in the high and late Middle Ages and interpreted to audiences clerical and lay. One of the most colourful of the tales was the account of Thomas's father Gilbert, his supposed visit to Jerusalem and marriage to a Saracen princess who was then converted to Christianity. The story, which apparently originated within a hundred years of Becket's death,[8] also found its way into the sermons of medieval preachers, who found the tale prophetic and exemplary of Thomas's sanctity.[9]

Prophecies relating to Becket's death were contained in the writings of Benedict of Peterborough, who was present in the church at the time of the martyrdom, was first custodian of the shrine and compiled the most important and influential collection of the miracles.[10] Writing about three years after Becket's death, in 1173–74, Benedict relates prophecies that showed that the future glory of Canterbury had been predicted by a monk of Jerusalem ten years before the martyrdom itself, and that an inhabitant of Argentam [i.e. Strasbourg] had a supernatural prophecy of the martyrdom before the news actually reached the town.[11]

These prophecies about Becket's birth and death, heralded by dreams and

---

6 George Greenaway, 'Introduction', in *The Life and Death of Thomas Becket*, ed. and trans. George Greenaway (London: The Folio Society, 1961), p. 28.

7 *The Life and Death of Thomas Becket*, p. 35.

8 Paul A. Brown, *The Development of the Legend of Thomas Becket* (Philadelphia: University of Pennsylvania, 1930), p. 257.

9 See Roberts, pp. 164, 189.

10 Barlow, p. 4.

11 Brown, p. 257.

portents,[12] were closely associated with the development and spread of the cult of the martyred archbishop. Originating in the earliest *Lives* and becoming a part of the hagiographical *corpus*, they made Thomas of Canterbury one of the major saints in the medieval English church.

It is significant, I think, that despite the historical circumstances of Becket's career in the service of the king and subsequent martyrdom in the cause of ecclesiastical liberties, the earlier prophetic traditions about Becket were not especially political. They served the purposes of hagiographical devotion and of the creation and diffusion of the cult of the saint. Not so the second group of Becket prophecies, which were associated with the sanctification of the monarchy and meet the definition of 'political prophecy' offered by Rupert Taylor in his study of the genre published in 1911: 'applying to any expression of thought, written or spoken, in which an attempt is made to foretell coming events of a political nature' and which take some 'literary form'.[13]

As examples of these Becket 'political' prophecies I shall cite two of the most prominent: first, those prophecies that relate to the reign of Edward III and which are contained in an alliterative poem written c.1356 in the vernacular, and second, those prophecies many of which are in Latin and concern the ampulla of holy oil allegedly found in the Tower of London by Richard II to be used for anointing kings of England.[14] As we shall see, these Becket prophecies are a useful means for viewing the condition of the fourteenth- and fifteenth-century monarchy.

The poem *Saint Thomas of Canterbury* survives in two manuscripts, giving parts of a longer piece which dealt with the travels of Thomas Becket. In it we read that Becket left Rome for Pisa, where he found masons at work on a tower of alabaster near a neglected shrine of the Virgin. In Pisa, Becket called the attention of the master workman to the shrine of the Virgin and contributed to its becoming a place of pilgrimage. There were subsequent stops in Basel, where, when he went into the church to celebrate mass, he discovered that his missal was missing and had probably been left in Rome. At a loss for what to do next, the author goes on to describe how a wonderful book fell upon the altar. The poem continues that, after obtaining a bridle to replace one that had been stolen while he was in the church, Becket went on to Avignon where, kneeling and kissing the ground, he prophesied that the place would some day be the seat of the papacy.

The material in the poem that relates most particularly to English affairs

---

12 Brown, p. 258.

13 Taylor, p. 2.

14 Taylor, p. 58. On political prophecies relating to Becket, see Rossell Hope Robbins, 'Poems Dealing with Contemporary Conditions', in *A Manual of the Writings in Middle English 1050–1500*, vol. 5, ed. Albert E. Hartung (New Haven: Connecticut Academy of Arts and Sciences, 1975), pp. 1528, 1722.

begins with Becket's arrival at Poitiers from Avignon. His host was a burgess of the town who was asked by Becket to identify the owner of a castle he saw under construction. Informed that the castle was being built at the command of King Charles, Becket begins to prophesy:

> There shall come, he said, two Boars from England and ruin the tower and the town, of whom one shall do much damage to the king and put him to flight, and the other pasture himself in the choicest fields of the kingdom. The people who heard these wonderful words reported them to King Charles, but he declined to cease the work 'for drede of a boar'. The Boar, said Thomas, shall be born of French and English blood and shall be matchless on earth. Thomas then went out into the fields and bade the masons build three crosses. At the first cross the King of France, said he, shall fall and lose his crown, at the second Archbishops and other church dignitaries shall die, at the third the crown shall fall in a battle of beardless boys.[15]

Another version of the poem goes on and in rather vivid detail describes the Boar's career in France, mentioning the burning of Abbeville and the battles of Mountjoy, Caen, Calais and Valois. There is then a prophecy of an invasion of the Boar's realm by a king from the North and the Boar's revenge at Berwick. After the capture of Berwick, a battle is predicted at Boulogne during which a two-headed Bird with an army of fifty thousand men sides with the enemy. There then follows an account of the capture of Paris and the defeat of the Bird. Afterwards, said Becket, the Boar shall win Milan, Lombardy, and the Bird's three crowns. He shall go on crusade to the Holy Land, whence (it appears) he is not to return. After his departure, the land is to be ruled by women or to be laid desolate by a pestilence. Edmund of Abingdon, who had not previously been mentioned, interrupts the proceedings and remarks on the lateness of the hour. An angel in blue orders Becket to close the book, from which it appears he had been reading, and carries the book up to Heaven. The poem closes as Becket and his companions resume their journey.[16]

Scholars have long noted the links between these prophecies and the wars of Edward III. In the version which mentions two Boars, these apparently stand for Edward III, who lived from 1312 to 1377, and his eldest son, Edward the Black Prince (1330–76); the one Boar of a second version is Edward III. Taylor examines the complex strands of the English prophetic tradition to show the borrowings from other well-known prophecies. Thus the two-headed Bird, for example, probably stands for the Holy Roman Emperor, who is referred to as the Eagle in another prophecy on the French wars, *The Prophecy of the Lion, the Lily, and the Son of Man*. The Eagle from the East at first comes to the aid of the Son of Man (Edward III in one interpretation) but

---

[15] Taylor, p. 59. From the version in Bodleian Library, MS Hatton 56.
[16] Taylor, pp. 59–60. From the version in Cambridge University Library, MS Kk.1.5.

loses his crown to the Lily (France). When the Lily lost it, the Son of Man was crowned with it. In this prophecy, the Son of Man takes the cross and makes a crusade to the Holy Land.

Becket was also linked to Edward III in the *Prophecy* of John of Bridlington, one of the most widely circulated prophecies of the fourteenth century,[17] which held that Edward III's accession in 1327 after the deposition of his father Edward II, had been earlier revealed to St Thomas, archbishop of Canterbury at a time when there was discord between Henry II and Henry, his eldest son and crowned heir.[18] Edward III had a long association with Canterbury, which he usually visited at least once a year. In 1353 he presented the cathedral with a gold statue of St Thomas at a cost of £40, one of many visits and gifts to Canterbury which continued to the end of his life.[19]

I turn now to the second of the Becket 'royal' prophecies, which is the well-known account of the holy oil of St Thomas of Canterbury. This prophecy, which had close associations with the accession of the Lancastrians in 1399, probably originated in its complete form as early as c.1340, but there is an earlier reference to it in a papal letter of 1318 in a reply to inquiries made on behalf of Edward II asking if the King should be anointed with the oil of St Thomas and if such unction would be beneficial.[20] According to the prophecy, the Virgin Mary appeared to the exiled Thomas of Canterbury as he was praying in the church of St Colombe in Sens. The Virgin presented Thomas with a golden eagle which contained a stone flask filled with oil and informed Thomas that the oil was to be used for the anointing of future (but unspecified) kings of England. The prophecy goes on to detail rather specific events. Thus, the king first anointed with the oil would recover Normandy and Aquitaine, without the use of force, and would be *maximus inter reges*. This same king would build many churches in the Holy Land, driving the pagans from Babylon, where many churches would also be built. Carrying the eagle in the royal bosom would ensure victory over one's enemies and the prosperity of the kingdom. The remainder of the prophecy provides details about the immediate disposal of the eagle and the oil, to be delivered in a leaden vase to William, a monk of St Cyprian of Poitiers.

The prophecy attests to the well-established association of Thomas Becket with visions that foretold distant events. Becket's earliest biographers, as we have seen, had described prophecies that related to Becket's birth and death and to his contemporaries. The prophecy of the holy oil, as T. A. Sandquist

---

17 On John of Bridlington, see Taylor, pp. 51–2, and A. G. Rigg, 'John of Bridlington's *Prophecy*: A New Look', *Speculum*, 63 (1988), 596–613.

18 See Livingston Corson, *A Finding List of Political Poems Referring to English Affairs of the XIII. and XIV. Centuries* (orig. publ. 1910, repr. New York: Burt Franklin, 1970), p. 35.

19 See W. M. Ormrod, 'The Personal Religion of Edward III', *Speculum*, 64 (1989), 849–77 (pp. 858–60).

20 See Walter Ullmann, 'Thomas Becket's Miraculous Oil', *Journal of Theological Studies*, 8 (1957), 129–53.

has observed, 'sheds valuable light upon the saint's posthumous reputation and also reveals something about the intellectual milieu of later medieval England'.[21] The prophecy appears in numerous manuscripts, with a broad geographical dispersion, and was widely popular during the fifteenth century.

It was in 1399, however, that the Becket prophecy reappeared in its fullest form and saw its fulfilment in the accession of Henry IV. The St Alban's chronicler Thomas of Walsingham, in his *Annales Ricardi Secundi et Henrici Quarti*, takes up the account of the fate of the golden eagle and the holy oil. I quote from Sandquist's summary:

> According to Walsingham the golden eagle lay hidden for a long time in the church of St. Gregory. At length the secret was revealed to a certain unnamed holy man. This discovery took place during the reign of Edward III when Henry, first duke of Lancaster, was fighting 'in those parts,' presumably near Poitiers. The holy man gave the treasure to the duke of Lancaster who in turn presented it to Edward, eldest son of King Edward III. It was intended that the oil would be used at the unction of the Black Prince. Walsingham notes that at the time of the discovery it was hoped that the Black Prince would be the king designated in the prophecy but that this hope proved false for the prince died before his father. When the Black Prince received the eagle he placed it in the Tower of London in a locked chest. A search was made for the eagle before the coronation in 1377 but it could not be found. Thus Richard II was not anointed with the oil of St. Thomas.[22]

The saga continues. Apparently Richard II was something of an antiquary and in 1399, while rummaging around in several chests in the tower (so Walsingham describes), he found one so securely locked that he ordered it to be broken open. We can well imagine what was in this chest! Therein the king found the eagle containing the ampulla of holy oil together with the 'writing' of the blessed martyr Thomas. Having learned of the powers of the holy oil, Richard asked Thomas Arundel, Archbishop of Canterbury, to anoint him with it, but his request was denied. Nonetheless, Richard was reported to have carried the treasure around with him to ward off all dangers. Finally, following the king's expedition to Ireland and his return late in the summer of 1399, the eagle and the holy oil were taken from him at Chester Castle by Archbishop Arundel, who informed the king that it was now clear whom the divine will favoured for anointing with the oil of St Thomas. The oil was intended for the coronation of Henry IV.[23]

The Becket prophecy is here linked with the accession of Henry IV and is therefore best known in the context of the Lancastrian usurpation. Nonethe-

---

[21] T. A. Sandquist, 'The Holy Oil of St. Thomas of Canterbury', in *Essays in Medieval History Presented to Bertie Wilkinson*, ed. T. A. Sandquist and Michael R. Powicke (Toronto: University of Toronto Press, 1969), pp. 330–44 (p. 333).

[22] Sandquist, p. 337.

[23] Sandquist, pp. 337–8.

less, it clearly had pre-Lancastrian origins, as mentioned earlier. While 'the claim to have received unction with the oil of St Thomas put the Lancastrian succession under the patronage of Canterbury's and England's premier saint in the most public and unambiguous manner',[24] the prophecy does not thereafter appear to have been exploited by either Henry IV or his successors in support of their dynasty.[25] The oil of St Thomas continued to be used in the English coronation rite until at least 1483 and probably until 1509.[26] While the prophecy clearly had its attractions for contemporaries as the prolific manuscript tradition attests, perhaps the best assessment of its significance lay in the rivalry of the English kings with the sacerdotal attributes of the French monarchy. It has been suggested that the prophecy probably represents the English desire to have an oil for the unction of their kings with as miraculous an origin as the oil of Clovis. In this context Marc Bloch may well have had the last word as he dismissed the prophecy as 'une médiocre imitation de la Sainte Ampoule',[27] a verdict borne out by the overwhelmingly important role played by the oil of Clovis in French history. As Walter Ullmann observed: 'The miraculous oil of Thomas Becket was not destined to have so great a future.'[28]

Ullmann's verdict was probably true for England, but in Wales, and in the Welsh language, the prophecy of Becket and the holy oil took on new life in another chapter in the transmission and significance of this tale. In a version of the prophecy in MS Peniarth 50, a manuscript of the fifteenth century in the National Library of Wales, the Welsh redactor added an introduction that provides an Arthurian background to the story of Thomas Becket receiving the oil from the Virgin Mary. Thus King Arthur receives a similar ampoule from the Virgin at Glastonbury. The oil is lost and is not heard from again until Thomas Becket went to Sens.[29] Dr C. Lloyd-Morgan, in her article 'Prophecy and Welsh Nationhood', has described in great detail the complexity of this Arthurian prehistory of the oil of St Thomas and the sources used by the Welsh redactor. For the purposes of our story here, what is significant is how the popular Becket prophecy came to serve the purposes of

---

[24] Christopher Wilson, 'The Tomb of Henry IV and the Holy Oil of St Thomas of Canterbury', in *Medieval Architecture and Its Intellectual Context: Studies in Honour of Peter Kidson*, ed. Eric Fernie and Paul Crossley (London: Hambledon Press, 1990), pp. 181–90 (p. 186).

[25] Sandquist, p. 344.

[26] Wilson, p. 189.

[27] Quoted by Sandquist, p. 336.

[28] Ullmann, p. 133.

[29] See the articles by Dr Ceridwen Lloyd-Morgan on the Welsh text of the prophecy of the holy oil: 'Darogan yr Olew Bendigaid: Chwedl o'r Bymthegfed Ganrif', *Llên Cymru*, 14 (1981–82), 64–85 and 'Prophecy and Welsh Nationhood in the Fifteenth Century', *Transactions of the Honourable Society of Cymmrodorion* (1985), 9–26. I am most grateful to Dr Lloyd-Morgan for sending me copies of her articles, and to Dr Catherine McKenna for assistance with the Welsh text.

Welsh nationhood in the fifteenth century. Minor adjustments were also made in the text when translating the Becket story itself into Welsh. The 'Reges anglorum' become 'brenhinoedd yr yns honn' (kings of this island). References to 'England' are changed to 'yr ynys honn' (this island), or 'Ynys Prydain', the 'island of Britain' of Welsh Arthurian tradition. As Dr Lloyd-Morgan concludes:

> It is ironic, and a testimony to the skill of the redactor, that a prophetical tale once used in a foreign context should be adapted to carry a very different political message in Wales. From its continental beginnings, where it became part and parcel of the French monarchy, to 14th century England where it could be related to quite different political objectives, the legend of the holy oil finally in its Welsh form is transformed into a lament for the loss of Welsh independence and a hope that one day the English yoke will be thrown off.[30]

St Thomas of Canterbury again became a symbol of opposition to the monarch in the Henrician Reformation until his cult was officially proscribed in 1538. For our final example of Becket prophecies, we turn to those associated with the flood of anti-royal propaganda in the 1530s, when prophecy came to be linked with political protest. As Susan Brigden observed in her study of London and the Reformation: 'Prophecies were circulating, foretelling disaster for the perpetrators of change, and giving hope of the return of the old order. Such prophecies, hallowed by age, were widely believed. Where they told of events which were imminent they were the more emotive and dangerous.'[31] The Tudors addressed the problem by various means: by investigation, by counter-prophecies, and finally in 1542 by statute defining prophecy itself as a felony and treasonable act.

By the sixteenth century, a confusion of prophetical texts had proliferated and been altered to serve various purposes, resulting in a confusion of meanings and disguises.[32] The organisation and nature of these prophecies have been discussed at considerable length in recent works by Keith Thomas, Sharon L. Jansen, and Alistair Fox, among many others.[33] Suffice it to say, for

---

[30] 'Prophecy and Welsh Nationhood', p. 26.

[31] Susan Brigden, *London and the Reformation* (New York: Clarendon Press, 1989), p. 214.

[32] Sharon L. Jansen, *Political Protest and Prophecy under Henry VIII* (Woodbridge: Boydell, 1991), p. 12. An older survey of the subject is by Madeleine Hope Dodds, 'Political Prophecies in the Reign of Henry VIII', *Modern Language Review*, 11 (1916), 276–84. For selected poems of political prophecy, see *Medieval English Political Writings*, ed. James M. Dean (Kalamazoo, MI: Medieval Institute, 1996), pp. 1–29.

[33] See Keith Thomas, *Religion and the Decline of Magic* (New York: Scribner, 1991), and Alistair Fox, 'Prophecies and Politics in the Reign of Henry VIII', in *Reassessing the Henrician Age: Humanism, Politics and Reform 1500–1550*, ed. Alistair Fox and John Guy (Oxford: Blackwell, 1986), pp. 77–94. On the possible connections between the rhetoric of monstrosity and the widespread prophecies of the sixteenth century, see Kathryn M. Brammall, 'Monstrous Metamorphosis: Nature, Morality, and the Rhetoric of Monstrosity in Tudor

the purposes of our present discussion, that the prophecies relating to Becket drew on a variety of traditions. Galfridian prophecy (from Geoffrey of Monmouth, regarded as the real source of political prophecy in England) emphasised animal symbolism. Echoes of the image of a boar and his tusks from the well-known prophecy of Thomas Becket resonated in the parodies of the rebels in the Pilgrimage of Grace.[34] Sybilline prophecy used alphabetic references, usually the initial of a name. The monks of Furness, in a case to which I shall turn presently, had a saying 'that A B and C [probably standing for Anne Boleyn and Cromwell] should sit all in one seat, and should work great marvels', and that afterwards 'the decorate rose shall be slain in his mother's belly'.[35] Prophecies also clustered around and cited as authorities famous figures of British prophecy including Becket himself.

Evidence in the *State Papers* attests to the attitude of the Tudor regime to the threat posed by political prophecies, which were increasingly seen as reflective of popular opinion.[36] During the investigation in 1537 of the monks of Furness, who appear to have supported the rebels in the Pilgrimage of Grace, an accusation was brought against the monk John Broughton that he had prophesied: 'in England shalbe slaine the decorat rose in his mothers bely', by which he meant, 'Your Grace shall die by the handes of preestes for their churche is your mother and the church shall sley Your Grace.' Broughton's prophecy about the murder of the rose in his mother's belly drew from prophecies popularly attributed to Thomas Becket, whose murder was supposed to have been foreshadowed by the prediction that 'the son shall slay the father in the womb of the mother', or that Becket, a father of the Church, would be slain by Henry II, a son of the Church, in front of the altar, the Mother Church. Broughton's 'red rose' was the monarch Henry VIII who would be killed in 'his mother's belly', the Church.[37] Broughton's prophecy was also echoed in the final lines of 'The Marvels of Merlin', one of the many prophecies that circulated in the 1530s:

> When the childe smytes the mother,
> The father shall hym distroye;
> The fluddes floing in Brettyn
> Shall cause an Interdiction.[38]

England', *Sixteenth Century Journal*, 27/1 (1996), 3–21. On the connections between history, prophecy, and the apocalyptic tradition, see Katharine R. Firth, *The Apocalyptic Tradition in Reformation Britain 1530–1645* (Oxford: Oxford University Press, 1979).

[34] Jansen, p. 56.

[35] Madeleine H. Dodds and Ruth Dodds, *The Pilgrimage of Grace 1536–1537 and the Exeter Conspiracy 1538*, 2 vols (London: Frank Cass, 1971), I, 81.

[36] See Fox, 'Prophecies and Politics', pp. 77–8.

[37] See Jansen, p. 44.

[38] Quoted in Jansen, p. 93.

Becket's death at the hands of King Henry II boded ill for the sixteenth-century King Henry VIII in the contemporary interpretation of these lines: 'when the child (Henry) attacks his mother (the Church), the father (the Pope) would destroy him'.[39] Furthermore, the reference in the prophecy to 'floods flowing in Britain' was a topical reminder of the heavy rains of 1535 that were interpreted by many as a sign of God's vengeance. As for the 'Interdiction' in the passage, by 1535 a bull interdicting all religious services in England had been formulated – all this well before the condemnation of Becket and the suppression of the cult of Becket in 1538.

Becket was also identified with another example of prophecy as anti-government propaganda, 'The Sayings of the Prophets', a series of brief prose paragraphs, each paragraph a 'saying' attributed to a reputed prophet. The roster of the 'prophets' is long and varied, but besides Becket, there are others who were by now familiar in the history of English political prophecy: Merlin, John of Bridlington, Thomas of Erceldoune, and Bede. The texts share a common theme, i.e., a mysterious king who is destined to win the Holy Cross and is, moreover, destined to be Henry's successor and replacement. By the end of the 1530s, at least one version of the 'Sayings' had abandoned Henry altogether, but a 1540 version focused on Edward as the long-awaited deliverer to succeed Henry.[40]

Prophets and prophecies, as I mentioned in my introduction to this essay, were not lightly dismissed. The Tudors recognised a formidable threat in these prophecies and mounted a counter-offensive, utilising the same weaponry of prophecy. Nor was St Thomas of Canterbury absent from these texts by Tudor propagandists, a testimony to the popularity and power of England's martyred Archbishop. As an example, Thomas Gibson, a printer and pamphleteer known to Hugh Latimer,[41] sent a re-interpreted version of the 'Sayings' to Thomas Cromwell in 1538 that purported to show that it was in fact King Henry VIII himself who was the predicted saviour of his people and the conqueror who would win the Holy Cross. In an initial reference to Becket's reputation for prophecy, the text begins:

> Thes be the namys of the sayntes and doctoures
> That speke of hym that shall wynne the Holy Crosse.
> Furst Sent Thomas of Canterbery calleth hym
> the virgyn kyng of bewtye.[42]

The glosses of Thomas Gibson to the 'Sayings of the Prophets' are one example of the response of the Tudors to the flood of prophecies that threatened the regime. Thomas Becket figured in yet another of these examples in

---

[39] Jansen, p. 93.
[40] Jansen, pp. 110–11.
[41] Jansen, p. 58.
[42] Quoted in Jansen, p. 113.

1537, in a work called *The fall and evill success of rebellion* by the rather obscure Yorkshire poet Wilfrid Holme, who argued that Henry VIII had fulfilled Merlin's prophecies and indeed those of others:

> This is the Britishe Lion by Sibilla prophesied
> This is the Egle surmounting, which Festome hathe notified,
> This is the kyng anoynted, which S. Thomas specified,
> This is the three folde Bul which Siluester magnified,
> This is the King which S. Edward in words glorified,
> Which shuld win Jerusualem with all the holy land.[43]

Ultimately, the Tudor propaganda machine was inadequate to the threat posed by political prophecy and resorted, by the Act of 1542 (33 Henry VIII, c.14), to law. The statute 'made it felony without benefit of clergy or sanctuary to erect tales and prophecies of a political nature'.[44] In fact, as Jonathan K. Van Patten has shown, opposition to the King which sometimes took the form of magic and political prophecy brought about a change and expansion of the law of treason from protection of the King's person to the protection of the King's policies. As Van Patten observed: 'The prophecies constituted treason by words because they denied that the King was not the rightful head of the Church.'[45]

Whether specific or more general, the political prophecies that opposed Henry's policy shared certain common themes: namely the desire to see the King put down and the Church of Rome regain its power. The struggle for religious and political supremacy in England took place on many levels, not least of all in the realm of magic and prophecy. We have seen how Tudor propagandists resorted to prophecy and legends as a way of validating the policy of the Crown. Their use of 'a subtle form of magic . . . to effectuate the religious reformation in England'[46] also called for the physical erasure of the Pope's and Becket's names from the service books of the English church. Striking of the name was seen as a strike against the person. On 16 November 1538, King Henry VIII decreed: 'that from henceforth the said Thomas Becket shall not be esteemed, named, reputed, nor called a saint . . . and that from henceforth the days used to be festival in his name shall not be observed, nor the service, office, antiphons, collects, and prayers in his name read, but erased and put out of all the books'.[47] Instructions to expunge the

---

43 Quoted in Jansen, p. 58.

44 Cited by Fox, 'Prophecies and Politics', p. 93.

45 Van Patten, p. 19. Further on the law of treason, see Lacey Baldwin Smith, *Treason in Tudor England: Politics and Paranoia* (Princeton: Princeton University Press, 1986).

46 Van Patten, p. 24.

47 See *Tudor Royal Proclamations*, ed. Paul L. Hughes and James F. Larkin, 3 vols (New Haven: Yale University Press, 1964–69), I, 270–6.

Pope's name from all service books had been issued in a letter to bishops in June 1535.[48]

The actions taken by the Crown in the 1530s purging the name and image of Thomas Becket exemplify a remarkable propaganda effort which supported the goals of the Henrician Reformation and required its thorough and effective enforcement. To King Henry VIII and the supporters of the sixteenth-century Reformation, Thomas Becket represented the cause of the liberties of the Church and resistance to the King, a cause that was perceived as a threat and called for prompt eradication. That Becket was tied to political prophecies that were hostile to the Crown was one reminder too many of Henry II's 'turbulent priest'. The twelfth-century saint became a new martyr to sixteenth-century Reformation politics.

What then can we conclude in this survey of prophecy, hagiography, and St Thomas of Canterbury, and what does this have to say about how we can assess prophecy as a medium for a medieval view of the future? While prophecy, by definition, looks to the future, it is very much a creature of the past and present and the historical circumstances which create it. The prophecies that grew up about Becket himself coincided with the growth and diffusion of the cult of the martyred Archbishop. These prophecies in turn came to make Becket in the popular imagination a repository of visions about the future. The Becket prophecies of the fourteenth and fifteenth centuries that were associated with the sanctification of the monarchy and the legitimising of royal authority reflected an image of Becket that was useful in the context of late medieval English politics. By the sixteenth century, however, political prophecies revived and emphasised the image of Becket as opponent to the King. The similarity between Becket and Henry II in 1169–70 and St Thomas of Canterbury and Henry VIII in 1538 was only too obvious, and dangerously prophetic.

Of all these Becket prophecies, there was one as yet unmentioned, that I close with. Such was the prophecy that came to the bishop of Exeter as he grieved over Becket's death: 'Truly he is dead, but his power lives on.'[49]

---

[48] Geoffrey R. Elton, *Policy and Police: The Enforcement of the Reformation in the Age of Thomas Cromwell* (Cambridge: Cambridge University Press, 1972), p. 232.
[49] Beryl Smalley, *The Becket Conflict and the Schools* (Oxford: Blackwell, 1973), p. 190.

III

PROVIDING FOR FUTURES

The French Aristocracy and the Future, c.1000–c.1200

MARCUS BULL

THE aristocracy has long been one of the most popular subjects among historians working on the Middle Ages. Particular attention has been paid to regions within or bordering the area that corresponds to modern France, and most work has been on the period between the late Carolingian era and c.1200.[1] An important feature of the study of the elites of the central medieval period is that scholars have not limited themselves to the idea of aristocrats as historical performers within various social, economic, political, and institutional settings. There has been an awareness that our understanding of these people requires us to consider what they thought as well as what they did; their identity was as much a function of their mental universe – their *mentalité* – as it was an aggregation of all the ways in which they behaved. Given this interest in the realm of ideas – understood in a broad sense as not simply a body of considered positions but also a complex of instincts, assumptions, and emotional reactions – it is valid to ask whether and to what extent the aristocrats of the eleventh and twelfth centuries directed their minds to the future. A useful starting point is that pondering the unknowability of things to come can amount to an opportunity to express a deep-rooted sense of self. Furthermore, the tensions created by the conflict between the unpredictability of the future and the impulse to control and contain it may lead to the forceful articulation of ideas that would otherwise not surface so clearly in the historical record. In other words, a consideration of attitudes towards and attempts to control the future has the potential to open up insights into the world of lords and knights and, more importantly, their notion of their place within it.

For the purposes of this discussion, the primary focus will be on the aristocracy in various parts of what is modern-day France and Belgium. Some refer-

---

[1] For an excellent overview that surveys the trends in recent scholarship, see Constance B. Bouchard, *Strong of Body, Brave and Noble: Chivalry and Society in Medieval France* (Ithaca, NY: Cornell University Press, 1998).

ence will also be made to Anglo-Norman conditions where they offer supporting evidence; the experience of the elites of post-Conquest England was in many respects a series of variations on basic themes found in northern France.[2] The term 'aristocracy' is used to avoid thorny issues about the origins and nature of the nobility, and the relationship between it and knighthood.[3] 'Aristocracy' has the merit of being an inclusive term that can cover both high-status nobles and lesser knights. The cut-off point is reasonably precise in that it turns on whether someone had the means or opportunity to equip himself with the accoutrements of a mounted warrior, and in the process to subscribe to a range of behaviours and attitudes that proclaimed membership of a social elite. On the other hand, the term takes us away from anachronistic notions of closed castes, for in this period there was a good deal of blurring at the lower margins of arms-bearing society. One qualification of the word 'aristocracy' is in order: for the purposes of this discussion the term will effectively be shorthand for adult males. This is not to argue that their mental world was wholly detached from that of women of the same social levels, nor that women did not have their own points of entry into thoughts about the future. Rather, it is useful to concentrate on the men for the simple reason that they dominate the picture of aristocratic society that is projected by the sources, just as they dominated the social environments in which their consciousness of status was forged and expressed.

There are several problems to confront when considering whether and how the aristocracy in eleventh- and twelfth-century France conceived of and planned for the future. In the first place, the sources upon which we can draw seldom lead us directly to the ideas of nobles and knights. Instead we are

[2] Comparisons between French and Anglo-Norman conditions may usefully be pursued through David Crouch, *The Image of Aristocracy in Britain, 1000–1300* (London: Routledge, 1992); Judith A. Green, *The Aristocracy of Norman England* (Cambridge: Cambridge University Press, 1997). There is also much of interest in Charlotte A. Newman, *The Anglo-Norman Nobility in the Reign of Henry I: The Second Generation* (Philadelphia: University of Pennsylvania Press, 1988).

[3] There is a very extensive bibliography on the nobility of this period. For a valuable survey, see Thomas N. Bisson, 'Nobility and Family in Medieval France: A Review Essay', *French Historical Studies*, 16 (1989–90), 597–613. Important studies in English include Jane Martindale, 'The French Aristocracy in the Early Middle Ages: A Reappraisal', *Past and Present*, 75 (1977), 5–45; Constance B. Bouchard, 'The Origins of the French Nobility: A Reassessment', *American Historical Review*, 86 (1981), 501–32; Theodore Evergates, 'Nobles and Knights in Twelfth-Century France', in *Cultures of Power: Lordship, Status, and Process in Twelfth-Century Europe*, ed. Thomas N. Bisson (Philadelphia: University of Pennsylvania Press, 1995), pp. 11–35. Germany provides many points of comparison: see John B. Freed, 'Reflections on the Medieval German Nobility', *American Historical Review*, 91 (1986), 553–75. For knighthood and chivalry, the conclusions of the leading French scholar in this field, Jean Flori, are usefully set out in his *Chevaliers et chevalerie au moyen âge* (Paris: Hachette, 1998). Many of the scholarly orthodoxies surrounding knighthood have been energetically attacked by Dominique Barthélemy, 'Qu'est-ce que la chevalerie, en France aux Xe et XIe siècles?', *Revue historique*, 290 (1994), 15–74.

faced with a range of mediations, and thus distortions, due to the fact that monks or clerics produced the great majority of the written evidence, and did so in accordance with their own needs and perspectives. In addition, few historians would now subscribe to the once common view that examples of vernacular literature – verse epics, lais and romances – invariably offer up a clearer picture of aristocratic culture, one that throws light on what the Latin sources must in their very nature obscure. This is not to say that these sources are not of enormous value.[4] But the language in which a text was written is in itself no indicator of its proximity to the minds of the lay elites.

Given the difficulty of detecting an aristocratic 'voice' in our sources, a more secure approach must be to work outwards from what we can establish about nobles and knights as historical actors; this involves extrapolating from their lived experience to an appreciation of the ideas and values that informed their actions. Here we are on firmer ground, for we are undeniably much better informed about these sorts of men than we are about other categories within lay society such as peasants, townspeople, and women and children of all classes. This is so both in relation to the aristocracy as a collectivity and with regard to the number of those whom we can identify as named individuals located more or less precisely in space and time. A further problem then emerges, however, in that the various types of source provide uneven and incomplete representations of aspects of these men's lives. They tend to the episodic and the exceptional when set against all that must have filled an adult lifetime. For example, a charter might capture one of the solemn highlights of an aristocrat's career, the day he gave some property to a religious community.[5] But few people had the resources or the freedom from familial responsibilities to do this on more than a handful of occasions. A miracle story might record a lord or knight on pilgrimage, an act that was in its nature a break from routine and an opportunity to effect a profound, if temporary, change in both one's status and the manner in which one was perceived by others.[6] And a historiographical text such as a chronicle or annal

---

[4] For a recent example of the effective mobilisation of vernacular material in the context of historical debates, see Linda M. Paterson, *The World of the Troubadours: Medieval Occitan Society, c.1100–c.1300* (Cambridge: Cambridge University Press, 1993). See also Jean Flori, 'La notion de chevalerie dans les chansons de geste du XIIe siècle: Étude historique de vocabulaire', *Moyen Age*, 81 (1975), 211–44, 407–45.

[5] Numerous recent studies have drawn on charter evidence in their analyses of the ideas underpinning aristocrats' relationships with the churches that they supported. For a range of perspectives, see Constance B. Bouchard, *Sword, Miter, and Cloister: Nobility and the Church in Burgundy, 980–1198* (Ithaca, NY: Cornell University Press, 1987); Stephen D. White, *Custom, Kinship, and Gifts to Saints: The 'Laudatio Parentum' in Western France, 1050–1150* (Chapel Hill, NC: University of North Carolina Press, 1988); Barbara H. Rosenwein, *To Be the Neighbor of Saint Peter: The Social Meaning of Cluny's Property, 909–1049* (Ithaca, NY: Cornell University Press, 1989); Megan McLaughlin, *Consorting with Saints: Prayer for the Dead in Early Medieval France* (Ithaca, NY: Cornell University Press, 1994).

[6] A detailed study of the aristocracy's place in miracle stories is much to be desired. There

might record an aristocrat operating as a warrior. The trappings of warfare and the language of conflict were central components of aristocratic identity, but fighting itself, especially that between members of the arms-bearing elites, was something done as little as possible; these men tended to talk a good fight rather more often than they exposed themselves to the unpredictable hazards of real warfare.[7] Overall, then, the sources give us a view of aristocratic life that downplays the mundane by highlighting the unusual. The problem here is not simply one of incomplete information, for we can assume that it was in and through their day-to-day routines, their domestic behaviour governed by familiarity and habit, that lords and knights developed many of their notions about who they were and what they believed in – in other words, laid the foundations for possible reflections on what the future might bring and how best to plan for it.

When we examine what the sources do have to tell us about the French aristocracy, and how scholars have interpreted the material, a further difficulty presents itself. A striking lesson to emerge from the regional studies that followed in the wake of Georges Duby's pioneering book on the Mâconnais is that it is impossible to frame conclusions that apply consistently across both space and time.[8] While it is possible to detect patterns of social, economic and political change that were broadly similar across several regions, there were numerous subtle but significant differences in relation to, for example, the spread and importance of feudal tenures, the development of banal lordship, the impact of urban growth and changes in the rural economy, and the relationship between ideas surrounding nobility and the ideological loading, if any, that attached to knighthood.[9] In addition, as the experience of the Anglo-Norman aristocracy helps to make particularly clear, another variable was the extent to which rulership impinged on aristocrats' lives, either as a restricting force or as an opportunity for advancement through service and

is a good deal of material relating to lords and knights in Pierre-André Sigal, *L'Homme et le miracle dans la France médiévale (XIe–XIIe siècle)* (Paris: Cerf, 1985); Constanze Rendtel, *Hochmittelalterliche Mirakelberichte als Quelle zur Sozial- und Mentalitätsgeschichte und zur Geschichte der Heiligenverehrung untersucht an Texten insbesondere aus Frankreich*, 2 vols (Düsseldorf: doctoral dissertation, Freie Universität Berlin, 1985). See also C. Caitucoli, 'Nobles et chevaliers dans le *Livre de miracles de sainte Foy*', *Annales du Midi*, 107 (1995), 401–16; Marcus G. Bull, *The Miracles of Our Lady of Rocamadour: Analysis and Translation* (Woodbridge: Boydell, 1999).

[7] For an important recent study of aristocratic attitudes towards violence, see Matthew Strickland, *War and Chivalry: The Conduct and Perception of War in England and Normandy, 1066–1217* (Cambridge: Cambridge University Press, 1996).

[8] Georges Duby, *La Société aux XIe et XIIe siècles dans la région mâconnaise*, 2nd edn (Paris: École Pratique des Hautes Études, 1971).

[9] For useful synopses of the findings of regional studies, see Jean Flori, *L'Essor de la chevalerie XIe–XIIe siècles*, Travaux d'histoire éthico-politique, 46 (Geneva: Droz, 1986), pp. 20–35, 119–41; Jean-Pierre Poly and Eric Bournazel, *The Feudal Transformation 900–1200*, trans. Caroline Higgitt (New York: Holmes & Meier, 1991), pp. 9–45, 87–118.

patronage. The point to note here is that factors of this sort – the nature of what a lord or knight owned, his place within the power structures that oper- ated in his local environment, his economic opportunities, his sense of social status, and the people to whom he owed deference and obedience – were among the central elements of aristocratic self-perception and identity. These considerations governed how aristocrats behaved towards each other and how they positioned themselves relative to other groups. By extension they must have had a profound effect on the mental universe in which ideas about the past, present, and future had to be forged.

Compounding these difficulties there is also the possible argument that attentiveness to the future was not a quality that contemporaries routinely read into aristocratic behaviour and values. The issue at stake here is the extent to which we may read the commonplaces of moralising literature as distillations of the ways in which different groups of people were perceived. Without doubt the clichés of medieval Christian moralists did violence to the complexities of life, but there is a case for saying that like all good carica- tures they succeeded in registering some of the dominant and readily recog- nisable features. The vice that was most future-minded was avarice, which was most commonly associated with merchants. Avarice was the stick with which to beat those whose livelihoods depended on long-term planning, hoarding, lending, and speculation.[10] On the other hand, the vice that was most typically ascribed to members of the aristocratic elite was pride.[11] The manifestations of pride resided overwhelmingly in the realm of the immedi- ate: display, appearance, and demeanour were the concerns of those whose aspirations seemed to extend no further than the short term. Aggressiveness was seen as symptomatic of the same failing. Moreover, the behaviour that could expose lords and knights to imputations of pride had the potential to negate any regard for the future, for status was often achieved and expressed through social exchanges that emphasised consumption and the ability to bestow. Men who valued largesse, as both givers and receivers, were – or wanted to appear – qualitatively distinct from the burgesses whose impulse to save and plan they often liked to disparage.[12] It goes without saying that there was an enormous amount of over-simplification inherent in a moralising schema such as this. But the fact that the accusation of pride stuck so easily and repeatedly to the aristocracy points to a contemporary vision of a group that put present advantage and gratification before thoughts for the morrow.

One way to resolve these problems is to focus on some feature of aristo-

---

[10] John W. Baldwin, *Masters, Princes, and Merchants: The Social Views of Peter the Chanter and his Circle*, 2 vols (Princeton: Princeton University Press, 1970), I, 261–5.

[11] Lester K. Little, 'Pride Goes before Avarice: Social Change and the Vices in Latin Chris- tendom', *American Historical Review*, 76 (1971), 16–49 (pp. 31–7).

[12] But see Ad Putter, *'Sir Gawain and the Green Knight' and French Arthurian Romance* (Oxford: Clarendon Press, 1995), pp. 230–43.

cratic experience, and with it its particular body of source material, that combined aspects of the exceptional and the familiar. When these two apparently opposed and mutually exclusive entities are placed in close proximity, the result can be creative tensions and responses to new problems that throw light on otherwise obscure issues. Values, instincts, and habits that would not normally be addressed in the written record can become much easier to detect as new conditions force them to be aired, contested, modified, or reaffirmed. Crusading fits the bill in this regard. A study of the sources bearing on the first century of the crusade movement – for example, the various accounts of Pope Urban II's speech at the Council of Clermont in November 1095 and the papal bulls which launched the Second and Third Crusades – offers a useful point of entry into broader aspects of aristocratic thinking and behaviour.[13] It should be emphasised that crusading does not enjoy some privileged methodological status as the only possible key to the problems that we have identified, but it commends itself for a number of compelling reasons.

First, there is the fact that whereas most of our sources for the aristocracy amount to clerics and monks talking *about* lords and knights, crusading throws up instances of the Church talking *to* these people. The nature of the dialogue that took place emerges from a comparison with other occasions when there was communication between the two groups. For example, the ecclesiastics who promoted the Peace and Truce of God movements in the late tenth and eleventh centuries certainly had messages to get across to the aristocratic perpetrators of violence about restraint and moral reform.[14] But these messages were not always clear and did not have the same impact on all the regions of France. Similarly, the ways in which a crusade message was propagated and acted upon differed from the dynamic evident in the spread of Gregorian Reform ideals.[15] Reformers had ambitious agendas that repaid unhurried persuasion; to get lay people to reconsider their relationship with the Church, their power over ecclesiastical property and personnel, and their sense of moral self, was normally a matter of patient reiteration and constant reinforcement that measured meaningful change in generations. In stark contrast, the delivery of a crusade message was of necessity in the nature of a

---

[13] For an excellent study of this body of material, see Penny J. Cole, *The Preaching of the Crusades to the Holy Land, 1095–1270* (Cambridge, MA: Medieval Academy of America, 1991).

[14] See the articles by many leading scholars assembled in *The Peace of God: Social Violence and Religious Response in France around the Year 1000*, ed. Thomas Head and Richard Landes (Ithaca, NY: Cornell University Press, 1992). See also Herbert E. J. Cowdrey, 'The Peace and Truce of God in the Eleventh Century', *Past and Present*, 46 (1970), 42–67.

[15] The scholarship on the Gregorian Reform is vast. For an excellent treatment, with full bibliographical orientation, see Colin Morris, *The Papal Monarchy: The Western Church from 1050 to 1250* (Oxford: Clarendon Press, 1989). See also Gerd Tellenbach, *The Church in Western Europe from the Tenth to the Early Twelfth Century*, trans. Timothy Reuter (Cambridge: Cambridge University Press, 1993).

short, sharp shock – something to be effected in ways that facilitated immediate comprehension and direct response. The sense of urgency that in the case of the First Crusade was imparted by the rhetorical power of Urban II's appeal and by the novelty of what he was proposing was increased in the preaching of the Second and Third Crusades – the twelfth-century expeditions that attracted the largest numbers of recruits – because these were responses to disasters in the East that begged prompt and effective action.[16] In order to get people to act, the promoters of crusading had to engage with their audience's value systems and aspirations with particular vigour and clarity. A result of this is that there is the clear potential in the crusade sources to detect traces of that audience's beliefs about the future and its place in it.

Second, the challenges that faced those who promoted crusades, and the rhythms of crusading's institutional development, mean that we have been left a quite coherent and well-defined source base that is rooted in an evolving movement of interconnected ideas and practices.[17] On one level the immediate context of the material might seem to set it apart, for crusading was just one, very distinctive, facet of aristocratic activity. The numbers of lords and knights that we can roughly estimate went on crusades amount to a minority of the available arms-bearing adult males: crusading was something for some of the people some of the time. But, more importantly, the language and content of crusade documents often stepped beyond the specifics of crusading to draw on a substantially wider range of experiences that was more inclusive. The sources' use of analogy, metaphor, imagery, and association mean that they articulated ideas that had the potential to resonate with any member of the aristocracy, whether or not he was actually emboldened to take the cross. A corollary of this is that many of the sources for the preaching of the crusades – specifically those relating to the big international expeditions – transcend regional difference. They are evidence for attempts to mobilise people from many different areas within France and elsewhere. It is therefore reasonable to conclude that they focused predominantly on what was shared among the target audience – ideas and associations that were abstracted to the point at which the sorts of differences of experience that were mentioned earlier would be submerged beneath the common ground. Texts such as crusade encyclicals were carefully drafted exercises in achieving relevance irrespective of the location of the end audience; preachers on the ground could add local colour in order to increase their listeners' sense of recognition and approval, but the core around which they worked had to be messages of universal application. It follows from this that it is legitimate to

16 For the launching of these crusades, see Jonathan S. C. Riley-Smith, *The Crusades: A Short History* (London: Athlone Press, 1987), pp. 2–17, 93–8, 109–10.
17 For an attempt to downplay the institutional coherence and capacity for development of twelfth-century crusading, see Christopher J. Tyerman, *The Invention of the Crusades* (London: Macmillan, 1998), pp. 8–29.

frame generalisations about aristocratic values and ideas on the basis of these sources because to do so is to work with the grain of contemporaries' searching after common denominators.

Finally, crusades permit us to examine aristocrats' behaviour in a setting that was formed out of and around an informed understanding of these men's particular capabilities and attributes. It may seem odd to characterise crusading as a distinctively aristocratic activity, for lords and knights were always a minority of those who responded to the preaching of the cross: they made up perhaps no more than 10–15% of the total numbers on the larger expeditions.[18] As early as the First Crusade the Church discovered that the linking of military rhetoric to ideas of pilgrimage and penance attracted the enthusiasm of many types of people who normally took no active part in the conduct of warfare, with the result that many non-combatants attached themselves to campaigns. Armies that included women, children, the poor, and clergy were much more microcosms of western European society in motion than they were elite forces of specialist warriors permitted to function in isolation.[19] What is more, the blurring of the composition of crusade armies was not simply the result of the Church's difficulties in patrolling the boundaries of the enthusiasm generated by its preaching. Many of the lower-status crusaders took part as the servants of the lords and knights – masters whose emerging ideal of knight errantry belied the hard fact that they needed the skills of others to survive, to keep their knightly apparatus in good condition, and to look after their horses. To this extent, then, the aristocratic colouring of crusading was a highly selective registering of observable conditions. On the other hand, lords and knights did fashion the experience of crusading out of all proportion to their relative numbers. They believed they were the natural leaders and best-trained fighters, and they acted accordingly. In addition, notions of social hierarchy and professional expertise were clung to with particular force and, if anything, reinforced when disparate groups of people from different parts of Latin Christendom found themselves thrown together in unfamiliar and stressful conditions. A corollary of this is that much of the material bearing on the preaching of crusades focused principally on the aristocracy, and in the process reinforced the notion that there was – or ought to

---

18 Calculations of the total numbers on crusades and the relative size of different elements are fraught with difficulty. For recent discussions of the problem with regard to the First Crusade, see Jean Flori, 'Un problème de méthodologie: La valeur des nombres chez les chroniquers du moyen âge (A propos des effectifs de la première Croisade)', *Moyen Age*, 99 (1993), 399–422; John France, *Victory in the East: A Military History of the First Crusade* (Cambridge: Cambridge University Press, 1994), pp. 2–3, 14–15, 122–42.
19 Walter Porges, 'The Clergy, the Poor, and the Non-Combatants on the First Crusade', *Speculum*, 21 (1946), 1–23; Randall Rogers, 'Peter Bartholomew and the Role of "The Poor" in the First Crusade', in *Warriors and Churchmen in the High Middle Ages: Essays Presented to Karl Leyser*, ed. Timothy Reuter (London: Hambledon Press, 1992), pp. 109–22.

be – a discreet body of distinctive and positive ideas, images, and associations that adhered to this group of people.

What, then, are some of the most important features of the crusade sources in the context of aristocratic self-perception, and how can they help us to identify the ways in which lords and knights addressed the future? Perhaps the single most recurrent and powerful motif found in the texts derives from their use of simile and metaphor based on the experience of family relationship. This was applied in a number of connected ways. In the first place, the propagators of crusades attempted to tap into the emotional strength of impulses associated with membership of family groups in order to help potential crusaders reach a personalised understanding of the just cause of what was being proposed to them. According to Baldric of Bourgueil's version of Urban II's speech at Clermont, the pope drew attention to the travails of eastern Christians suffering persecution at the hands of the Muslims by describing the victims as his audience's blood-brothers. Those oppressed, he argued, were born of the same womb in the sense that they too were children of Christ and of the Church.[20] This argument reveals the potential difficulty of pushing hard at the boundaries between figurative language and literal understanding, but the fact that Baldric believed that the pope could argue in these terms points to the value of even strained appeals to familial experience. In later crusades preachers found it simpler, and probably more effective, to apply the language of fraternal bonding to the Latins now living in the East; to present these people as brothers in need, as, for example, Pope Alexander III did in his encyclical *Inter omnia* (1169), was to encourage in the crusader a personal stake in the affairs of people who might otherwise seem very remote.[21]

Other responses could also be elicited by appeals to family consciousness. An effective way in which to condemn warfare between Christians, and by extension to highlight the different moral loading of crusading against the infidel, was to evoke the particular horror of conflict that set brother against brother.[22] More broadly, the language of family relationship could be exploited to encourage in would-be crusaders the idea that they represented the community of all Christians, and that once on campaign they ought to feel bound by a sense of common purpose and mutual responsibility: they were sons of the Church, brothers of one another. In addition, crusade promoters found, as the movement began to span generations, that they could

20 Baldric of Bourgueil, 'Historia Jerosolimitana', *Recueil des historiens des croisades: historiens occidentaux*, 5 vols, ed. Académie des Inscriptions et Belles Lettres (Paris: Académie des Inscriptions et Belles Lettres, 1844–95) [hereafter *RHC Occ*], IV (1879), 9–111 (pp. 12–13).
21 Alexander III, 'Epistolae et privilegia', *Patrologiae cursus completus: series latina*, ed. Jacques P. Migne, 221 vols (Paris: the author, 1844–64), CC (1855), 69–1318 (cols 599–600).
22 For example Fulcher of Chartres, *Historia Hierosolymitana (1095–1127)*, ed. Heinrich Hagenmeyer (Heidelberg: Carl Winter, 1913), p. 136; Baldric of Bourgueil, pp. 14–15.

appeal to family pride and a predisposition to construct forbears as role models. A notable example of this technique is *Quantum praedecessores* (1145, reissued 1146), the encyclical that launched the Second Crusade. In it Pope Eugenius III recalled the achievements of the first crusaders, men described as the fathers of the present generation; those alive today were encouraged to follow their example in order to establish their own credentials as good sons possessed of nobility and moral worth.[23] According to Robert the Monk, Urban II had appealed to a feeling of being connected to the past by evoking memories bound up with belonging to a large group – the ancestral Franks epitomised by Charlemagne and Louis the Pious.[24] By the time of the Second Crusade, however, the focus could be much tighter. Many crusaders did indeed have fathers or other relatives with crusading traditions; others could be made to feel as if this were the case.[25]

In arguing in these terms, those preaching crusades were quite deliberately exploiting the importance of the family in the aristocratic imagination. Some care needs to be taken in establishing what we understand by 'family'. It is well known that there was no strictly equivalent term in our period; the Latin *familia* meant household rather than a domestic unit created by bonds of blood or marriage. Moreover, the composition of an aristocrat's family was not an *a priori* given but the result of choices about the relative strength of the bonds that he felt with various others around him and about the implications of those bonds for how he ought to act. In these circumstances, it is unsurprising that the aristocratic family in the central medieval period has been one of the most contentious areas of scholarly debate in recent decades. To simplify matters enormously, at the heart of the problem is the validity of the model constructed in particular by Georges Duby and Karl Schmid. According to this schema, around the year 1000 the large, 'horizontal' kinship groupings of earlier centuries – *Sippen* in the useful technical jargon of German scholars – broke up into narrow, 'vertical' *Geschlechter*, or lineages. The norm became the small dynastic unit that was largely defined by the central position within it of a single dominant male who located himself in a sequence of patrilineal succession. As Constance Bouchard has observed, much of the problem is that family size and shape fluctuated operationally: different contexts such as property inheritance, pious benefaction, feuding and socialising encouraged correspondingly different configurations, none of

23 Erich Caspar, 'Die Kreuzzugsbullen Eugens III.', *Neues Archiv der Gesellschaft für ältere deutsche Geschichtskunde*, 45 (1924), 285–305 (pp. 302–3).

24 Robert the Monk, 'Historia Iherosolimitana', *RHC Occ*, III (1866), 721–882 (pp. 727–8).

25 See Jonathan S. C. Riley-Smith, 'Family Traditions and Participation in the Second Crusade', in *The Second Crusade and the Cistercians*, ed. Michael Gervers (New York: St Martin's Press, 1992), pp. 101–8.

which was necessarily the most 'real' version of the family.[26] On the other hand, blood and marriage relationships were so important to aristocratic identity that nobles and knights needed some stable points of reference – some markers to help them to delineate what their family was at least most of the time. It is possible to argue that the family shape that was becoming progressively more common over the course of our period, and consequently more potent as the site of familial emotionalism, was the patrilineal structure, often though not always reinforced by primogenital inheritance that transmitted the lion's share of the patrimony to the eldest son.[27] An important characteristic of the narrow lineage is that for those within such a patrilinear unit – and especially the privileged members in the father-son chain – the family was an entity that stretched back in time in order to define and legitimate itself. Indeed, this was an essential part of its self-perception. This sort of chronological reach, a built-in sense of the value of the long term, created a framework within which strategies for future survival and success could be formulated.

One way in which this perspective found expression was in genealogical narratives.[28] This statement might at first glance seem paradoxical, for accounts of the deeds of past generations would seem on the surface to be little more than exercises in looking backwards. But in fact these reconstructions of the past do contain important lessons for attitudes towards the future because they were grounded in the perspectives and needs of the present, which functioned as the bridging point between what had been and what ought to be. This becomes clear from a reading of a text such as Fulk Réchin's accounts of his predecessors as counts of Anjou, written in the later 1090s.[29] Fulk tells us at the beginning of his work that his aim was to relate how his

---

[26] Constance B. Bouchard, 'Family Structure and Family Consciousness among the Aristocracy in the Ninth to Eleventh Centuries', *Francia*, 14 (1986), 639–58. See also the same author's 'The Structure of a Twelfth-Century French Family: The Lords of Seignelay', *Viator*, 10 (1979), 39–56.

[27] For a different view, see Amy Livingstone, 'Kith and Kin: Kinship and Family Structure of the Nobility of Eleventh- and Twelfth-Century Blois-Chartres', *French Historical Studies*, 20 (1997), 419–58.

[28] For discussions of this type of material, see Léopold Genicot, *Les Généalogies*, Typologie des sources du moyen âge occidental, 15 (Turnhout: Brepols, 1975); Georges Duby, 'French Genealogical Literature', in his *The Chivalrous Society*, trans. Cynthia Postan (London: Arnold, 1977), pp. 149–57; Fernand Vercauteren, 'A Kindred in Northern France in the Eleventh and Twelfth Centuries', in *The Medieval Nobility: Studies on the Ruling Classes of France and Germany from the Sixth to the Twelfth Century*, ed. and trans. Timothy Reuter, Europe in the Middle Ages: Selected Studies, 14 (Amsterdam: North-Holland, 1978), pp. 87–103; Jean Dunbabin, 'Discovering a Past for the French Aristocracy', in *The Perception of the Past in Twelfth-Century Europe*, ed. Paul Magdalino (London: Hambledon Press, 1992), pp. 1–14.

[29] 'Fragmentum Historiae Andegavensis', *Chroniques d'Anjou*, ed. Paul Marchegay and André Salmon (Paris: Jules Renouard, 1856), pp. 375–83. See Dunbabin, pp. 5–6.

forbears had acquired their *honor* – the word is rich in connotations – and held on to it up to his own time, and then how he too had done the same. The sense of present informing the construction of the past further emerges in the passage in which Fulk deals with Ingelgerius, the man whom he believed had been the first count back in the ninth century; in recording that this man had been given the title of count by Charles the Bald, Fulk inserts a dig at the king of his own day, Philip I, who had made off with his wife some years earlier. The privileging of the present is also evident in the importance that Fulk attaches to the honour that had been paid him by Pope Urban II when he had visited the count's domains in the spring of 1096. A man with a question mark hanging over the legitimacy of his status and power – he had been involved in a long and divisive dynastic struggle with his brother Geoffrey back in the 1060s[30] – could feel secure in his present circumstances and by extension reflect on the accumulated achievements of forbears whose actions established a blueprint for continued prosperity and recognition. Implicit in Fulk's text are the sentiments later made explicit by, for example, John of Marmoutier in his history of the counts of Anjou (*c.*1170) that was dedicated to Fulk's great-grandson King Henry II.[31] The lives of Henry's predecessors were held up as a mirror to equip him to imitate the good and shun the bad. Ancestors were exemplars out of which one created a moral programmatic to govern future action. The mechanisms of dynastic success that genealogical texts such as those by Fulk and John adumbrated – principally the shrewd acquisition of property, the use of advantageous marriages, warlike energy, patronage of the Church, physical presence, moral correctness, and the cultivation of loyalty – were incontestable and timeless verities. And their timelessness meant that they became an important site of aristocratic ideas about the future.

Any discussion of aristocrats' families inevitably leads into a consideration of their attitudes towards property, for the two were inextricably linked. This point was not lost on those who promoted the crusade message. For example, the passage in Baldric of Bourgueil's account of Urban II's speech that was noted earlier moves from the description of the eastern Christians as bloodbrothers to a vivid evocation of the injury that was being done to these people by virtue of the fact that foreign lords had usurped their inheritances and driven some of them away.[32] Some of the dispossessed, Baldric has Urban say, were being sold into slavery; in other words, the status and sense of permanence that enjoyment of their property should bring were now turned upside down. The Christians found themselves subject to floggings; thus the

---

[30] Olivier Guillot, *Le Conte d'Anjou et son entourage au XIe siècle*, 2 vols (Paris: Picard, 1972), I, 102–16.

[31] 'Historia Abbreviata Consulum Andegavorum', *Chroniques d'Anjou*, ed. Paul Marchegay and André Salmon (Paris: Jules Renouard, 1856), pp. 351–63. See Dunbabin, p. 11.

[32] Baldric of Bourgueil, p. 13.

normal power relations that attached to lordship and propertied wealth were perversely inverted. And many of the victims had been forced into exile; that is to say, the anchoring effect of being possessed of land, and the grounding of self expressible through the increasingly common toponymic formula that made someone N *de* X, had been cruelly negated. Ideas surrounding property did not only have the potential to stimulate an aristocrat's sympathy for people in the East. More importantly still, the language of proprietorial right was exploited to demonstrate the special status of the Holy Land, which became conceived of as Christ's patrimony. Some of the most powerful expressions of this view were made by St Bernard of Clairvaux, perhaps the most effective communicator of crusading ideas in the whole history of the movement. In one letter intended to arouse interest in the Second Crusade, for example, he skilfully emphasised the connection between the Lord and his land by repetition of the Latin *suam*; Christ had made the Holy Land distinctively his by honouring it with his birth, by his preaching and performance of miracles there, and by the consecrating effect of his death and resurrection.[33] Once again, the intention was to equip the crusader to recognise and internalise the nature of the just cause – in this instance by mining the rich vein of impulses and assumptions that turned the matter-of-fact possession of property into a leitmotiv of personal value.

Looking beyond the crusades to the wider picture of aristocratic experience, it is easy to find abundant evidence for the importance attached to property – not only as an economic resource that underpinned power but also as a representation and repository of social identity. For example, it is noteworthy that genealogical texts such as Lambert of Ardres's history of the counts of Guines include careful descriptions of how a family's property base was built up over the generations.[34] In other words, aristocrats' ideas concerning property extended beyond practical considerations about their rights and incomes; they also spoke to how these men related to space as an enabler of identity, and to how they were able to achieve an understanding of themselves through their position in the environment around them. A good way to demonstrate the significance of this point is to look at the various meanings that could attach to the control of castles, which were the supreme symbol of what could be gained from the control of an area of land and of the people living on it.[35] The number of castles increased enormously in the

---

[33] Bernard of Clairvaux, *Opera*, ed. Jean Leclercq, Charles H. Talbot, and Henri Rochais, 8 vols (Rome: Editiones Cistercienses, 1957–77), VIII: *Epistolae*, ed. Jean Leclercq and Henri Rochais (1977), p. 312; cf. Robert the Monk, p. 729.

[34] Lambert of Ardres, 'Historia comitum Ghisnensium', *Monumenta Germaniae Historica, Scriptores*, ed. Georg H. Pertz and others (Hanover, Weimar, Berlin, Stuttgart, and Cologne: various imprints, 1826–), XXIV (1879), 550–642.

[35] For French castles in this period, see Gabriel Fournier, *Le Château dans la France médiévale* (Paris: Aubier Montaigne, 1978). For conditions in the British Isles, which provide many valuable points of comparison and contrast, see Norman J. G. Pounds, *The*

eleventh and twelfth centuries. Indeed, their proliferation is one of the most convincing pieces of evidence in support of the view that there was a profound transformation in the nature and structure of the aristocracy beginning around 1000 – the 'feudal transformation' or 'revolution' of much recent scholarship.[36] Castles were symptoms of dynamic change, and for this reason the opportunity presents itself to search in them for clues about the reactions of lords and knights to their surroundings, and by extension their ideas about the future.

A note of caution needs to be sounded, for an examination of castles necessarily splits aristocratic society into two unequal parts. On one side of the divide we have the minority of richer, more powerful individuals who achieved control of a castle by building it themselves, through inheritance, or because they had particular qualities of leadership and reliability that meant that men who were even more powerful were prepared to delegate control of a fortification to them. On the other side we have the large majority of arms-bearers who could not afford their own castle or who lived in regions in which the local prince was able to control what was built and who was allowed to share in the power that these structures brought. The differential implicit in this distinction was potentially enormous, and contemporaries had no illusions about the special level of power that castles brought those in the minority. For example, Bernard of Angers noted in the 1010s how the monks of Conques had feared Count Raymond of the Rouergue's plans – in the event unrealised – to build a fortification on a ridge overlooking their abbey. Raymond had a good enough reputation with the monks, but this project stood to transform their relationship, for, as Bernard observed, the castle would have equipped the count to use violence in the subjugation of those who did not offer their allegiance to him and in the building up of his lordship.[37] To this extent, then, there might seem to be a case for saying that castles can only take us into the ideas and behaviour of privileged *domini*, an elite within an elite. On the other hand, it must be remembered that castles were the site of a host of social transactions that were more inclusive and brought different levels of the aristocracy together even as they reasserted the pecking orders that set the lord and his family apart. In these places knights could observe the trappings and possibilities of the higher status to which they might themselves aspire. Castles crystallised ambition. Interestingly,

Medieval Castle in England and Wales: A Social and Political History (Cambridge: Cambridge University Press, 1990); Michael W. Thompson, *The Rise of the Castle* (Cambridge: Cambridge University Press, 1991).

[36] The notion of a 'feudal transformation' has been vigorously contested by Dominique Barthélemy, 'La mutation féodale a-t-elle eu lieu?', *Annales: Economies, Sociétés, Civilisations*, 47 (1992), 767–75. But see the response by Thomas N. Bisson, 'The "Feudal Revolution" ', *Past and Present*, 142 (1994), 6–42.

[37] *Liber Miraculorum Sancte Fidis*, ed. Luca Robertini, Biblioteca di medioevo latino, 10 (Spoleto: Centro italiano di studi sull'alto medioevo, 1994), pp. 165–6.

Orderic Vitalis observes that one of the priorities of some of the 'new men' who rose through service of King Henry I of England in the early decades of the twelfth century was to build fortified residences – that is to announce their new status through the appropriation of the messages about power, status, and wealth that castles sent out.[38]

If we therefore treat castles as a point of entry into the thought world of the aristocracy as a whole, we can begin to identify various factors that reveal how they spoke to ideas about the future. In the first place, castles were exercises in attempted permanence. As such they became the concretisations of the social structures and economic conditions that made them possible. At the beginning of our period many fortifications were made of wood; they were often very modest structures that could even be disassembled and moved. But by the later decades of the eleventh century stone was taking over as the material of choice for the main architectural features (although wood, of course, remained indispensable for superstructures and ancillary buildings). In this way fortifications were better able to communicate the same sorts of ideas about durability that would have been conveyed by church buildings.[39] Lambert of Ardres tells the revealing story of how back in the mid-eleventh century his forbear Arnulf I built the *donjon* of Ardres and then arranged for a stone set in a gold mounting to be buried in a secret place on the site, with the intention that it should lie there forever.[40] It does not particularly matter whether or not this story was based on truth, for its significance lies in the symbolic rooting of the castle in the ground as an expression of powerful assumptions about the possibilities surrounding the fashioning of the future.

One important consequence of the transition from wood to stone was that castles became very expensive. Detailed evidence for the costs involved only begin to become available in the different conditions of the thirteenth century, but it is reasonable to suppose that an eleventh- or twelfth-century lord building a castle typically needed to spend the equivalent of several years' income. As we noted earlier, these men were more consumers than savers. When they had to find large lump sums – as when, for example, they were planning to crusade – they were often forced to sell, lease, or pledge precious family property. So the fact that such large investments in castle construction were made is striking – the more so in that castles were not usually one-off projects but rather constantly evolving environments that were

---

[38] Orderic Vitalis, *The Ecclesiastical History*, ed. and trans. Marjorie Chibnall, 6 vols (Oxford: Clarendon Press, 1969–80), VI (1978), 16, 468. For a statement of the confidence that possession of strongholds brought aristocrats, see *The Gesta Normannorum Ducum of William of Jumièges, Orderic Vitalis, and Robert of Torigni*, ed. and trans. Elisabeth M. C. van Houts, 2 vols (Oxford: Clarendon Press, 1992–95), II (1995), 92.

[39] Xavier Barral i Altet, 'Le paysage architectural de l'an Mil', in *La France de l'an Mil*, ed. Robert Delort and Dominique Iogna-Prat (Paris: Éditions du Seuil, 1990), pp. 169–83 (pp. 174–6).

[40] 'Historia comitum Ghisnensium', c. 109, cited in Fournier, p. 289.

added to and improved upon generation by generation. These sorts of investment only make sense if we see in them a projection into the future of a lord's ambitions and insecurities. A lord without a sense of future time could never have embraced the full potential of his habitat. This point is reinforced if we consider that castles were excellent arenas for aristocratic attempts to generate and control change. There is plenty of evidence for lords moving populations into or near their castles, setting up markets there, and making space in them for the founding of new churches.[41] That is to say, the castle equipped the lord to effect a vision of the future on his own terms – an ambition that could seem realistic because it would be attempted within the manageably small social and economic environment that the castle animated. In essence a castle was the expression *par excellence* of power; and it is as he ponders this power, its possibilities and limitations, that we can readily imagine an aristocrat addressing questions about what the future held.

When the promoters of crusades drew on ideas and images derived from aristocratic experience of the family and of possession of property, they did so in order to build towards the central strand of their appeal, which was the holding out of spiritual rewards to those who took the cross and submitted themselves to the rigours of the campaign. Whatever the exact formulation at any given point – the notion that crusading was a particularly efficacious form of penance, or the more ambitious offer of the remission of sins made possible by God's limitless mercy[42] – the core of the crusade message was always an invitation to the audience to submit itself to a series of negotiations that was governed by an implicit chronological sequence. First, a lord or knight should reflect on his past actions. He should then reach a clear verdict on his past life by locating himself in the present on what amounted to a scale that measured sinfulness, conceptualised as a more-or-less quantifiable entity. And finally he was to project that sense of moral positioning into the future by pondering its implications for his fate in the afterlife. In other words, attention to what would happen to the soul was the force behind the enthusiasm for what Guibert of Nogent, in a much-quoted phrase, described as the 'new means of gaining salvation'.[43]

Here too we find that ideas present in crusading discourse are to be found in other aspects of aristocratic culture. Indeed, it is in the evidence for how lords and knights made provision for the spiritual welfare of themselves and members of their families that we find the most overt and routine articulations of ideas linked to the future. This is so because many charters that

---

[41] See, for example, the evidence for the castles of Ardres, Vendôme, Vihiers, Vignory, Appoigny, Pirmil, La Ferté-Hubert, and Merckem assembled in Fournier, pp. 288–91, 294–6, 297–8, 306, 308–9, 317, 325–6, 327.

[42] For the nature of the indulgence, see Jonathan S. C. Riley-Smith, *What Were the Crusades?*, 2nd edn (London: Macmillan, 1992), pp. 4–6, 57–63.

[43] Guibert of Nogent, 'Gesta Dei per Francos', *RHC Occ*, IV (1879), 117–263 (p. 124).

recorded benefactions of religious institutions included reflections on the circumstances which had led an aristocrat to decide to give some of his property, on the transient nature of human achievement in this life, and on the infernal punishments that sinners could expect when they died.[44] The economy of exchange that the charters expounded was one rooted in the idea that the giving of property or rights, the confirmation of a predecessor's gifts, or the resolution of a property dispute with a church would win the aristocrat the intercessory support of the monks or clerics whom he was supporting and of the saints with whom they identified. The aim was to increase one's chances of an eternal future that was to be played out in an environment that some documents constructed as a projection and perfection of conditions recognisable in this life – a heavenly kingdom or homeland in which an anthropomorphic deity presided over a hall in which he heard petitions and made judgements, and in which the blessed dwelt in the habitations of Luke 16. 9.

In studying the language of the charters we find ourselves confronted by one of the problems mentioned earlier, in that these texts are in the first instance reflections of the thought-world of monks and clerics rather than of the laymen who appear in them. Moreover, in assessing how far aristocratic understanding of these ideas can be retrieved from these documents, we must avoid any neat conversion formula which requires that the metaphorical and allegorical interpretations of religious were simply translated into literal meanings as far as lords and knights were concerned. On the other hand, the fact that similar statements about the afterlife appear in many thousands of charters written in many different areas is compelling evidence that what we are seeing is something much more than monastic or clerical ventriloquising. Rather, charters are a route into the hopes and fears of aristocrats. This is confirmed by the fact that ideas about the spiritual future were inextricably bound up with other priorities that we have already identified. The family group was the typical unit of pious benefaction, even when an individual was acting as principal; relatives would witness donations or be expected to confirm them later, and if a donor specified whose souls were to be prayed for, those so favoured would in most instances be members of his family, living or dead. In addition, the wherewithal to give, and through it the opportunity to win friends in heaven, was precisely that property resource which contributed to a family's sense of itself and formed the material basis of its aspirations for its future in this world. In other words, ideas about the next life could not be played out in a detached space within the realm of the imagination. They were simply a different inflection of the basic elements that shaped elitist self-awareness – in other words, one way to entertain notions of the future by means of a projection of lived experience.

In conclusion, we can see that those who devised and spread crusade

---

[44] Marcus G. Bull, *Knightly Piety and the Lay Response to the First Crusade: The Limousin and Gascony, c.970–c.1130* (Oxford: Clarendon Press, 1993), pp. 179–91.

appeals showed a shrewd appreciation of the sensibilities and needs of their aristocratic audience. It would be wrong to see this simply in terms of the clever use of language and imagery to 'package' ideas. Beneath the rhetoric there was real substance, not least because crusade preachers were faced with a potentially very delicate balancing act that required a careful understanding of those with whom they were communicating. Their task was to persuade people that they should disregard the many sound reasons for staying at home, and voluntarily submit themselves to something that was unquestionably and extremely long, expensive, dangerous, and stressful. Moreover, the reactions that preachers wanted to elicit had to reconcile two apparently conflicting ways of behaving, for they intended a crusader to combine very different sets of ideas and instincts: an emotionally expressive response based on an empathetic identification with the suffering of others or the dishonour done to the Lord through injury to his property; and a considered calculation – a form of sober cost-benefit analysis – that could sustain a sense of purpose in the weeks and months, if not years, between the taking of the cross and departure. Preaching a crusade was an exercise in teaching reflectivity. And reflectivity resides as much as anything in pondering the choices that lie ahead. The sources for crusading suggest that crusade preachers were able to recognise in their audiences pre-existing mental frameworks that made the insertion of their own ideas about the future possible. This was so because a range of associations and images that derived from the essentials of aristocratic identity – the family and property – amounted to the means whereby a lord or knight could locate himself in time, and devise strategies for the future.

In perpetuum: the Rhetoric and Reality of Attempts to Control the Future in the English Medieval Common Law

PAUL BRAND

WHEN Chief Justice Mettingham gave judgment in Michaelmas term 1300 in favour of Ralph de Frecheville and against the dean and chapter of Southwell after the verdict of a grand assize (a jury of twelve local knights) in a long-running action about the advowson of the Nottingham-shire church of Bonney, it was (as we learn from three surviving independent reports of what was actually said in court) that Ralph was to retain the advowson 'to himself and his heirs quit of the chapter and their successors *to the end of time (a remenaunt de mond)*'.[1] A similar form of words was also used by William of Brunton, one of the justices of the 1302 Cornish eyre, in his final judgment in an action of right for land, again after the verdict of a grand assize in favour of the existing tenant.[2] The official plea roll enrolment of the first of these cases uses only the rather less colourful form of words, that 'Ralph . . . is to hold the said advowson to himself and his heirs quit of the said chapter and their succcessors *in perpetuity*', but even these words clearly also stress the finality of the judgment being given.[3] A similarly definitive form of words seems also to have been used in the judgment given in the Common Bench in 1287 in an action of right claiming the Suffolk manors of Semer and Groton brought by John of Creake and his two fellow-coheirs against the abbot of Bury St Edmunds, after the victory of the demandants' champion in judicial combat (trial by battle). This awarded the manors to the claimants 'to hold to themselves and their heirs quit of the said abbot and his successors

---

[1] Bodleian Library, Holkham MS, Miscellaneous 30, fol. 17v; British Library, Additional MSS 31826, fol. 323v and 37657, fol. 48v (not here specifically ascribed to Mettingham); *Novae Narrationes*, ed. E. Shanks and S. F. C. Milsom (London: Selden Society, 80, 1963), p. 163. The phrase does not appear in the report in Lincoln's Inn, Hale MS 174, fol. 12v.
[2] *Year Books 30 & 31 Edward I*, ed. Alfred J. Horwood (London: Rolls Series, 1863), p. 119.
[3] Public Record Office, Court of Common Pleas, CP 40/105, m. 29.

in perpetuity'.[4] Again these are the words of the enrolment. If we also possessed a report of the words spoken by the presiding justice in court, we might well discover that he had used a similar form of words to those used by Mettingham and Brunton.

Such words were, however, by no means the common currency of judgments. They were a distinctive feature of actions of right, legal actions in which the grand assize or trial by battle were the methods of proof, and in which legal procedure allowed multiple possibilities of delay. What was at stake in these cases was which of these two parties had the 'greater right' to the property concerned. In other kinds of case, where the stakes were less high, the judgment was merely that the demandant 'recover seisin' of the land claimed or that the demandant 'take nothing by his writ', words which are deliberately much less definitive. It was only in actions of right that English courts and English judges wanted to stress the finality of the judgment given, the fact that this judgment had indeed determined for all time the question of entitlement as between the parties and their heirs and successors, and so the rhetoric of the judgment was of an unchanging future whose shape was to be determined for ever by the present, definitive decision.

A similar picture of an essentially static future, but one whose shape was determined in its essentials by the agreement of the two parties, even if it derived some of its force from the fact that it was backed up by the authority of the king's courts, also underlay, indeed was specifically invoked by the name of, the 'final concord'. This court-prepared and court-authorised type of written agreement (normally about land or other types of real property) is found in England from the reign of Henry II onwards (the earliest dates from c.1170). Final concords purported to bring an end to litigation between two parties but from an early stage were also used as a way of registering noncontentious agreements. They also regularly used the language and rhetoric of permanence: the grants or quitclaims that they register are to X and his heirs 'in perpetuity'. Indeed, as *Bracton* puts it, the final concord is so called precisely 'because it puts an end to litigation'.[5]

Final concords and judgments in actions of right could be even more definitive than they at first sight appeared. The general doctrine of the English legal treatise *Bracton*, which was originally written in the 1220s and 1230s,[6] seems to be that both final concords and final judgments in actions of right were binding not just on the parties to the judgment or final concord

---

[4] *The Earliest English Law Reports, vol. II*, ed. Paul Brand (London: Selden Society, 112, 1996), p. 297.

[5] *Bracton*, ed. George E. Woodbine, rev. and trans. Samuel E. Thorne, 4 vols (Cambridge, MA: Harvard University Press, 1968–77), IV, 353.

[6] Paul Brand, 'The Age of Bracton', in *The History of English Law: Centenary Essays on 'Pollock and Maitland'*, ed. John Hudson, Proceedings of the British Academy, 89 (Oxford: Oxford University Press, 1996), pp. 65–89.

concerned but also on third parties if those third parties (however good their potential claim to the property) had failed to put in their claim to the property concerned before the judgment was given or the final concord delivered to the parties.[7] Fairness allowed some minor exceptions to this rule, of which the most important were where the person with the claim was incompetent (because below the age of majority or not in possession of full mental faculties) or unable (because detained in prison or physically outside the country) to register his claim at the time of the delivery of judgment or the making of the final concord.[8] Later law was more restrictive on this point. Although the precise details of the process of change have yet to be ascertained, by the third decade of the fourteenth century the generally accepted rule seems to have been that final concords and judgments were binding on third parties only where they had led to a transfer of possession of the property from one party to another by the local sheriff acting with the authorisation of the court, a process which would serve to provide proper notice of the final concord or judgment to any third party. The third party also now had a period of a year and a day after the judgment or the making of the final concord to register his claim.[9] But provided property was transferred in this way by a judgment or a final concord and no claim was made within the limitation period, the judgment or final concord still retained its power to exclude the claims of third parties.

Final judgments in actions of right and final concords might use the language of 'eternity' or at least 'perpetuity'. They did not, and could not, in reality necessarily control the future, other than in a negative way. They did exclude the rights of those against whom judgment was given or who had quitclaimed or surrendered their rights by final concord and (in the right circumstances) of those who had possessed rights but had failed to register their claims. They could not, and did not, stop those awarded property or given property by a final concord in turn transferring it to someone else; nor did they provide any safeguard against third parties wrongfully acquiring the property from a subsequent possessor. The mere possession of a final concord or fact that a definitive final judgment had once been given in relation to a particular piece of property did not stop argument about the validity of transactions which had occurred after the making of the judgment or concord. Thus, despite the forward-looking rhetoric of the final concord and final judgment, their real importance was in controlling the past, in cutting off claims based on the history of the property prior to their making, rather than in controlling the future. The final concord (though not the final judgment) only did more than that, as will be seen, when it also attempted, like other

---

7 *Bracton*, IV, 354–6. But there seems to be no trace of this doctrine in the earlier legal treatise *Glanvill*, completed between 1187 and 1189.
8 *Bracton*, IV, 354–8.
9 *YB 7 Edward III*, fol. 37 (Trinity, pl. 41).

types of deed, to make active plans for the future descent of the property concerned.

The grant of property to a man 'and his heirs' 'in perpetuity', whether by charter or by final concord, looks, at first sight, to be the strongest example of a disposition whose purpose is to control the future for an indefinite, indeed potentially infinite, period of time. It certainly does so in a negative sense. The promise of warranty given on behalf of the grantor and his heirs that is the normal accompaniment of such a grant did, indeed, have the effect of obliging the grantor and his heirs into the indefinite future to come to the defence of the title to the land if litigation was brought against its owner and also to provide a substitute of the same value if the land was then lost to the claimant. This warranty also had the effect of preventing the grantor and his heirs from making their own claim to the land, unless it had been forfeited by the death of the owner without heirs, or his commission of a felony, or his denial of the existence of the tenurial bond between them. But it did *not* control the future of the property in any more positive sense, for it did not ensure that the land really did pass to the grantee's heirs in perpetuity. Even if the grant was specifically phrased as being one 'to the grantee *and his heirs*', there was nothing to stop the grantee (or indeed any of his heirs) granting away all or any part of the land to a third party and thereby disinheriting *his own* heirs. When *Glanvill* was written at the end of the reign of Henry II, there were still some limits on the ability of the owner of land to disinherit his heir apparent. These had all disappeared by the second decade of the thirteenth century and they did not reappear thereafter.[10] The generally accepted explanation for this among legal historians is that it was a byproduct of the owner's ability to bind his heirs in perpetuity by a warranty clause, whether or not they had inherited any assets from him. However, another factor at work seems to have been the development of English legal thought about the nature of the interest of the heir apparent during his ancestor's lifetime. Since the actual identity of an heir could only be discovered at the moment the current tenant of the land died (for an heir apparent *may* always die before his ancestor), no-one (as the maxim puts it) can be the 'heir' of a living person (*nemo est heres viventis*): the identity of the heir is uncertain right up until the moment of the ancestor's death. As an early fourteenth-century law report puts it, all the son and heir apparent has during his father's lifetime is an 'expectation of right' (*une biaunse de dreit*) and not an actual 'right'. In this particular context, the conclusion drawn was that for this very reason he could not during his father's lifetime effectively renounce his right to succeed

---

10 F. Pollock and F. W. Maitland, *The History of English Law before the Time of Edward I*, 2nd edn reissued, 2 vols (Cambridge: Cambridge University Press, 1968), II, 308–13; S. F. C. Milsom, *The Legal Framework of English Feudalism* (Cambridge: Cambridge University Press, 1976), pp. 121–32.

to the land.[11] But it is perhaps precisely because English medieval law did not see the heir or heir apparent possessing any 'right' during his father's lifetime that it also did not develop any mechanism allowing him to act to protect that right, that legitimate expectation, when his ancestor in effect disinherited him.

More scope for controlling the future devolution of land was offered to grantors of land from at least 1200 onwards by the form of grant later to be known as the entail. In its earliest and simplest form, the grant in *maritagium*, the entail took the form of a grant made on marriage to a particular woman (commonly the daughter of the grantor) and the husband she was marrying and to their issue (the heirs of their bodies, their children). Such grants implicitly excluded inheritance of the land granted by any collateral heirs of the grantees (brothers, sisters, uncles and aunts, etc.). By the early thirteenth century we find a number of variants on this: grants made to a particular individual (whether male or female) and the heirs of their body not specifically associated with marriage and grants made to a husband and wife and the heirs of the body of the husband (or of the wife), allowing for the succession to the land of the children of a second or other marriage. By the middle of the thirteenth century (but not before) there had also developed a further variant, though one which seems at first to have been very uncommon, restricting inheritance in such grants to an individual or a couple's *male* issue.[12] The grant might specifically spell out that if the grantee(s) died without issue, the land was to revert to the original grantor or his heirs or might grant the reversion to some third person. If the charter was not specific, the presumption was that it was the grantor's intention that the land should revert to him. A further complication not mentioned in *Glanvill* but whose existence was traced back by Maitland to the final decade of the twelfth century was the inclusion in such grants of provisions for 'remainders'. These stipulated that even if the original grantee(s) did die without issue, the land was not to revert immediately but was to go to someone else, commonly a brother or sister of the original grantee, and their issue, and only if they in turn died without issue was it to revert to the grantor.[13] In practice it was possible to include any number of such remainders in a grant. A good mid-thirteenth-century example is the settlement made (in this case by means of a final concord) in 1258 by Edward of Westminster, Henry III's artistic adviser, providing for most of Edward's property in Westminster, Southwark, Stepney and Bengeo to be held by his mistress Katherine of Ely for life with successive remainders over to her (or rather their) son Odo and his issue, to his brother Nicholas

---

11 BL, Hargrave MS 375, fol. 34r.

12 For early examples of such grants, see *Calendar of Inquisitions Post Mortem*, i, no. 587; PRO, CP 40/17, m. 16 and JUST 1/1322, m. 10d.

13 F. W. Maitland, *Collected Papers*, ed. H. A. L. Fisher, 3 vols (Cambridge: Cambridge University Press, 1911), II, 174–81.

and his issue, to his brother Thomas and his issue with a final remainder over to the 'right heirs' of Katherine.[14]

For most of the thirteenth century, however, the ability of the original settlor who established such an entail to control what happened to the property after he had granted it was a limited one. *Provided* the original grantee and his heirs remained in possession of the land, the land did apparently retain its original characteristic of being inheritable only by the descendants of the original grantee or grantees. In 1275 an action of formedon in the descender was brought to enforce the right of succession under an entail of the grandson of the original grantee,[15] and in 1278 an action of formedon in the reverter was brought to enforce a right of reversion under an entail after the death without issue of the grandson of the original grantee. These two actions provide clear evidence that in the early part of the reign of Edward I property settled in this way was still thought to be held under the rules of descent laid down by the entail in the third generation.[16] It is not, however, wholly clear how long the land so granted retained this special characteristic. The *maritagium* as described in *Glanvill* retained its special characteristic of exemption from homage (and the *liberum maritagium* its special characteristic of exemption from all other services as well as homage) until the third heir had inherited the land: the great-grandson or great-grandchild of the original donee.[17] It is a plausible guess that these variants on the *maritagium* may also have shared this general characteristic of their progenitor in respect of the rules of inheritance.

But grantee(s) in tail and their descendants were generally also able for most of the thirteenth century to defeat the intentions of the original grantor and also the claims of their own descendants and of reversioners and remaindermen by granting or selling all or any part of the land held under the entail.[18] From early in the thirteenth century (if not before) this became legally possible once issue was born to the original grantee. It was this that fulfilled the 'condition' imposed by the original grant and turned the grantee(s) into a full owner of the property. Legislation of 1285 about such gifts (the statute of Westminster II, c. 1) stated that the existing rule allowed alienation (the granting or selling of the entailed property) once issue was

---

14 PRO, CP 25(1)/283/14, no. 344.
15 *John fitzJohn v. Edmund earl of Cornwall*: PRO, CP 40/9, m. 54d.
16 *Robert fitzWalter v. William de Valence*: PRO, CP 40/27, m. 132.
17 *The Treatise on the Laws and Customs of the Realm of England commonly called Glanvill*, ed. G. D. G. Hall (London: Nelson, 1965), pp. 92–4 (VII, 18).
18 This seems to be the implication of the pleading in the cases of *Henry son of Simon v. John Smith alderman of the guild of St Nicholas of Newport Pagnel* in the 1247 Buckinghamshire eyre (PRO, JUST 1/56, m. 13); of *Henry Aky v. William son of Nicholas de la Marine* in the 1268–69 Gloucestershire eyre (PRO, JUST 1/275, m. 52); and was argued by one side in the case of *William le Chanu v. Baldwin de Akeny* in the 1272 Cambridgeshire eyre (PRO, JUST 1/84, m. 13d).

born and (at least by implication) whether or not that issue was still living when the grant took place.[19] Earlier cases suggest that this had previously only been one possible understanding of the general rule.[20] Some lawyers and judges had held that alienation was permissible only if the issue was still living when the grant took place;[21] others had allowed alienation even before the birth of issue provided that issue was then born and that issue then survived the original grantees.[22] But, whatever the precise interpretation adopted, the essential point is clear: for most of the thirteenth century the original grantor only controlled the devolution of land granted in fee tail once issue had been born to the original grantee(s) if the original grantees did not attempt to upset his arrangements. In practice, therefore, control of the devolution of entailed property was something shared between the original grantor and the current holder of the land.

Chapter 1 of the statute of Westminster II of 1285 (*de donis conditionalibus*) deliberately set out to alter the existing balance of power as between the original grantor of an entail and the grantee and the grantee's issue, and thereby significantly enhanced the ability of the original grantor to determine the future devolution of entailed land.[23] The statute adopted as its guiding principle that 'the will of the donor as clearly expressed in the charter of gift is to be observed in future'. It also spelled out the main consequences of this: that those to whom tenements were so given would not in future have the power to alienate the tenement so given in such a way that it did not pass after their death to their issue or revert to the donor if issue failed. Legal historians have taken different views about just how long the statute intended to make the entail inalienable. Plucknett's view was that the original intention was to keep entailed land inalienable for four generations (until the third heir inherited) but that the text of the statute had been clumsily amended at a late stage to make land inalienable only in the hands of the first grantees;[24] Milsom thought that from the first the statute was intended to make entailed

---

[19] *Statutes of the Realm*, ed. A. Luders and others, 12 vols (London: Record Commission, 1810–28), i. 71–2.

[20] For a case where the rule seems to have been accepted in this form by the courts, see *Adam de la Rivere v. Edmund Spigurnel and Clarice his wife* in the 1281 Wiltshire eyre (PRO, JUST 1/1005, part I, m. 13). It was also the interpretation of the rule argued for by two of the serjeants in the report of an unidentified formedon in the reverter case of the 1280s in BL, Royal MS 10.A.V, fols 93r–v.

[21] See *the prioress of Heynings v. Thomas Duthty and his wife Cecilia* heard in the Common Bench in 1287 (PRO, CP 40/69, m. 129d) and *Nicholas of Redesdale v. Robert son of William le Provost of Little Peatling* heard in the Common Bench in 1292 (PRO, CP 40/95, m. 65: reported in BL, Additional MSS 5925, fols 84r–v and 31826, fol. 67r).

[22] This seems to be the view adopted by Justice Saham in the unidentified case of the 1280s reported in BL, Royal MS 10.A.V, fols 93r–v and the initial view of Serjeant Ashby in a reported case of 1292 (see previous note).

[23] *Statutes of the Realm*, i. 71–2.

[24] T. F. T. Plucknett, *Legislation of Edward I* (Oxford: Clarendon Press, 1962), pp. 131–4.

land inalienable only in the hands of the original grantees;[25] Simpson believed that it was intended to make the entail inalienable for longer than one generation but did not specify for just how long.[26] The plea rolls indicate that the courts were in practice relatively quick to adopt the position that entailed land was to be inalienable not just in the hands of the original grantees but also in the hands of at least the first generation of issue. Grandchildren regularly brought actions of formedon in the descender from at least 1292 onwards[27] and the use of this action by grandchildren probably implies that entailed land was considered subject not just to the special rules of inheritance laid down by the entail but also to the statutory restrictions on alienation for at least the first two generations of the grant, that is to say, while it was in the hands both of the original grantee(s) and of the first heir in tail. That this was indeed the courts' understanding of the statute is made clear by a reported case of 1302 in which a grandson sued to revoke an alienation made by the son of the original grantees in tail.[28] In a well-known case of 1312 (*Belyng v. Anon.*) Bereford, C.J. claimed that it had been the intention of the legislators to keep the entailed land inalienable until the fourth heir (the great-grandson) inherited under the entail (the same point as that at which the *maritagium* lost its special characteristics), but this was said in passing in a case where the real issue at stake was whether or not the second generation holding entailed land could lawfully alienate.[29] The length of time for which the entail ought to remain inalienable still remained a matter of debate and doubt in the 1340s, but the choice seems then still to have been between inalienability only in the hands of the first generation or in the hands of the first two generations, though not any longer.[30] However, by the early fifteenth century the courts seem to have come to the view that the special characteristics of the entail lasted not just for two (or even four) generations but indefinitely and thus that a grantor could keep land within the family and in the hands of descendants of the original grantees for ever. How and when they came to this view is the subject of current research by Professor Joseph Biancalana of the University of Cincinnati School of Law.

[25] S. F. C. Milsom, *Historical Foundations of the Common Law*, 2nd edn (London: Butterworth, 1981), pp. 175–6.

[26] A. W. B. Simpson, *A History of the Land Law*, 2nd edn (Oxford: Clarendon Press, 1986), pp. 82–3.

[27] *Roger Imayne v. William de Pyrye and wife Juliana*: PRO, CP 40/95, m. 65.

[28] *John le Poer v. William le Poer:* reported in YB 30 & 31 Edward I, pp. 15–17; BL, Additional MSS 31826, fol. 180v and 37657, fol. 192r, Harley MS. 25, fol. 25v, Stowe MS 386, fol. 167v and LI, Miscellaneous MS 738, fol. 31v; the case is enrolled on PRO, CP 40/144, m. 152.

[29] *YB 5 Edward II*, ed. W. C. Bolland (London: Selden Society, 31, 1915), p. 177; *YB 5 Edward II*, ed. W. C. Bolland (Selden Society, 33, 1916), p. 226; Simpson, *History of the Land Law*, pp. 83–4; Milsom, *Historical Foundations of the Common Law*, p. 177.

[30] *Select Cases in the Court of King's Bench, vol. III*, ed. G. O. Sayles (London: Selden Society, 58, 1939), p. cxx.

Professor Biancalana is also working on the origins of the legal device that in turn made this development tolerable: a collusive form of litigation (the collusive common recovery) which from shortly after the middle of the fifteenth century in effect allowed those holding under entails to break those entails and freely alienate the land, though collusive common recoveries were evidently sometimes just used to resettle land differently within the same family or even to use it as collateral for a loan of money.

As has been seen, English medieval law was notably reluctant to anticipate the future by giving rights (even of a limited and subordinate type) over property held in full ownership (fee simple) to the heir apparent of the current tenant. It was not always that reluctant to anticipate the future: indeed, over the course of the thirteenth century there was a growing willingness to provide present protection for the future rights of the reversioner or remainderman entitled to take possession after the death of a tenant for life. Life tenancies were created in two different ways. A majority came into being by the operation of the law. The Common Law generally gave the widow a life interest in one-third of the lands her late husband had held at any time during their marriage (dower), and the widower (provided his late wife had borne him at least one child) a life estate in the whole of his wife's lands (curtesy). A minority of life estates were created by individual grants or as part of wider settlements of land.

The earliest form of immediate protection for the rights of the reversioner was that provided through the action of waste. From early in the thirteenth century it was possible for a reversioner to secure a royal prohibition addressed to a local sheriff ordering him to stop a doweress making 'waste, sale or exile' of the 'lands, men, rents, houses, woods or gardens' she held in dower and, if she still continued doing this, to bring her to court to answer for her actions.[31] The reversioner's future interest in the land and what was on the land was thereby protected against the doweress's failure to maintain the buildings on her holding or her destruction or removal of them; against her selling or cutting down trees there apart from those required for the repair of buildings or the erection of fences or for use as firewood; against her either manumitting the villein tenants on her lands or forcing them to abandon their holdings through excessive demands; and even (in the first half of the century at least) against her selling off any of the land she held in dower. A similar mechanism seems also occasionally to have been used to prevent or punish waste committed by tenants who held for life by grant[32] and even by

---

[31] *Bracton*, III, 405–6; *Early Registers of Writs*, pp. 16, 53 (Hib. 51; CC 64–66). For an early example, see *Curia Regis Rolls*, 18 vols so far published (London: HMSO, 1923–99), vi, 42.

[32] *Curia Regis Rolls*, ix, 20–1 (=*Bracton's Note Book*, pl. 1371); PRO, CP 40/15, m. 90 (allegedly based on statute and without any prior prohibition).

curtesy tenants.[33] The existence of an action of waste against both these latter categories was specifically confirmed by legislation enacted in 1278 (the statute of Gloucester, c. 5). This also increased the punishment for those convicted of waste: damages to triple the value of those assessed by the jury and loss of the property where the waste had taken place.[34]

A different clause of the same statute (statute of Gloucester c. 7) also gave an immediate remedy to the reversioner if a doweress attempted to grant away for any period longer than her own life any of the property she held in dower, a right to implead the grantee and secure the immediate forfeiture of the land.[35] Hitherto the reversioner normally had to wait until the doweress died before he could take legal action to recover such land.[36] Henceforth he could take immediate action that in effect anticipated his own right of reversion to the land. The statute said nothing about grants by other kinds of life tenant but soon came to be extended to them as well. The first two alienees of tenants for life by grant impleaded by reversioners in 1282 and 1284 specifically objected that the statute did not cover their case and secured an adjournment of their cases for judgment,[37] but writs continued to be issued thereafter and forfeitures successfully claimed by reversioners. From 1288 onwards actions also began to be brought, again allegedly based on the statute of Gloucester, to secure the immediate forfeiture of land alienated by curtesy tenants as well.[38]

A second late thirteenth-century statute (the statute of Westminster II of 1285, c. 3) added a further protection for the rights of the reversioner.[39] Hitherto, when life tenants were impleaded for land, they had been entitled to ask for the assistance of the reversioner in the defence of their title through the procedure known as aid-prayer. But if the tenant for life (whether collusively or otherwise) neglected to do this and even went so far as to fail to appear (which would lead to judgment awarding the land by default to the claimant) or simply surrendered the land to the claimant, the reversioner had no remedy until the life tenant died. The new provision did not go so far as to give the reversioner the right to intervene under all circumstances, but it did give him the right to ask the court to be 'received' to defend the land whenever the life tenant was in the process of losing it by default or surrendering it

---

[33] For two allegedly statutory actions brought against such tenants in 1277, see PRO, CP 40/19, mm. 38, 66.

[34] *Statutes of the Realm*, i. 48.

[35] *Statutes of the Realm*, i. 48.

[36] From at least 1220 onwards there was a special form of writ of entry to allow him to do exactly that: for what seems to be the earliest example, see *Curia Regis Rolls*, ix. 252.

[37] *John Bufford v. master of the Templars*: PRO, CP 40/46, m. 30d; *Walter of Amersham v. Humphrey de Boun earl of Hereford*: PRO, CP 40/53, m. 43.

[38] The earliest case is *John of Shrewsbury and his wife Alice v. William son of Deodatus of Tyringham*: PRO, CP 40/70, m. 65d.

[39] *Statutes of the Realm*, i. 74.

to the claimant: a further manifestation of the way in which the reversioner was increasingly being treated as having a substantial current interest in the land during the tenure of a life tenant.

It was, however, at this point that the line was drawn and very largely remained drawn. The reversioner after the life estate was given rights; the reversioner or remainderman after a fee tail estate was not, nor (generally) was the issue in tail. This does not mean, however, that reversioners, remaindermen and heirs in tail did not try to gain such rights. A particularly strong case could be made for treating as life tenants those persons to whom land had been given in tail but who had no issue and now no possibility of issue: for example, where land had been given to a husband and wife and their issue where no issue had been born and the husband was now dead. A plaintiff tried to bring the statutory action of waste against a widow (and her second husband) in just such circumstances in 1302, treating the wife as being for these purposes no more than a tenant for life, but once the defendants had shown that the wife was the sole survivor of grantees in tail the case was dismissed.[40] In 1287, there was also at least one attempt by a reversioner to extend still further the already extended provisions of the statute of Gloucester to claim the immediate forfeiture of land alienated in fee by a tenant in tail (again apparently when there was no possibility of issue now being born and by treating and describing the tenant as a tenant for life). Again this was not successful.[41]

There are also a number of reported cases from the years around 1300 when it was the issue in tail (the heir apparent of the current tenant in tail) who tried to have the courts 'receive' him to defend title to land. In a case of 1300 Thomas of Tidmarsh was about to lose by default land that had been granted to him and his late wife Hawise and their issue. It was their son John who asked the court to receive him to defend the land as the 'son and heir' of Thomas to whom the land was to descend after the death of his father.[42] The claimant resisted this attempt at least in part on the predictable grounds that John could not claim to be the 'son and heir' of his father during his father's lifetime. It was only descent that 'made' an heir, and it was still possible that Thomas would outlive John and thus John would never inherit the land. The court seems to have sided with the claimant but did not have to give a definitive ruling as the claimant died while the case was still pending. In a 1302 case, Walter de Pagrave claimed land against Thomas of Tilney, and Thomas

---

[40] *YB 30 & 31 Edward I*, pp. 45–7 (also reported in BL, Additional MSS 31826, fol. 171r and 37657, fols 192r–v and Stowe 386, fol. 167r and in Cambridge University Library, MS Ee. 6.18, fol. 63r): the case is *Henry de Boys v. John Taylor of Tytherlegh and his wife Margaret* (PRO, CP 40/144, m. 162d).

[41] *Nicholas of Redesdale v. Robert son of William le Provost of Peatling*: PRO, CP 40/68, m. 64d.

[42] *Joan widow of John of Tidmarsh v. Thomas of Tidmarsh*: PRO, CP 40/133, m. 11; reported in BL, Additional MSS 31826, fols 167r and 327r, 37657, fols 12r–v and 5925, fols 52r–v.

defaulted after an unfavourable jury verdict had been given locally.[43] Thomas's son then came to court and showed the charter which had granted the land to Thomas and his issue, and asked to be received to defend the land. The court held that as long as Thomas was alive his son had no 'estate' in the land (no right which the court would protect); all he had was a '*byaunce*' (an 'expectation') and so could not be received. But the arguments for the 'receipt' of the issue in tail were evidently felt to be strong ones. In a further case heard in 1307 Margery and Edith, the daughters of Thomas Pykehorn, were suing Agnes the widow of Thomas Pykehorn, probably their step-mother, for four acres at Corley in Warwickshire. When she defaulted and the land was about to be adjudged to the claimants, John, the son of Thomas Pykehorn (apparently their half-brother) asked to be received to defend his right under an entail which had granted the land to his late father and Agnes and their issue, and this time the court did allow this.[44]

Most of the time English medieval courts and their lawyers and judges (like lawyers, judges and courts anywhere) were thinking and arguing about things that had happened in the past: specific occurrences which might or might not qualify as wrongs for which legal redress might be obtained; the past history of a holding which might or might not justify a current claim to that holding or the like. But part of the time at least, they were thinking about past attempts to control and plan for the future, or what might be construed as such, and were making decisions about how far future expectations of various kinds merited current protection. One particularly important context in which they did this was in connection with the granting and settlement of rights in land, a potentially permanent form of property. As we have seen, English legal doctrine at an early date set its face against any attempt to safeguard the expectations of the heir apparent to land held in 'fee simple', land held in something like full ownership. Initially, also, the courts gave relatively little protection to the expectations of heirs and reversioners of entailed land, despite the fact that the deeds creating fee tail interests in land looked as if they were specifically intended to create and safeguard such rights. The legislation of 1285 led to the safeguarding of such expectations and the honouring of the intentions of the original grantor for at least the first two generations of the entail, and by the early fifteenth century had come to safeguard these interests and honour the grantor's intentions for the land in perpetuity. But this was to give too much control to the dead and by the middle of the fifteenth century entailed land was again becoming alienable by each generation. Even at their fullest, the protection offered to future

---

43 BL, Additional MS 37657, fol. 164v.
44 *Margery and Edith daughters of Thomas Pykehorn v. Agnes widow of Thomas Pykehorn of Corley*: PRO, CP 40/163, m. 155 (reported in *Year Books 33–35 Edward I*, ed. Alfred J. Horwood (London: Rolls Series, 1879), pp. 497–501 and BL, Hargrave MS 375, fols 182v–183r).

expectations under entails by English law never (or at least rarely) exceeded the right to upset after the event (and perhaps many years later) attempts to thwart the purposes of the original grantor. Only in the case of the expectations of the reversioner after life tenancies can we see English law whole-heartedly, and with increasing thoroughness from the early thirteenth century onwards, take measures to safeguard that future interest and to protect it in the present even in ways that anticipate the future, the time when the reversioner becomes entitled to the property. It is always difficult to draw a line between those expectations which merit full legal protection ('rights') and those expectations which are recognised as having moral force but not as meriting any kind of legal enforcement ('mere expectations'). Where the line is drawn owes something to politics and popular sentiment, something to the internal discourses of lawyers and the courts, and it is often difficult to disentangle the complex relationship between these two worlds and their mutual influence. But English law by the fifteenth century did end up giving much greater weight to future expectations and much greater scope for grantors of entailed property at least to control its future devolution: a much closer fit between rhetoric and reality than had been the case in 1200.

The King's Conundrum:
Endowing Queens and Loyal Servants, Ensuring Salvation, and Protecting the Patrimony in Fourteenth-Century France

ELIZABETH A. R. BROWN

ALTHOUGH the word 'future' does not figure in the title of this paper, three words imply a span of time beyond the present which greatly concerned the kings of France in the fourteenth century: endowment, salvation, and patrimony.[1] Kings endowed their queens and favoured servants because they envisioned a time to come, after their own deaths, when these people

[1] This paper is based in part on a paper I delivered at the Caltech-Weingart Humanities Conference on Family and Property in Traditional Europe, at the California Institute of Technology in Pasadena in 1981. In 1982 the paper was published in typescript as a Humanities Working Paper (no. 71) by the Division of the Humanities and Social Sciences at the California Institute of Technnology (Pasadena) as *Royal Marriage, Royal Property, and the Patrimony of the Crown: Inalienability and the Prerogative in Fourteenth-Century France*. For their advice and help on that paper, I again thank the late John F. Benton (who organised the meeting) and Donald W. Sutherland, and Michel Bur. The paper also employs material I presented in a paper entitled 'Queens, Regencies, and Regency Power in Thirteenth- and Fourteenth-Century France', at the Annual Meeting of the American Historical Association in Washington in 1982. I am grateful for their questions and remarks to my fellow panellists and commentators, Robert-Henri Bautier, Brigitte Bedos Rezak, Thomas N. Bisson, Andrew W. Lewis, Claire R. Sherman, Gabrielle M. Spiegel, and Charles T. Wood. I also utilise the central chapters of an as yet unpublished monograph dealing with the adultery affair of 1314, on which Richard C. Famiglietti and Andrew W. Lewis have offered invaluable criticism and suggestions. I have profited from the paper that Michael D. Gordon presented in Naples on 12 April 1980, at the IV Congresso internazionale of the Società italiana di Storia del dritto, 'Royal Power and Fundamental Law in Western Europe, 1350–1650: The Crown Lands'; I appreciate Professor Gordon's kindness in sending me a copy of his essay. Research for this article was supported in part by a grant from the International Research & Exchanges Board (IREX), with funds provided by the National Endowment for the Humanities, the United States Information Agency, and the United States Department of State, which administers the Russian, Eurasian, and East European Research Program (Title VIII). I am as always grateful for the assistance of the staffs of the

would find themselves vulnerable, deprived of the protection and wealth they enjoyed while the kings, their husbands and masters, lived. As to salvation, kings attempted to guarantee it for themselves through lavish gifts and pious endowments, to be effected after their earthly deaths. Such royal interest in salvation was similar to that of their subjects, who were also intent on purchasing paradise, and on protecting their spouses. But kings were different from their subjects in having at their disposal far greater wealth to guarantee their speedy entry into heaven, and to provide for their wives and servants. Thus, at least, it appeared. But, unlike their subjects, kings confronted the conundrum central to my title. The property that was ostensibly theirs was not theirs to dispense as they wished; rather, it belonged to the kingdom and the crown, and thus to the descendants who, one after another, would successively replace the reigning king on the throne. By investing extravagantly in their own salvations, kings imperilled their successors' ability to rule. By immoderately indulging their wives and favourites, they betrayed the interests of their figurative spouse, the kingdom they governed.

As responsible rulers and public persons, kings were bound to defend the patrimony of the crown that never dies. The more they did so, the more their subjects admired and respected them. Royal prudence and parsimony, after all, meant for subjects freedom from taxation. Yet as caring husbands and masters, as Christians eager for eternal bliss, the kings had obligations and needs that ran counter to the responsibilities of their office. In wrestling with these conflicting pressures, kings had to weigh their desire for renown, widespread popularity, and their subjects' future prayers for their salvation against natural impulses to care for their own and take measures themselves to advance their prospects for eternal bliss. In the end, natural proclivities generally triumphed over more exalted aims. Note, however, how handily lofty goals could be enlisted in the service of human cravings when one king succeeded another. One ruler's endowments and gifts, made for perfectly defensible reasons, could appear to (or be made to appear by) his successor profligate and irresponsible. The successor could elevate his own reputation for rectitude by presenting them as rather embarrassing lapses on the part of the previous ruler. The successor could then invoke his responsibility to his subjects, to the crown, and to the kingdom, in quashing the grants. This, of course, provided him with resources with which he could endow his own loved ones

Columbia University Libraries and the New York Public Library, and the Archives nationales and the Bibliothèque nationale de France.
I use the following abbreviations: AD – Archives départementales; AN – Paris, Archives nationales; BNF – Paris, Bibliothèque nationale de France; BM – Bibliothèque municipale; Fawtier – Robert Fawtier, with Jean Glénisson and Jean Guerout, *Registres du Trésor des chartes*, vol. 1, *Règne de Philippe le Bel* (Paris: Imprimerie nationale, 1958); Guerout – Jean Guerout, *Registres du Trésor des chartes*, vol. 2, *Règnes des fils de Philippe le Bel*, part 1, *Règnes de Louis X le Hutin et de Philippe V le Long* (Paris: S.E.V.P.E.N., 1966).

and servants, and make bequests to further his salvation. Such strategies provoked inventive responses. Desire to ensure the stability of gifts and endowments stimulated flights of absolutist rhetoric, and led to the invention of diplomatic practices and tactics expected to guarantee the permanence of donations, and thus curb the inexorable dialectic created by conflicting royal capacities. Such practices and formulae helped elevate the status and power of the monarchy, although they were generally ineffective in protecting the individuals they were devised to assist.

Here I shall consider four topics as I elaborate on these general observations. I shall advance no overarching thesis but rather comment on what was one of the persistent and fundamentally unresolvable problems of the medieval and early modern French monarchy. I focus on fourteenth-century France. There the relentless dialectic of what I term royal successional proprietary antagonism commenced to function in earnest during the reigns of Philip the Fair (1285–1314) and his sons Louis X (1314–16), Philip V (1316–22) and Charles IV (1322–28). I shall begin by discussing theory, and by emphasizing the absence of clear principles at the beginning of the fourteenth century, the failure of kings and their counsellors to delineate and explicate the nature of the king's responsibility to his soul, his family, and his realm, and the lack of useful definitions of such critical concepts as patrimony, domain, and inalienability. In showing how the kings of France used principles of inalienability to benefit themselves, I shall discuss Philip V's legislation on the subject and his efforts to revoke alienations and reunite alienated property to the royal domain. Then I shall turn to the alienations he himself made. I shall propose that Philip V's reign saw the crystallisation and first clear manifestation of the dialectic. This resulted, I believe, from Philip's acumen in grasping the nature of the problem manifested in Louis X's treatment of their father's dying wishes (which in part benefited Philip himself), and also from Philip's quite special relationship with his wife, Jeanne of Burgundy and Artois, and the problems created by the death of their only son in February 1317. It was Philip V who elaborated diplomatic and formulaic mechanisms introduced by his father for other purposes, in hopes of ensuring that his provisions would bind his successors and that the arrangements he decreed would endure into the future, beyond his lifetime. His elaborate strategies had some, but by no means complete, success. Having discussed their effectiveness, I shall end by commenting briefly on the repercussions of Philip V's tactics, as his successors attempted to guarantee their ability to control the future from their graves, and on the long-term effects of the absolutist formulae he devised and employed.

1. Inalienability in Theory and Practice: The Background

The idea of the king as spouse of the kingdom, and hence bound to protect the realm's endowment, does not seem to have been articulated before Lucas de Penna enunciated it in the mid fourteenth century.[2] Still, even if the notion had not been expressed at the beginning of the century, lawyers were familiar with Roman legal principles protecting certain categories of property from alienation, and specifically limiting the husband's right to dispose of his wife's dowry.[3] Such notions were analogous to Roman ideas regarding the emperors' obligations to the fisc, although, as concerned themselves, the emperors were adept at gaining control of whatever property they needed.

[2] For background, see Filippo E. Vassalli, 'Concetto e natura del fisco', *Studi Senesi nel Circolo giuridico della R. Università*, 25 (1908), 67–121, 177–231 (p. 198); and Robert Descimon, 'Les fonctions de la métaphore du mariage politique du roi et de la république, France, XVe–XVIIIe siècles', *Annales: Economies – Sociétés – Civilisations*, 47 (1992), 1127–47; cf. Ernst R. Kantorowicz, *The King's Two Bodies: A Study in Mediaeval Political Theology* (Princeton: Princeton University Press, 1957), pp. 214–16; for later developments of the idea, see ibid., 222; and Paul Saenger, 'Burgundy and the Inalienability of Appanages in the Reign of Louis XI', *French Historical Studies*, 10 (1977–1978), 1–26 (pp. 19–21). Françoise Barry comments on the implications of the principle of inalienability for kings' gifts to queens, in *La reine de France* (Paris: Éditions du Scorpion, 1964), pp. 425–9, esp. 425–6 (where she discusses Jean du Tillet and the provision of the Justinian Code that he invokes, on which see below). Jacques Krynen briefly discusses the principle, in *L'Empire du roi: idées et croyances politiques en France, XIIIe–XVe siècle*, Bibliothèque des histoires (Paris: Gallimard, 1993), pp. 153–9. See also the useful discussion of the 'domaine', in the preface to *Ordonnances des Roys de France de la Troisiéme Race [. . .]*, ed. by Eusèbe-Jacob de Laurière *et al.*, 22 vols and *Supplément* (available in the Cabinet des manuscrits of the BNF) (Paris: Imprimerie royale *et al.*, 1723–1849), XV, iv–xij (esp. pp. v–vj, on Philip V and Charles IV).

[3] Kantorowicz, *King's Two Bodies*, pp. 168–92, 221–3, 347–58; Gaines Post, *Studies in Medieval Legal Thought: Public Law and the State 1100–1322* (Princeton: Princeton University Press, 1964), pp. 416–19. In the Roman law, note particularly D.,23,5,4, 'Lex Iulia, quae de dotali praedio prospexit, ne id marito liceat obligare aut alienare, plenius interpretanda est, ut etiam de sponso idem iuris sit quod de marito'; also D.,23,3,2, 'Rei publicae interest mulieres dotes salvas habere, propter quas nubere possunt'; and D.,23,3,9,3, 'sed quia non puto hoc agi inter virum et uxorem, ut dominium ad eum transferatur'; D.,23.3,75, 'Quamvis in bonis mariti dos sit, mulieris tamen est, et merito placuit, ut, si in dotem fundum inaestimatum dedit'; and D.,23,3,37, 'Non enim alias perit mulieri actio, quam si nuptiae secutae fuerint: nam si secutae non sunt, manet debitor mulieri obligatis'; although note D.,23,3,7, 'Dotis fructum ad maritum pertinere debere aequitas suggerit'; and D.,23,5,17, 'Fundus dotalem maritus vendidit et tradidit: si in matrimonio mulier decesserit et dos lucro mariti cessit, fundus emptori avelli non potest'. Pierre Noailles provides a guide to the complexities of imperial legislation on this subject, in 'L'inalienabilité dotale et la Nouvelle 61', *Annales de l'Université de Grenoble*, 30 (1918), 451–509, and 31 (1919), 161–218. See also Saenger, 'Burgundy and the Inalienability of Appanages', p. 20 n. 75, referring to Cod.,5.3.15.; and Susan Treggiari, *Roman Marriage: Iusti Coniuges From the Time of Cicero to the Time of Ulpian* (Oxford: Clarendon Press, 1991), esp. pp. 323–64 (pp. 331, 360, 362). I am grateful to Paul Brand for his counsel on the Roman law.

The distinction drawn in Roman law between the prince's patrimony, which the emperor could use as he required, and the sacred patrimony of the fisc, which was the empire's and hence inalienable, appealed to and was often cited by apologists at the end of the sixteenth century and later, who argued that the kings of France were entitled to dispose of a private domain, separate from the domain of the realm – even though, in July 1607, Henri IV declared that because the kings of France 'contract with their crown a sort of marriage commonly called holy and politic, through it they endow [the crown] with all the lordships which they can possess as individuals'.[4]

As to ecclesiastical property, the Roman law considered it sacred and bound to be preserved intact. Following this line of thinking, in the thirteenth century Bracton presented the Church's property as God's and

---

4 Henri IV's edict united to the crown all the property he possessed before his accession: *Recueil général des anciennes lois françaises*, ed. Athanase-L. Jourdain, P. Decrusy, and François-A. Isambert, 29 vols (Paris: Belin-le-Prieur and others, 1821/22–33]), XV, 328–30 ('la cause la plus juste de laquelle réünion a pour la plus part consisté en ce que nosdits prédécesseurs se sont dédiés et consacrés au public, duquel ne voulans rien avoir de distinct et séparé, ils ont contracté avec leur couronne une espèce de mariage communément appellé saint et politique, par lequel ils l'ont dottée de toutes les seigneuries qui à tiltre particulier leur pouvoient appartenir, mouvantes directement d'elles, et de celles lesquelles y estoient jà unis et rassemblées, la justification de ce grand et perpétuel dot se peut aisément recueillir d'une bonne partie desdictes unions, et spécialement la très illustre remarque qu'en fournit la ville capitale de la France auparavant le domaine particulier du très noble et très ancien tige de nostre royalle maison. De sorte que s'il y a eu des réünions expresses, elles ont plustost déclaré le droict commun, que rien déclaré de nouveau en faveur du royaume'). François-Jean-Marie Olivier-Martin discusses the controversy that preceded this edict, and the arguments advanced by opposing legists, in 'La réunion de la Basse-Navarre à la couronne de France', *Anuario de Historia del Derecho español*, 9 (1932), 249–89. He does not treat the protagonists' different interpretations of the Roman law, nor comment on the importance of Roman precedent in their arguments, topics that deserve investigation. See esp. BNF, fr. 16673–75 (papers of Auguste Galland), esp. fr. 16674, fols 10r–16r (Jacques de la Guesle, 1590, elaborated in his published *Remontrance*, for which see BNF, 8° Lf90.8), 29r–34r (René Choppin, 8 November 1594; Choppin's position was doubtless affected by his desire, as a former *Ligueur*, to win Henri IV's favour). Robert Descimon considers the episode, in 'L'union au domaine royal et le principe d'inaliénabilité. La construction d'une loi fondamentale aux XVIe et XVIIe siècles,' *Droits: revue française de théorie juridique*, 22 (1995), 79–90. He seems to me to exaggerate the prevalence of the notion of a double domain in the sixteenth century. Jean Bodin, for example, mentions 'la diuision du domaine en public & particulier' found 'generalement en tous les Iurisconsultes & Historiens', but his discussion, which focuses on France but includes comments on other countries, treats only 'le domaine public': *Les Six Livres de la Repvbliqve [. . .]* (Paris: Jacques du Puys, 1578), pp. 628–34. Later commentators who endorsed the idea include Louis Carondas le Caron, in *Recueil des anciens edits et ordonnances du Roy, concernant les Domaines, & Droits de la Couronne. Avec les Commentaires de Loüis Carondas le Caron [. . .]* (Paris: Thomas Charpentier, 1690), pp. 1–2, 5–6; and François de Paule Lagarde, *Traité historique de la souveraineté du Roi, et des droits en dépendans, A commencer à l'établissement de la Monarchie*, 2 vols (Paris: Durand, 1754), I, 26–30, 42–3. See below, n. 100, for Guy Coquille. I thank Alfred Soman for his counsel on these issues.

declared it sacred and inalienable, whereas he considered 'the things of the fisc' merely quasi-sacred. Some fiscal attributes, such as peace and justice, were inalienable because they were essential to the crown and affected public utility. Others, such as landed estates, simply strengthened the crown and could thus be transferred.[5] Other English texts, and other authorities, papal as well as legal, insisted on the duty of rulers not to alienate any of the *res Corone*. In England and elsewhere oaths expressing this obligation were incorporated into the coronation ceremony.[6]

Medieval French theorists were vague about what if any actual limitations on royal authority an obligation to refrain from alienating entailed. Giles of Rome, who dedicated his treatise *De Regimine Principum* to Philip the Fair before his accession in 1285, defended hereditary monarchy by arguing that since fathers generally loved their firstborn most of all their children, the king would pay particular attention to the kingdom (and, presumably, its property) when he knew that the child he most cherished would inherit it. The king's council, Giles opined, would see that the king was not defrauded and that the kingdom's revenues increased. These comments are exceedingly nebulous. One could hardly expect more from a theorist who considered the king *dei minister* and *quedam animata lex*, who believed that rulers should give generously and live magnificently,[7] and whose treatise was composed for a

---

5 Bracton, *On the Laws and Customs of England*, ed. G. E. Woodbine, trans. and rev. Samuel E. Thorne, 4 vols (Cambridge, MA: Selden Society and Harvard University Press, 1968–77), II, 57–8 (fol. 14); cf. Kantorowicz, *King's Two Bodies*, p. 186.
6 The London collection of the *Leges Anglorum* (c.1200) states, 'Debet uero de iure rex omnes terras et honores, omnes dignitates et iura et libertates corone regni huius in integrum cum omni integritate et sine diminutione obseruare et defendere, dispersa et dilapidata et amissa regni iura in pristinum statum et debitum viribus omnibus reuocare': *Die Gesetze der Angelsachsen*, ed. Felix Liebermann, 3 vols (Halle: Max Niemayer, 1903–16), I, 635–6 (II, 1, A2 and A8), and esp. p. 635 n. c; Kantorowicz, *King's Two Bodies*, pp. 234–5; Robert S. Hoyt, 'The Coronation Oath of 1308: The Background of "Les Leys et les Custumes" ', *Traditio*, 11 (1955), 135–257 (pp. 249–50). Fleta's reading of Bracton's statement shows that by Edward I's time, the opinion voiced in the London collection was widely approved: *Fleta, Volume III, Book III and Book IV*, ed. and trans. H. G. Richardson and G. O. Sayles (London: The Selden Society, 1972), p. 12. For the English coronation oath, see *inter alia*, E. H. Kantorowicz, 'Inalienability: A Note on Canonical Practice and the English Coronation Oath in the Thirteenth Century', *Speculum*, 29 (1954), 500–1. I am grateful to James Ross Sweeney for sharing with me the fruits of his valuable work on Hungary; see esp. his 'The Problem of Inalienability in Innocent III's Correspondence with Hungary: A Contribution to the Study of the Historical Genesis of *Intellecto*', *Mediaeval Studies*, 37 (1975), 235–51. Adhémar Esmein provides background, in 'L'inaliénabilité du domaine de la Couronne devant les États Généraux du XVIe siècle', in *Festschrift Otto Gierke zum Siebzigsten Geburtstag [...]* (Weimar: Hermann Böhlaus, 1911), pp. 361–2.
7 Aegidius Romanus, *De Regimine Principum Libri III* (Rome: Stephan Plannck, 1482), 1.1.12; 1.2.12, 19; 1.4.3; 2.3.3; 3.2.5, 9, 19. Giles's ideas are similar to those that a counsellor of Charles V, Jean le Fèvre, abbot of Saint-Vaast of Arras expressed in 1376, during negotiations with the English: 'il avoit semblable affection [a son ainsné fils le Dalphin] que ses peres avoit eu a lui et ses predecesseurs avoient eu a leurs enfanz, lesquelz avoient laissié leur

young man whose grandfather, the sainted Louis, had (to Simon de Mont-fort's dismay) issued the Mise of Amiens.[8] Giles was certainly aware of the general presumption that rulers were bound to preserve the kingdom's patri-mony, but he devised imaginative arguments to defend the king's right to alienate property to benefit the Church – and thus provided a line of reason-ing that could be used to justify endowments of many sorts. In one of his trea-tises he considered the following question: 'Since kings and princes commonly, at their coronations, are accustomed to swear not to alienate the possessions and immovable property pertaining to their crown, whether they violate this oath if they bestow some of this property on the church'.[9] After lengthy and complex analysis, he concluded (unsurprisingly) 'that the king does not in fact alienate property as long as the property pertains to the unity of the kingdom and as long as it remains under the patronage and protection of the kingdom'. Indeed, an oath prohibiting alienation of holdings to the church would, Giles said, be *indebitum*, contravening as it would 'the love and devotion that princes should be bound to show to churches'.[10]

royaume tout enterin sens diminucion de ressort et souverainneté chascun apres soy aux rois'. See Édouard Perroy, 'Un discours inédit de Jean le Fèvre, abbé de Saint-Vaast et con-seiller de Charles V (8 décembre 1376),' *Mémoires de l'Académie des sciences, lettres et arts d'Arras*, 4th ser., 2 (1943), 81–90 (p. 88). I discuss the possible influence of Giles of Rome's pronouncements on Philip the Fair, in 'The Prince Is Father of the King: The Character and Childhood of Philip IV of France', originally pub. in *Mediaeval Studies*, 49 (1987), 282–334, and in 'Persona et Gesta: The Image and Deeds of the Thirteenth-Century Capetians. 3. The Case of Philip the Fair', originally pub. in *Viator*, 19 (1988), 219–46. These essays are reprinted with original pagination (and corrections) in Elizabeth A. R. Brown, *The Monar-chy of Capetian France and Royal Ceremonial* (Aldershot: Variorum, 1991), nos. IV–V.

8   For the Mise of Amiens, see *Foedera, conventiones, litterae, et cujuscunque generis acta publica inter reges Angliae et alios quosvis imperatores, reges, pontifices, principes, vel communi-tates ab ingressu Guilielmi I. in Angliam, A.D. 1066, ad nostra usque tempora habita aut tractata*, ed. Thomas Rymer and Robert Sanderson, and Adam Clarke and Frederick Holbrooke, 4 vols in 7 parts (London: Record Commission, 1816–69), I¹, 433–4; and Charles T. Wood, 'The Mise of Amiens and Saint-Louis' Theory of Kingship', *French Historical Studies*, 6 (1970), 300–10.

9   'cum reges et principes communiter in sua coronatione prestare consueuerunt iuramen-tum de non alienandis possessionibus nec immobilibus bonis ad suam coronam spectantibus an prestetur huic obuia iuramento si de huiusmodi bonis aliqua ipsis ecclesiis largiantur': BNF, lat. 6786, fol. 22r (a fifteenth-century manuscript that belonged to Jacques-Auguste de Thou and then to Colbert); this question is edited with some readings that differ from those of this manuscript (esp. 'An huic iuramento obsistat'), in *Primvs Tomvs Opervm D. Aegidii Romani Bitvricensis Archiepiscopi, Ordinis Fratrvm Eremitarvm Sancti Avgvstini* (Rome: Anto-nius Bladus, 1655), following (and separately paginated with) 'Liber de Renunciatione Papæ', fols 36v–38r, with the title 'Determinatio, Quomodo Reges circa bona ad coronam pertinentia possunt liberalitatis opera exercere'. On Giles's ideas, see Post, *Studies*, p. 289.

10   'Quod non alienantur bona a rege quamdiu pertinent ad vnitatem regnj et quamdiu subsunt patrocinio et protectioni regni. Quod si rex expresse Iuraret quod nichil de immo-bilibus bonis ad suam coronam pertinentibus nec quantum ad fructum nec vtilitatem / Nec quantum ad Iudicium et potestatem largietur ecclesiis dicemus Quod esset indebitum iura-mentum': BNF, lat. 6786, fol. 41r; in Giles's *Opera*, fol. 38r.

As Giles' comments show, France was not isolated from developments elsewhere. It was common knowledge that coronation oaths often included promises not to alienate. Perhaps it was this that inspired the royal counsellor Pierre de Cuignières to proclaim at Vincennes in 1329 (in the king's presence) that 'the king at his coronation swore not to alienate the rights [*jura*] of the kingdom, and to revoke any alienations that have been made'.[11] As his critics immediately pointed out, Pierre was twisting the truth. One adversary carefully (and accurately) rehearsed the clauses of the actual oath and rightly declared that the king had sworn 'these things and no others, saving the reverence of Lord Peter, who said that [the king] swore an additional oath'.[12] In fact, no French king made any such undertaking before Charles VI was consecrated in 1380. In the oath he apparently swore on that occasion, what was protected were the *superioritas*, the *iura*, and the *nobilitas* of the crown, not its territories. Nonetheless, invoking the oath, in 1402 and 1413 Charles VI pledged not to alienate lands except to endow members of his lineage – a rather grand exception.[13] Not until the ordonnance of Moulins of 1566 did

11 'cum Rex in sua Coronatione juravisset jura Regni non alienare, & alienata, ad se revocare, si per Ecclesiam aut quemcumque alium erant aliqua usurpata, Rex tenebatur per juramentum ad se illa revocare': Pierre-Toussaint Durand de Maillane, *Les libertez de l'Église gallicane, prouvées et commentées Suivant l'Ordre & la Disposition des Articles dressés par M. Pierre Pithov, Et sur les Recueils de M. Pierre Dupuy, Conseiller d'État*, 5 vols (Lyon: Pierre Bruyset Ponthus, 1771), III, 425–503 (pp. 456–7) (Libellus of Cardinal Pierre Bertrand, bishop of Autun; the discourse of Pierre de Cuignières, delivered at Paris on 8 December 1329, was reported by Pierre Roger, bishop elect of Sens, in the speech he gave at Vincennes on 22 December following; useful information regarding the tract is found in the introduction written by Brunet in 1731, in ibid., pp. 425–43); the passage is cited imprecisely in Esmein, 'Inaliénabilité', pp. 362–3 n. 3. On the interchanges and the assembly, see Olivier Martin [sic, for François-Jean-Marie Olivier-Martin], *L'Assemblée de Vincennes de 1329 et ses conséquences: étude sur les conflits entre la juridiction laïque et la juridiction ecclésiastique au XIVe siècle*, Travaux juridiques et économiques de l'Université de Rennes, Premier Supplément (Rennes: Bibliothèque universitaire, 1909), esp. pp. 69–83, on the protagonists. F. M. Powicke discusses the pervasiveness of the belief that a commitment not to alienate was implicit in coronation oaths, in 'The Oath of Bromholm', *English Historical Review*, 56 (1941), 529–48 (pp. 535–8).

12 Addressing the king, Pierre Roger, bishop elect of Sens, declared, 'Modo, præcharissimè, attendatis, si vos in coronatione vestra jurastis ista, & non plura, scilicet [. . .]. Ista jurastis, & non plura, salvâ reverentiâ Domini Petri, qui vos unum alium jurasse dicebat': Durand de Maillane, *Libertez*, III, 477–8; cf. Esmein, 'Inaliénabilité', pp. 362–3 n. 3. In the speech he gave before the king in Paris on 29 December 1329, Cardinal Pierre de Bertrand insisted on the king's pledge at his coronation 'privilegium canonicum servare Ecclesiæ': Durand de Maillane, *Libertez*, III, 481–2. Like Giles of Rome, he argued that the king 'non abdicat à se cum Deo, & Ecclesiæ dat. Quia *Domini est terra*, &c. tale enim dare non est, nisi reddere Deo & Ecclesiæ quod suum est'. On the traditional French coronation oath and its development, see Elizabeth A. R. Brown, *'Franks, Burgundians, and Aquitanians' and the Royal Coronation Ceremony in France*, in *Transactions of the American Philosophical Society*, 82[7] (Philadelphia: American Philosophical Society, 1992), esp. pp. 38–42, 78–9, 83–4, 89, 96, 100, 119–20, 104.

13 *Ordonnances*, VIII, 484–6; X, 82–3. Charles did not exclude donations to ecclesiastical

formal royal legislation ban alienation, and even this ordonnance contained exceptions.[14]

Philip the Fair's lawyers were happy to invoke the doctrine of inalienability to benefit the monarchy. It was useful in dealing with foreign powers. Around 1300 one of Philip's counsellors argued against the Aragonese that the king of France could not diminish the limits of the kingdom or make the Val d'Aran 'totally exempt from the realm of France'. The minister compared the king of France to the pope and the emperor, 'who cannot completely exempt from their power an episcopal see or a county or anything else that is subject to them'.[15] The king also used the principle to reap from his subjects

establishments, as others had done: ibid., III, 140, 162–4 (1357), 225 (1358), 442–3, 466–7 (1360). I am grateful to Richard A. Jackson for his counsel on the French oath: see esp. his 'Les manuscrits des *ordines* du couronnement de la bibliothèque de Charles V, roi de France', *Le Moyen Age*, 82 (1976), 67–88 (pp. 87–8), and *Vive le Roi! A History of the French Coronation Ceremony from Charles V to Charles X* (Chapel Hill: University of North Carolina Press, 1984; trans. [by Monique Arav] as *Vivat Rex: histoire des sacres et couronnements en France*, [Strasbourg: Association des publications près les Universités de Strasbourg, 1984]), pp. 76–7, 241 n. 28 (Fr. ed., pp. 74–5). We disagree, however, on the question of whether Charles VI actually swore an oath of inalienability: my reasoning and evidence are presented in Elizabeth A. R. Brown and Richard C. Famiglietti, *The Lit de Justice: Semantics, Ceremonial, and the Parlement of Paris (1300–1600)*, Beiheft 31 of *Francia*, Deutsches Historisches Institut Paris (Sigmaringen: Jan Thorbecke, 1994), pp. 37–8 esp. n. 24. See also the penetrating analyses of Esmein, 'L'inalienabilité', pp. 362–3 n. 3; and of Saenger, 'Burgundy and the Inalienability of Appanages', pp. 3 n. 8, 6 nn. 19–20, 19 n. 74, 20 n. 75.

14 'Le Domaine de notre Couronne ne peut être aliéné qu'en deux cas seulement; l'un pour apanage des puisnés mâles de la Maison de France; auquel cas y a retour à notre Couronne par leur déceds sans mâles [. . .]; l'autre pour l'aliénation à deniers comtans pour la nécessité de la guerre, après Lettres patentes pour ce décernées & publiées en nos Parlemens: auquel cas y a faculté de rachat perpétuel': [Louis François du Vaucel], *Essai sur les apanages ou Mémoire historique de leur établissement [. . .]*, 2 vols (n.p., n.d.; probably Paris, 1780/92), I, 251. At the beginning of the ordonnance, Charles IX declared that 'à notre Sacre nous avons entr'autres choses promis & juré garder & observer le Domaine & patrimoine roial de notre Couronne, l'un des principaux nerfs de notre état, & retirer les portions & membres d'icelui qui ont été aliénés, vray moyen pour soulager notre peuple tant affligé des calamités & troubles passés': ibid. On the significance of the edict, see esp. Esmein, 'L'inalienabilité', pp. 368–81. Félix Aubert discusses the implementation of the principle of inalienability in the sixteenth century, before the edict of Moulins, in 'Le Parlement de Paris au XVIe siècle', *Nouvelle Revue historique de droit français et étranger*, 29 (1905), 737–90; 30 (1906), 55–83, 178–209 (pp. 193–200). For French kings' invocation of necessity to advance their own ambitions, see Saenger, 'Burgundy and the Inalienability of Appanages', p. 25, and Percy Ernst Schramm, *Der König von Frankreich*, 2nd edn, 2 vols (Weimar, 1960), I, 238; II, 140 n. 7.

15 'et rex Francie jus habeat imperii in regno suo quod a nemine recogno[s]cit se tenere; non potuit limites regni diminuere nec ipsam vallem a regno Francie facere exemtam totaliter, ut de papa et imperatore dicitur qui non possunt episcopatum vel comitatum vel quivis aliud subjectum a potestate sua totaliter exhimere': Philippe Lauer, 'Une enquête au sujet de la frontière française dans le Val d'Aran sous Philippe le Bel', *Bulletin du Comité des travaux historiques et géographiques, Section géographique* (1920), 17–38 (p. 30) (from an 'Informatio' prepared in connection with the *enquête*, preserved in BNF, Clairambault 1021, fol. 75).

profit both tangible and intangible. Like his predecessors, he gained loyalty as well as revenue by issuing pledges of inalienable annexation to the crown, which his subjects greatly valued.[16]

Theorists, like rulers, are notorious contortionists when dealing with principles that for one reason or another are inconvenient or embarrassing. In contrast, the royal chancery officials who, sometime during the reign of Philip V, collected the admonitory and scathingly critical texts (including the long version of the *Livres de Fauvel*) assembled in BNF, fr. 146, were not afraid to speak their minds and express views that many others shared.[17] As *dits* included in the manuscript made clear, the king was expected to be generous and openhanded, but to dispose only of his movable property, never of his inheritance. It is pure folly, one *dit* declares, to give away regions and lands bestowed on the king for the realm's defence and protection. Too much of the kingdom has been severed from it, making the realm weaker and the king poorer. From this – and here was the real rub – stem the taxes the king must impose when he goes to battle. As these verses show, subjects were primarily concerned to protect their purses. They wanted the king to live of his own and leave them in peace.[18] Their interest in the principle of inalienability

16 I comment on these letters, in 'Gascon Subsidies and the Finances of the English Dominions, 1315–1324', *Studies in Medieval and Renaissance History*, 8 (1971), 33–163 (pp. 110–14, 126–9, 154–63), and in an as yet unpublished monograph, *Corruption, Finance, and Reform in Fourteenth-Century France: The 'Reformatores Patrie Generales' in Languedoc, 1318–1319*, some conclusions of which Richard W. Kaeuper discusses in his *War, Justice and Public Order: England and France in the Later Middle Ages* (Oxford: Clarendon Press, 1988), pp. 308–9.

17 On the contents of this manuscript, BNF, fr. 146, the circumstances under which it was assembled, and the possible authors of the pieces it contains, see Elizabeth A. R. Brown, 'Représentations de la royauté dans les *Livres de Fauvel*', in *Représentation, pouvoir et royauté à la fin du Moyen Age: Actes du colloque organisé par l'Université du Maine les 25 et 26 mars 1994*, ed. Joël Blanchard (Paris: Picard, 1995), pp. 215–35, and eadem, '*Rex ioians, ionnes, iolis*: Louis X, Philip V, and the *Livres de Fauvel*', in *Fauvel Studies. Allegory, Chronicle, Music, and Image in Paris, Bibliothèque Nationale de France, MS Français 146*, ed. Margaret Bent and Andrew Wathey (Oxford: Clarendon Press, 1998), pp. 53–72.

18 *Six Historical Poems of Geffroi de Paris Written in 1314–1318, Published in their Entirety for the first time from MS fr. 146 of the Bibliothèque Nationale, Paris*, ed. and trans. Walter H. Storer and Charles A. Rochedieu, University of North Carolina Studies in the Romance Languages and Literatures, 16 (Chapel Hill: University of North Carolina, 1950), pp. 32 ('Avisemens pour le Roy Louys', lines 1061–5), 70–2 ('Un songe', lines 323–54). See as well the passages in *Fauvel*, the *dits*, and the metrical chronicle of BNF, fr. 146, that I list in my article, 'Représentation', pp. 222–3 n. 42. The attitude of representatives of towns to Philip V's attempt in 1321 to gain the realm's approval for the revocation of illegally alienated domain lands was typical. Fearful of having to contribute financially to the king's planned reform, the representatives declared that it was the king's responsibility to deal with the issue. See Elizabeth A. R. Brown, 'Subsidy and Reform in 1321: The Accounts of Najac and the Policies of Philip V', originally pub. in *Traditio*, 27 (1971), 399–430 (p. 419), reprinted with original pagination, in eadem, *Politics and Institutions in Capetian France* (Aldershot: Variorum, 1991), no. VIII. I deal with French attitudes to taxation in a number of studies,

was less pressing, but they knew perfectly well that a diminished domain increased the likelihood that they would have to pay. One solution to the dilemma would have been to provide the king with a landed estate separate from the kingdom's, as had happened in Roman times, but such a possibility was apparently not seriously considered until centuries later, only, in the end, to be rejected.[19]

including 'Cessante Causa and the Taxes of the Last Capetians: The Political Applications of a Philosophical Maxim', originally pub. in *Studia Gratiana* (*Post Scripta*), 15 (1972), 565–87; 'Taxation and Morality in the Thirteenth and Fourteenth Centuries: Conscience and Political Power and the Kings of France', originally pub. in *French Historical Studies*, 8 (1973), 1–28; 'Reform and Resistance to Royal Authority in Fourteenth-Century France: The Leagues of 1314–1315', originally pub. in *Parliaments, Estates and Representation*, 1 (1981), 109–37; and 'Customary Aids and Royal Fiscal Policy under Philip VI of Valois', originally pub. in *Traditio*, 39 (1974), 191–258; these articles are reprinted in Brown, *Politics*, as, respectively, nos. II, III, V and IX. See also Elizabeth A. R. Brown, *Customary Aids and Royal Finances in Capetian France: The Marriage Aid of Philip the Fair*, Medieval Academy Books, 100 (Cambridge, MA: Medieval Academy of America, 1992), esp. pp. 35–69. Rumours that Philip V had been poisoned were linked with the unpopular tax he had proposed to finance reform projects: Elizabeth A. R. Brown, 'The Ceremonial of Royal Succession in Capetian France: The Funeral of Philip V', originally pub. in *Speculum*, 55 (1980), 266–93 (p. 272), reprinted in Brown, *Monarchy*, no. VIII. See n. 31 below.

[19] On 21 December 1316, shortly before his coronation on 9 January 1317, Philip reintegrated into the administrative and judicial structure of the realm the property he held as count of Poitiers: *Ordonnances*, I, 627–8. When Philip was given Poitiers, the viscounty of Thouars (which had *ab antiquo* been attached to the county's *ressort*) was transferred to the *ressort* of Loudun. Having become king, in March 1318, Philip V restored the viscounty of Thouars to the *ressort* of the seneschalsy of Poitou, thus acceding to the request of the viscount 'ut, cum regnum Francie ad nos jure hereditario devolutum existat, quod dictum vicecomitatum ad ressortum Pictavense, prout esse solebat, ut est dictum, reducere et reponere vellemus': Paul Guérin, 'Recueil des documents concernant le Poitou contenus dans les registres de la chancellerie de France', *Archives historiques du Poitou*, 11 (1881) and 13 (1883), in vol. 11, pp. 177–8 (Guerout, no. 1736). These steps fully support the contention of the royal procurator in 1323 that Philip, Charles IV's 'Seigneur & frere est mort saisi & possesseur desdits Comté & terres comme Roi & non comme Comte': Du Vaucel, *Essai*, I, 137–40 (p. 139) (identified as 'Arrêt contre le Duc de Bourgogne au profit de Charles-le-Bel, touchant le Comté de Poitou, & six mille livres de rente qui avoient appartenu à Philippe-le-Long à cause de sa mere, & pour monstrer que filles ne succedent en Terres d'apanage. L'an 1322', which Du Vaucel found in MS 415 of Harlay's collection); cf. the Latin, 'quod licet dictus Dominus germanus noster Philippus, tempore quo erat Comes Pictaviensis, præmissa possedisset ut Comes, præmissa tamen, statim quod ipse fuit Rex desiit possidere ut Comes'. The procurator made this statement in contesting the claim of Philip V's eldest daughter Jeanne and her husband, the duke of Burgundy, to the property Philip possessed in Poitiers and Champagne before his accession. Philip apparently viewed his holdings in Champagne (which he had inherited from his mother) differently from his other lands, since until the end of 1317 he insisted that his property there should form part of his wife's dower: Besançon, AD du Doubs, B 24 (exemplification by Louis X, dated 1316, of Philip's act of June 1315); AN, JJ 53, fol. 41r, no. 91 (Guerout, no. 378) (February 1317); JJ 53, fol. 47r, no. 106 (Guerout, no. 394) (March 1317; with the heading 'pro domina Regina', and the rubric, 'donacio vinginti milium librarum terre facta domine Regine pro dotalicio

Philip V was well aware of the popularity of royal parsimony. He was a man of considerable intelligence and sensitivity, arguably the wisest and most politically apt of Philip the Fair's sons. When his brother Louis died at the age of 27 in 1316, Philip was 25 or 26. He had witnessed the troubles of the last year of his father's life, and his brother's brief but stormy reign. He had observed the variety of means Louis and his advisers had used to quiet opposition to the policies of Philip the Fair, and particularly his demands for taxes.[20] Philip needed all the wit and experience he possessed to deal with the difficult circumstances under which he became regent in 1316 and was crowned in January 1317. Many believed that Louis X's daughter Jeanne should have succeeded her father, and were prepared to defend her right to the crown. The problems with weather and crops that had plagued the kingdom since 1314 continued.[21] As usual, war with Flanders threatened, and Philip knew from his father's and brother's experiences that appeals to his subjects for revenue would be futile unless a clear and unquestionable military crisis materialised – and persisted.[22] Philip used various strategies to swell the treasury and win the support and loyalty of his subjects. One of the most important was to insist on and demonstrate his dedication to reform in general, and, in particular, to reclaiming rights, revenues, and territories that had been wrongly alienated.[23]

suo'; a copy of the act is in Besançon, AD du Doubs, B 24); AN, JJ 53, fols 148v–49r, no. 352 (Guerout, no. 649) (October 1317; with the heading 'pro domina Regina', and the rubric 'littere de ordinatione assignationis vinginti vnius Mille librarum terre pro dotalicio domine Regine'); Besançon, AD du Doubs, B 24 (24 December 1317); cf. the final assignment made in July 1319, which I shall discuss below. Nonetheless, in 1323 Philip V's daughter Jeanne and her husband Eudes, duke of Burgundy, were unable to obtain any part of Poitiers or Champagne. Charles IV pressed them, in addition, for money allegedly owed for the marriage settlement of Eudes's sister Marguerite, Louis X's first wife: AN, J 1036, no. 12. For Philip's coronation, see Elizabeth A. R. Brown, 'The Ceremonial of Royal Succession in Capetian France: The Double Funeral of Louis X', originally pub. in *Traditio*, 34 (1978), 227–71 (p. 267), reprinted with corrections in Brown, *Monarchy*, no. VII.

20 See Brown, 'Reform and Resistance'.

21 William Chester Jordan, *The Great Famine: Northern Europe in the Early Fourteenth Century* (Princeton: Princeton University Press, 1996), pp. 7–10, 18–20, 75–6, 167–71.

22 On Philip's accession, see Brown, 'Double Funeral', pp. 234–69. An anonymous chronicler of Paris described the rains that swept the kingdom and ruined the harvest in August 1320: A. Hellot, ed., 'Chronique parisienne anonyme de 1316 à 1339 précédée d'additions à la Chronique française dite de Guillaume de Nangis (1206–1316)', *Mémoires de la Société de l'histoire de Paris et de l'Ile-de-France*, 11 (1884), 1–207 (p. 62, no. 70). In August 1320 Philip V granted a privilege to the abbey of Essômes near Château-Thierry because of their 'Iacturas insuper / atque dispendia que hoc anno ex tempestatis seuitia permittente domino in terrarum et vinearum suarum fructibus totaliter pene consumptis / ipsos pertulisse cognouimus': AN, JJ 59, fol. 274r–v (fol. 274r), no. 508 (Guerout, no. 3230). In return, the monks were to celebrate a mass of the Holy Spirit annually for him and Queen Jeanne while they lived, and a mass of the dead for them after they died.

23 See, in general, Brown, 'Subsidy and Reform in 1321', pp. 419–24.

Philip began in March 1317 by reissuing an act that Philip the Fair had promulgated on 19 January 1311. In it Philip the Fair had authorised his fiscal officials to revoke abusive alienations of various offices, and of grain and wine.[24] This timid commencement was followed by a far more aggressive proclamation, which Philip V issued on 18 July 1318, with his council's approval. The king declared magnanimously that if he decided to bestow lands heritably or for life, he would do so from territory that had been forfeited to the crown. He promised that at its monthly meetings, his great council would review all such grants. It was not his intention, he proclaimed, to make any award 'from our domain or our heritage, except in cases where we should reasonably do so'. Sealing and writing offices, he asserted, 'are of our own domain'. The ordonnance thus distinguishes between property the king acquired accidentally, as it were, and property that was the king's 'domain' or 'heritage', which included rights and offices as well as lands. Another provision of the ordonnance forbade the sealing or execution of any letter contravening its provisions, and of any letter containing the phrase, 'non contrestant Ordenances' ('notwithstanding ordonnances').[25] Like many of the declarations in the charters he and his brother, following in their father's footsteps, issued to their subjects, these provisions seemed to manifest the king's prudence and self-restraint. As was true of those provisions, however, the king did not completely restrict his freedom to act. 'Reason', after all, is a slippery standard.

For the moment Philip was intent on demonstrating his rectitude. In mandates issued on 29 July 1318 (eleven days after promulgating the ordonnance), he stressed his wish to maintain justice and law, and to restore the good usages and customs of his great-grandfather, Saint Louis. He voiced amazement and consternation at reports he had heard about actions taken by his father and brother. Greatly deluded, they had made excessive and ill-advised grants, bringing grief and prejudice to king and kingdom, and defrauding and deceiving both themselves and himself, their successor. Therefore, after serious deliberation with great men of the realm, he was

---

[24] *Ordonnances*, I, 476–7, 634.

[25] *Ordonnances*, I, 657–60 (clauses 1, 15, 21–2), specifying (clause 15, p. 659), 'Et se il nous plest donner terres a heritage ou a vie, nous donrrons des dictes fourfaictures & en deniers aussi, au jour & en la maniere que il est contenu ci-dessus au premier article, & par nostredit Conseil. Et n'est par nostre entention que nous dongnons point de nostre demaine, ne de nostre heritage, se ce n'est au cas que nous le doions faire par raison. Et est a entendre que Seaulz et escriptures sont de nostre propre demaine'. Clauses 21 and 22 deal with the sealing of letters contravening the ordonnance. In a mandate he issued on 28 August 1316 (as 'Regis Francorum filius, Regens regna Francie & Navarre'), Philip lamented the terrible burden of debt that encumbered the treasury: ibid., I, 626. He then decreed 'quod omnes forisfacture, seu incursus, aut commissa, que nobis, & bonis hereditariis deinceps provenient, personis habentibus redditus perpetuos, vel ad vitam super thesauro predicto, in exonerationem, & acquitationem perpetuam predictorum reddituum assignentur'.

revoking all such gifts and other questionable arrangements regarding royal property. The property and rights given to many individuals, specified by name, were to be seized, and the individuals were to be required to justify their title. Note: revocation was ordered not because the property and rights pertained to the crown or kingdom and were therefore inalienable, but rather because they had been deviously obtained and fraudulently exploited.[26] The king issued another relevant ordonnance on 10 March 1321. Again bemoaning the land and rights belonging to his father, brother, and himself that had been alienated to the realm's detriment, he declared it 'more fitting' (*convenientius*) for such property to be restored to the kingdom's 'rights and domains' (*regni jura et domania*) than for it to remain with those to whom it had 'wrongly' (*male*) been transferred. General revocation was ordered, except of property granted to churches. Although terms like *domania* and *ab antiquo* were not precisely defined, the ordonnance set the stage for extensive investigation of royal lands and rights.[27]

---

[26] Ibid., I, 665–8; also in Léon Ménard, *Histoire civile, ecclésiastique et litteraire de la ville de Nismes [. . .]*, 7 vols (Paris: Hugues-Daniel Chaubert, 1750–58), II, *preuves*, 25–6. See also Charles-Victor Langlois, 'Registres perdus des archives de la Chambre des Comptes de Paris', *Notices et extraits des manuscrits de la Bibliothèque nationale et autres bibliothèques*, 40 (1917), 33–399 (pp. 107–20), who magisterially surveys Philip V's policies regarding alienation.

[27] Langlois, 'Registres perdus', pp. 110–14, esp. 112–13 n. 1. In executing this ordonnance, the king and his ministers stressed the pressures employed by those soliciting grants. Charles T. Wood discusses the significance of 'domain' in this period, in 'Regnum Francie: A Problem in Capetian Administrative Usage', *Traditio*, 23 (1967), 117–47 (pp. 123, 133 n. 38). Andrew W. Lewis emphasised the variety of significances possessed by the word *domanium* during the reign of Philip Augustus, in a paper presented at the annual meeting of the American Historical Association in 1982, 'The Capetian Royal Domain: Problems of Definition, Applicability, and Balance'. He pointed out that, in practice, in endowing their sons, the thirteenth-century Capetians treated the royal patrimony ('the principality of Hugues Capet'), differently from old and recent acquisitions (of which those considered strategically important constituted a special category). He concluded that the term royal domain should probably be eliminated 'from the general vocabulary on Capetian France'. Lewis also discusses the royal patrimony and the domain in his *Royal Succession in Capetian France: Studies on Familial Order and the State*, Harvard Historical Monographs, 100 (Cambridge, MA: Harvard University Press, 1981; trans. [by Jeannie Carlier] as *Le sang royal: la famille capétienne et l'état, France, Xe–XIVe siècle*, Bibliothèque des histoires [Paris: Gallimard, 1987]). A memorandum which Langlois believes ('Registres perdus', pp. 137–8) was written in the early fourteenth century distinguishes 'domain' (*domanium*) from 'forfeitures' (*forefacture*), which are divided into two categories: first, the forfeiture 'incorporata et que remanet incorporata cum effectu', and second that which is 'non incorporata vel incorporata que tamen non remanet cum effectu'. Donations of non-incorporated property were declared valid, but the other conclusions of the memorandum are unknown, since the text breaks off at this point. The edict of Moulins defined the domain of the crown as 'celui qui est expressément consacré, uni & incorporé à nostre Couronne, ou qui a été tenu & administré par nos Receveurs & Officiers par l'espace de dix ans, & est entré en ligne de compte': Du Vaucel, *Essai*, I, 251, and cf. René Choppin's reference to the possibility of alienating property 'quæ nondum Fiscali Patrimonio nexa sint nominatim, aut tacite confusa, redi-

Philip V and his ministers were accurately summarising royal policy when, in the spring of 1321, they declared that the king 'wanted for the common good to recover the domains of his land which had been wrongly given and alienated, whether by gift or exchange or in any other way, so that he and his successors would have less cause to ask the people for money'.[28] Representatives of the realm's towns may have attributed to him the desire to revoke all alienations, but their response to the king's request for counsel (and subsidy) showed that they were satisfied by the policy he had implemented and wished for no modification – particularly, it seems clear, since change would have involved taxation.[29]

Philip's attitude and policies regarding royal grants were conservative and responsible. His declarations might suggest that he himself had refrained from making any such awards. This was not the case. In his ordonnance of 10 March 1321 he confessed that he, as well as his brother and father, had harmed the realm by alienating royal rights. The grants that the ordonnance revoked, admittedly, were those that had been made 'badly' (*male*). Philip would surely have considered the bulk of his awards 'right' and 'reasonable', and thus concordant with the standards he had enunciated since his accession, standards that his subjects approved and endorsed. In view of his campaign for revocation, however, he might have wondered whether *his*

---

tuum possessione decenni', in *Renati Choppini Andegavi. I. C. Et in supremo Galliarum Senatu. Aduocati. De Domanio Franciæ Libri III.* (Paris: Michaël Sonnius, 1588), p. 386; Choppin's dedication to Christophle de Thou is dated 13 November 1572. In ibid., pp. 471–2, Choppin quotes the text of a memorandum he found in the Chambre des comptes, which describes in detail steps Charles IV took in the spring of 1322, shortly after the death of Philip V, against various individuals charged with having wrongfully acquired royal property and rights.

28 'Item les demaines de sa terre mal donnez ou alienez, soit en dons ou en eschanges ou en autre chose que ce soit, les veut ravoir pour le bien commun, et que il ait mains causes, ne li autres qui apres luy vendront, de despendre sur les peuples': Joseph Petit, Michel Gavrilovitch, Maury, and D.-A. Teodoru (with preface by Charles-Victor Langlois), *Essai de restitution des plus anciens mémoriaux de la Chambre des comptes de Paris*, Bibliothèque de la Faculté des Lettres de l'Université de Paris, 7 (Paris: F. Alcan, 1899), p. 148; on the declaration, see Charles H. Taylor, 'French Assemblies and Subsidy in 1321', *Speculum*, 43 (1968), 232–3; cf. Brown, 'Subsidy and Reform', pp. 416–17.

29 'Item, se ce seroit bon et profitable chose que ce qui a este dou demaine dou roy dou temps passe, s'il a este allienez, ou mis hors doudit demaine, et estrangez en aucunes personnes, par les predecesseurs dou roy, qui fust remis et appliquez audit demaine [. . .]. Item, as allienacion des demaines, li roys et ses nobles consaux sauront bien regarder se elles sont faites deuement, et sans deceipte, et que elles peussent estre faites; et se il voient que elles soient ensi faites, si leur plaist, si demeurent en icele maniere; si voient qu'elles soient faites induement [. . .], si soient rapelees et mises au noient, et rajonctes audit demaine': *Archives administratives de la ville de Reims. Collection de pièces inédites pouvant servir à l'histoire des institutions dans l'intérieur de la cité*, ed. by Pierre-Joseph Varin, 3 vols in 5, Collection de documents inédits sur l'histoire de France, 1st ser., Histoire politique (Paris: Crapelet, 1839–48), II[1], 273 (10 October 1321).

principles of 'rightness' and 'reasonableness' would be shared (or at least respected) by his successor. The question became increasingly important and pressing after the death of his only son in February 1317 (within two months of his own coronation). This made it likely that he would be succeeded by his brother Charles.[30] Likelihood became virtual certainty when Philip fell ill of a wasting disease during the summer of 1321.[31]

2. Philip V and Jeanne of Burgundy

Jeanne of Burgundy, Philip's wife, was the chief beneficiary of his largesse. Why Philip was as generous as he was to Jeanne is a matter for speculation, but a number of facts that are known about their relationship seem pertinent. Born late in 1290 or early in 1291, Philip was his parents' second son.[32] Jeanne, in contrast, was the oldest and for a number of years the sole child of Count Othon of Burgundy and Mahaut of Artois. Born late in 1287 or early in 1288, she was some three years older than Philip, and a year or two older than Philip's older brother Louis.[33] Anxious to obtain the county of Burgundy

---

[30] Brown, 'Double Funeral', pp. 237–8, 267–9. In ibid., p. 238 n. 46 I pointed out that the date of the son's birth is unclear, although I hypothesised that it occurred in mid-June of 1316. However, since messengers the countess of Poitiers sent to Edward II in England to announce the birth of her child did not reach the king until 7 August 1316, the son was probably born in July: *English Medieval Diplomatic Practice, Part I, Documents and Interpretation*, ed. Pierre Chaplais, 2 vols (London: Her Majesty's Stationery Office, 1982), II, 820–1, no. 408.

[31] Brown, 'Funeral of Philip V', p. 269. David Nirenberg offers a singular, anthropologically inspired reading of the last year of Philip's life and the circumstances of his death, in *Communities of Violence: Persecution of Minorities in the Middle Ages*, rev. edn (Princeton: Princeton University Press, 1998), pp. 43–68.

[32] An anonymous Parisian chronicle stated that Philip was 'en l'an de son aage xxj^{me}' when he died on 2 January 1322: Hellot, 'Chronique parisienne', p. 64, no. 77.

[33] In 1285 Jeanne's mother, Mahaut, married Othon, a widower, who was then forty-five: Jules-Marie Richard, *Une petite-nièce de saint Louis, Mahaut, comtesse d'Artois et de Bourgogne (1302–1329): étude sur la vie privée, les arts et l'industrie, en Artois et à Paris au commencement du XIVe siècle* (Paris: H. Champion, 1887), p. 5. Although the precise date of Jeanne's birth is unknown, the marriage agreement concluded on 2 March 1295 stated that Jeanne was then 'in aetate legitima ad contrahenda sponsalia constituta', and thus at least seven years-old: Urbain Plancher and Zacharie Merle, *Histoire générale et particulière de Bourgogne [. . .]*, 4 vols (Dijon: A. de Fay, 1739–81), II, *preuves*, lxxxxvii, no. CXXXXI. Mahaut and Othon had a son Robert, who was born and died before the birth of a second son named Robert; the second Robert arrived after Jeanne and Blanche (born in 1296): AN, J 682, no. 2, esp. membrane 10 (testimony of Charles of Valois). The second Robert was buried at the church of the Franciscans in Paris following his death in September 1317; in 1306 a tomb was made for the first Robert, who was buried at Poligny: I am grateful to Françoise Baron for this information; on the tomb of the second Robert, see Richard, *Mahaut*, pp. 316–17, and Françoise Baron, 'Robert d'Artois (+ 1317)', in *L'art au temps des rois maudits: Philippe le Bel et ses fils, 1285–1328*, exhibition catalogue (Paris: Réunion des Musées Nationaux, 1998), pp. 98–9,

and Artois for his lineage, Philip the Fair in 1291 began negotiations for Jeanne to marry one of his sons.[34] Owing to her father's indebtedness, in February 1295 Philip was able to conclude an exceptionally favourable contract, which effectively placed the county of Burgundy in his own hands.[35] The contract provided that Jeanne would marry one of Philip's two eldest sons. In announcing the terms, Jeanne's father Count Othon acknowledged his own interest (and indeed he profited handsomely) but he stressed even more the honour the match brought to him, and the exaltation it meant for his lineage. Othon declared that he would turn his daughter over to the king and would relinquish to him the county of Burgundy, making him its *verum dominum*. Even if Jeanne should die before the marriage (or afterwards should die childless), the lands were to be the property of the king of France.[36]

---

no. 48. A third son, Jean, was also buried at Poligny; his tomb was completed in 1315: see Richard, *Mahaut*, p. 315, and Baron, 'Jean de Bourgogne, fils de Mahaut d'Artois', in *L'art au temps des rois maudits*, pp. 97–8, no. 47. Baron here suggests that Jean died before Mahaut became countess of Artois in 1302, but if he did, it is puzzling that Mahaut did not have a tomb made for him when she had the first Robert's monument made in 1306. Since the testament Othon completed on 13 September 1302 contains no reference to Jean, it seems likely to me that he was born after that date, and perhaps after Othon died in March 1303. I thank Françoise Baron for discussing these questions with me. For Louis of France, see Anselme de la Vierge Marie (Pierre Guibours), *Histoire généalogique et chronologique de la maison royale de France*, continued by Du Fourny, 3rd edn, ed. les P. Ange and Simplicien, 9 vols (Paris: La Compagnie des Libraires, 1726–33), I, 92.

[34] For the text of the agreement of 9 June 1291, see *Acta Imperii, Angliae et Franciae ab a. 1267 ad a. 1313. Dokumente vornehmlich zur Geschichte der auswärtigen Beziehungen Deutschlands in ausländischen Archiven gesammelt und mit Unterstützung des Johann-Friedrich-Böhmer-Fonds herausgegeben*, ed. Fritz Kern (Tübingen: J. C. B. Mohr [Paul Siebeck], 1911), pp. 46–8. The many corrections and emendations in drafts of the agreement show the care with which it was negotiated: AN, J 255, nos. 122 and 146. The agreement was exemplified on 29 August 1317 (AN, J 408, no. 5), together with an act issued by Othon and Mahaut at Asnières on 9 July 1291, in which, at King Philip's request, they pledged to bestow on Jeanne at the time of her marriage to any of Philip's sons the *château* of Montrond (Jura, ar. Lons-le-Saunier, c. Champagnole). The act begins by declaring, first, that Mahaut and Othon were bound by the marriage contract to give with Jeanne the barony of Salins and its appurtenances to the value of 7,000 *livrées* of land; second, that if Jeanne did not marry the king's eldest son, Othon might retain for his lifetime 3,000 *livrées* of income and the *château* of Bracon (Jura, ar. Lons-le-Saunier, c. Salins-les-Bains); and, finally, that Montrond would be Jeanne's because Philip the Fair considered it part of the barony of Salins.

[35] AN, J 250 (Bourgogne IV), no. 3, an exemplification dated 29 August 1317 (attested by three notaries, and sealed with the seal of the court of Paris), and no. 4 (another copy of the exemplification, similarly dated and validated).

[36] At the same time Othon disseised himself of the county, and assigned it and its revenues to Philip the Fair: AN, J 248A, no. 5 (dated February 1295 at Paris). A supplementary agreement, dated 2 March 1295, confirmed the provisions: AN, J 250 (Bourgogne IV), no. 5; ed. in Plancher and Merle, *Bourgogne*, II, lxxxvii–xc, no. CXXXXI, and, less correctly, in *Corps universel diplomatique du droit des gens [. . .]*, ed. Jean Dumont, 8 vols (Amsterdam: P. Brunel, 1726–31), I[1], 292–94, no. DXXIX (taken from Estienne Perard, *Recveil de plvsievrs pieces cvrievses servant a l'histoire de Bovrgogne [. . .]* [Paris: Claude Cramoisy, 1564], pp. 574–9). In the act, Othon acknowledged receiving 100,000 l.p.t. as a deposit (*pro arris sponsalium*) and

Othon may have regretted the contract after the birth of a daughter (Blanche) in 1296, and even more after the arrival of a son (Robert) in 1300. He died, however, in March 1303, and Mahaut of Artois was apparently delighted with the marriage, which ensured her own close connection with the royal court – and did not involve her own precious county of Artois.

At some point Philip the Fair's eldest son Louis formally committed himself to marry Jeanne.[37] However, on 27 February 1300, he was contracted to Marguerite, daughter of Saint Louis' daughter Agnes, and Duke Robert II of Burgundy.[38] A formal ceremony of union between Louis and Marguerite occurred sometime between February and the beginning of August 1305, and the marriage was (in effect, again) solemnised at Vernon on 23 September 1305.[39] The way was thus cleared for the marriage of Philip and Jeanne,

he promised the king 400,000 l.p.t. should, because of him or his daughter, the marriage not take place. More clearly than the agreement of February, this contract provided that another daughter might be substituted for Jeanne should Jeanne die.

[37] In a bull that Philip the Fair obtained on 18 August 1305, Clement V declared, 'Sane petitio ex parte tua nobis exhibita continebat, quod [. . .] Ludovicus [. . .] cum Iohanna [. . .] sibi quarto gradu consanguinitatis coniuncta, absque dispensatione seu indulgentia dicte sedis, sponsalia per verba de futuro seu matrimonium per verba de presenti contraxit, et postmodum proprio super corpus Christi iuramento firmavit dictam Iohannam et non aliam, ea vivente, in coniugem se ducturum': Giulio Battelli, *Acta Pontificum*, Exempla Scripturarum Edita Consilio et Opera Procuratorum Bibliothecae et Tabularii Vaticani, 3 (Vatican City: Biblioteca Apostolica Vaticana, 1933), p. 16, no. 17; see also Bernard Barbiche, *Les actes pontificaux originaux des Archives nationales de Paris*, 3 vols, Index Actorum Romanorum Pontificum ab Innocentio III ad Martinum V Electum, 1–3 (Vatican City: Biblioteca Apostolica Vaticana, 1974–82), III, no. 2229. See also Bernard Barbiche, '*Litterae ante coronationem*: note sur quelques actes pontificaux originaux conservés aux Archives nationales de Paris', in *Palaeographica Diplomatica et Archivistica: Studi in onore di Giulio Battelli* [. . .], 2 vols, Storia e Letteratura raccolta di Studi e Testi, 139–40 (Rome: Storia e Letteratura, 1979), II, 269–71. Jean of Saint-Victor is the only historian known to me who mentions the commitment: *Recueil des historiens des Gaules et de la France*, ed. Martin Bouquet and others, 24 vols (Paris: Victor Palmé, H. Welter, Imprimerie nationale, 1738–1904) XXI, 647–8.

[38] Fawtier, no. 993 (AN, JJ 44, fol. 66r–v, no. 101), ed. in Plancher and Merle, *Bourgogne*, II, *preuves*, xcvii–iii, no. CXXXXIX, and in *Corps diplomatique*, I¹, 324–5, no. DLXVIII. Louis and Marguerite were to be married when they reached marriageable age (*annos nubiles*); Marguerite was about as old as Louis. Robert promised Philip the Fair that, with his daughter, he would give the king for his son and his son's needs 100,000 l.p.t.; a quarter of this would be paid on the day the marriage was solemnised 'in facie Ecclesie', and the rest in annual instalments of 15,000 l.p.t. Marguerite was to be given land worth 6000 l.p.t. a year unless she became queen, at which time her endowment was to be doubled.

[39] '[. . .] habita tantum super ipsa consanguinitate sedis dispensatione prefate, matrimoniali se vinculo copulavit, non attendens quod cum eadem Margarita propter publice iusticiam honestatis ex precedentibus sponsalibus seu matrimonio quamvis nullis exortam, contrahere non poterat nec debebat, absque sedis eiusdem licentia speciali': Battelli, *Acta Pontificum*, p. 17, no. 17. For the ceremony at Vernon, see *Chronique latine de Guillaume de Nangis de 1113 à 1300, avec les continuations de cette chronique de 1300 à 1368*, ed. Hercule Géraud, 2 vols, Publications de la Société de l'histoire de France, 33, 35 (Paris: Jules Renouard,

which was celebrated with great pomp at Corbeil in January 1307.[40] Triumphant at this success, Mahaut of Artois quickly negotiated another royal union by offering the huge cash settlement of 200,000 l.p.t. with her daughter Blanche. Blanche (then eleven) and Philip the Fair's third son Charles (then thirteen),[41] duly concluded a marriage contract on 23 September 1307,[42] and were married at Mahaut's fairytale château of Hesdin the following January.[43]

1843), I, 349; *Recueil des historiens*, XXI, 26 (Richard Lescot's continuation of Géraud de Frachet), and 645 (Jean de Saint-Victor); the Continuator of Guillaume de Nangis and Jean de Saint-Victor noted that the marriage was accomplished with papal dispensation. See also Barbiche, '*Litterae*', p. 273.

[40] On 19 December 1306 Mahaut of Artois confirmed her late husband's contract of 1295 with Philip the Fair; she pledged that she, her son Robert, and her daughter Blanche would accept its conditions on pain of forfeiting 200,000 l.t.: Fawtier, no. 301; Arras, AD du Pas-de-Calais, A 52; Besançon, AD du Doubs, B 23. For the marriage, see Richard, *Mahaut*, pp. 9–10; *Chronique de Guillaume de Nangis*, I, 356–7; *Recueil des historiens*, XXI, 647–8 (Jean de Saint-Victor); Arras, AD du Pas-de-Calais, A 53, nos. 2 and 3 (exemplifications of the royal act of January 1307 at Longpont and of a royal letter dated 20 January 1307 at Corbeil concerning Jeanne's dower, issued on 14 and 17 February 1309 by Pierre le Feron, *garde* of the *prévôté* of Paris); *Comptes royaux (1285–1314)*, ed. Robert Fawtier and François Maillard, 3 vols, Recueil des historiens de la France, Documents financiers, 3 (Paris: Imprimerie nationale, 1953–56), II, nos. 24015, 24036, 24038 (gifts of Philip the Fair to Jeanne, the first offered the day after her marriage), and no. 24055 (expenses for provisions taken 'à l'hospital de Corbueil aus noces Mons. Philippe' in royal accounts for 1 January to 1 July 1307).

[41] For Charles's birth on 18 June 1294, see Brown, 'Prince is Father', p. 317 n. 118; and J.-Robert de Chevanne, 'Charles IV le Bel et Blanche de Bourgogne', *Bulletin philologique et historique du Comité des travaux historiques et scientifiques* (1936–37), 313–50 (p. 315).

[42] AN, JJ 44, fols 4r–5v, nos. 1–3 (Philip the Fair's announcement of the terms of the treaty, dated September 1307; the counterpart of this act, issued by Mahaut on 23 September 1307; and Mahaut's pledge, made on the same day, to establish, before Christmas, additional guarantors for the payment of the dowry, on penalty of forfeiting 20,000 l.t.; all three acts are dated at Saint-Germain-en-Laye); see Fawtier, nos. 895–7. Fawtier's analysis of the marriage agreement (no. 895) indicates, following the text in AN, JJ 44, that Philip the Fair promised to given Blanche 10,000 l.t., but both Mahaut's counterpart and an exemplification of Philip's copy dated 17 February 1309 (for which see Arras, AD du Pas-de-Calais, A 53, no. 34) state clearly that Mahaut was assigning this sum to the king 'in augmentacionem dicte Dotis' or 'in dicte dotis augmentum'. Mahaut's pledge was made to Philip the Fair 'tanquam legitimo administratori dicti Karoli'; after the marriage was solemnised 'in facie Ecclesie' half the money was to be Charles's outright; the rest was to be spent on lands and revenues to support Blanche and their children. Following their marriage, Charles and Blanche were to ratify all agreements that had been made regarding the marriage of Philip and Jeanne of Burgundy. These guarantees were made in October 1308, although Mahaut of Artois had requested the king to have them executed the previous July: AN, JJ 40, fol. 165r–v, no. 41 (Fawtier, no. 383); Arras, AD du Pas-de-Calais, A 54, no. 21 (2801), and also A 54, no. 11 (2786) (a letter of Philip the Fair dated 28 July 1308, promising to have the couple ratify the agreements on 5 September). See Paul Marchegay, 'Documents relatifs au mariage du roi de France Charles IV' (preceded by Edgard Boutaric, 'Rapport sur une communication de M. Marchegay'), *Revue des sociétés savantes des départements*, 4th ser., 4 (1866), 437–41, and Jean Favier, *Un conseiller de Philippe le Bel: Enguerran de Marigny*, Mémoires et documents

Note 42 continues on next page with note 43.

Just how happy Jeanne's marriage to Philip was is impossible to say. It was certainly more prolific than those of Philip's brothers. Philip and Jeanne had their first child, a daughter Jeanne, in May 1308, and before the spring of 1313 at least three other daughters.[44] In contrast, Louis and Marguerite had no children before a daughter Jeanne was born on 28 January 1312.[45] Charles and Blanche at some point had a son and a daughter, but neither is known to have been born before January 1314.[46] Whatever the significance of the

publiés par la Société de l'École des Chartes, 16 (Paris: Presses universitaires de France, 1963), pp. 117–18.

[43] The itinerary of Philip the Fair shows that the king was at Hesdin (Pas-de-Calais, ar. Montreuil-sur-Mer) from 18 to 20 January 1308, during which time the wedding must have taken place: Robert-Henri Bautier and Elisabeth Lalou are preparing the itinerary for publication, working with the findings of Robert Fawtier and François Maillard, and I am grateful to them for permitting me to consult their files. On 18 January 1308 Philip the Fair confirmed the promise made to Mahaut (as her daughter Blanche's guardian) to assign Blanche lands in France worth 4,000 l.t. a year; they would lie within the territory which, the king said, he 'should [*debemus*] assess and assign' to his son; the lands would be Blanche's whether or not she had any children; the portion would be hers even if Charles died before receiving his assignment. Philip suggested that these details had been settled in the marriage contract, but the agreement of 23 September 1307 had left Blanche's dower rights vague. See the exemplification of the royal letter executed by Pierre le Feron, *garde* of the *prévôté* of Paris, on 17 February 1309, in Arras, AD du Pas-de-Calais, A 54, no. 2 (2758). The wedding preceded by about a week the marriage of Philip the Fair's daughter Isabelle to Edward II of England, for which see Brown, *Customary Aids*, pp. 16–20.

[44] Richard, *Mahaut*, pp. 9–10; for the birth of their only son in July 1316, see n. 30 above.

[45] Jeanne's birthdate is given by Bernard Gui: *Recueil des historiens*, XXI, 724; see also Brown, 'Double Funeral', pp. 234, 238. On 5 March 1312 Edward II of England, then at York, richly rewarded the usher of the queen of Navarre, Jeannot de Samoys, who brought him news of Jeanne's birth: London, British Library, MS Cott. Nero C VIII, fol. 85r.

[46] In the bull nullifying their marriage, issued on 19 May 1322, John XXII stated that the couple had had 'prolem tam masculinam quam femininam': *Jean XXII (1316–1334). Lettres secrètes et curiales relatives à la France extraites des registres du Vatican*, by Auguste-Léonel Coulon *et al.*, Bibliothèque des Écoles françaises d'Athènes et de Rome, ser. 1, 3 (Paris: Albert Fontemoing and others, 1906–), II, 92, no. 1419. Anselme assumes (*Histoire généalogique*, I, 96) that the child ('enfant', according to Anselme) of whose birth Philip of Poitiers learned on Saturday, 5 January 1314 (n.s.) was Charles's and Blanche's son Philip; the full financial account from which Anselme drew this information no longer survives. The 'enfant', in any case, died before 24 March 1322. For the death of Charles's and Blanche's daughter, Jeanne, on 18 May 1320, see Denis de Sainte-Marthe *et al.*, *Gallia Christiana* [. . .], 16 vols (Paris: Victor Palmé, 1729–1877), VII, 931; cf. Anselme, *Histoire généalogique*, I, 96 (assigning her death the impossible date 'le jour de la Pentecôte 17 may 1321'). When Jeanne was born is unclear; she was buried at Maubuisson. There seems little doubt that Blanche and Charles had at least one additional child, since Charles IV's third wife Jeanne and his successor Philip VI each made gifts to the abbey of Pont-aux-Dames at Crécy-en-Brie because two of Charles's children were buried there. Blanche may have had a child, possibly by Charles, after she was incarcerated for adultery; I discuss the evidence in the unpublished study cited in n. 1 above. Suffice it to say here that in the account of the royal succession, which he wrote in 1329, Pierre Jacob of Montpellier declared that after her imprisonment Blanche 'concepisset, & peperisset filium in carcere'; he noted the rumour

number of children Philip and Jeanne produced, Jeanne's relationship with her husband survived the adultery scandal that engulfed the royal court in the spring of 1324. Unlike her sisters-in-law, Marguerite and Blanche who were imprisoned as adulteresses at Château-Gaillard, Jeanne largely escaped its consequences. Although the censorious Philip the Fair had Jeanne confined at the castle of Dourdan, she was judged, found innocent, and liberated after Philip the Fair's death on 29 November 1314.[47] She was reunited at once with her husband, and her mother Mahaut of Artois later testified that from this time on the couple lived together 'in good peace, concord, agreement, and love, without strife, rancor, or hatred'.[48]

that Charles, her husband, 'eam in carcere cognouerat carnaliter'. He went on to say that when Charles died the son did not succeed to the crown (*dimisso illo filio*) 'in tanta obscuritate & dubietate iuris sui concepto, & maxime quia quando contractum fuit illud matrimonium banna non fuerant edita': Petrus Jacobus, *Avrea practica libellorum* [. . .] (Cologne: Geruinus Calenius, 1575), p. 281, no. 59. The Continuator of Guillaume de Nangis says that some believed Blanche 'a proprio comite [. . .] vel ab aliis impraegnata' (*Chronique de Guillaume de Nangis*, I, 418–19); the Continuator of Gérard de Frachet quite reasonably emended this to 'a proprio comite Marchiae dicebatur ab aliis impraegnata' (*Recueil des historiens*, XXI, 43 n. 7).

47 I discuss the various accounts of the affair in the unpublished study mentioned in n. 1 above. As I show there, the rhymed chronicle and the *dits* contained in BNF, fr. 146, insist repeatedly on Jeanne's innocence. In contrast, the Continuator of Guillaume de Nangis' Chronicle makes no judgment of his own and simply states that, although Jeanne was under grave suspicion at the beginning and was separated from her husband for a time (*aliquamdiu*), she was eventually cleared of suspicion and declared 'guiltless and completely innocent' (*inculpabilis et omnino innoxia*) by the Parlement of Paris, in the presence of the counts of Valois and Evreux: *Chronique de Guillaume de Nangis*, I, 406. The reticence of Jean de Saint-Victor is curious, since he ordinarily follows closely the rhymed chronicle of MS fr. 146. As regards this incident, Jean says that Jeanne was arrested 'because of certain suspicions' (*ex quadam suspicione*) but that 'nothing could be proved against her' (*sed nichil contra eam probari potuit*). He reports that she was detained for a long time (*diu*) at Dourdan, and that she was isolated from her husband; he omits the rhymed chronicle's description of the comforts she was given there. Nor does he say anything of the inquest which declared her innocent or of her restoration to Philip of Poitiers. This he leaves to the reader to deduce from his later comment that Philip of Poitiers had had 'one son of his wife when he was in Burgundy dealing with the cardinals' (in the summer of 1316): *Recueil des historiens*, XXI, 666. I consider the possibility that Philip the Fair's daughter Isabelle was involved in the revelation of the adultery affair, in 'Diplomacy, Adultery, and Domestic Politics at the Court of Philip the Fair: Queen Isabelle's Mission to the Court of France in 1314', in *Documenting the Past: Essays in Medieval History Presented to George Peddy Cuttino*, ed. J. S. Hamilton and Patricia J. Bradley (Woodbridge: Boydell, 1989), pp. 53–84.

48 '[. . .] et ante continue a tempore quo Nos et dicta consors Nostra fueramus matrimonialiter copulati usque ad nunc tempus presens fueramus continue et eramus in bona pace, concordia, societate et dilectione absque dissencione, rancore et odio, sicut scire poterant et illi qui Nos tunc temporis frequentarant': Denis-Charles, Marquis de Godefroy Menilglaise, 'Mahaud comtesse d'Artois: accusation de sortilége [sic] et d'empoisonnement, arrêt d'absolution, confédération des nobles du Nord de la France', *Mémoires de la Société des antiquaires de France*, 3rd ser., 8 (1865), 181–230 (pp. 203–4) (a royal decree of 9 October 1317 in

Such feelings as Mahaut attributed to Philip and her daughter would go far to explain Philip's generosity to Jeanne. But it is not clear that her words are trustworthy. What else would Mahaut have said of a daughter who had reigned as queen of France – particularly when she was defending herself against charges of using potions to bewitch her son-in-law? Just how Philip and Jeanne felt about each other is obviously impossible to determine. Philip often waxed eloquent about his sentiments toward Jeanne, but many of his statements are formulaic. He repeatedly referred to the 'sincere [*or* magne] dilectionis affectum' which she bore him,[49] to the 'faithful and natural con-

which Philip V declared his mother-in-law innocent of the charges of using philtres against him and Charles of la Marche and of poisoning Louis X).

[49] 'attendentes sincere dilectionis affectum quem ad nos gerit Carissima Consors nostra Iohanna Regina franc. & nauarre / causas que & Raciones plurimas efficaces nos ad assignandum Sibi dotalicium competens inducentes [. . .]. Et Si quod absit ante nostrum decessum facta non esset ad plenum assisia seu assignacio antedicta / per . . heredem uel . . Successorem in dicto Regno franc. volumus & concedimus / eam post nostrum decessum fieri efficaciter / integre et complete secundum formam & modum predictos / ac in locis superius declaratis / volentes ac etiam concedentes expresse / quod dicta . . Consors nostra / totale suum dotalicium Supradictum [. . .] cum tanta Munificencia et etiam tantis libertatibus / priuilegiis / ac honoribus teneat & possideat efficaciter & ad plenum / quemadmodum / et . . Regine predecessores eiusdem Consortis nostre / uidelicet Carissime domine / domina Maria / vel domina Clemencia / vel alie Regine franc. quecumque sint vel fuerint que nobilius tenuerunt sua dotalicia / et Res / ac loca sibi pro eis assignatas / retroactis possederunt temporibus / et adhuc tenent & possident et etiam hactenus tenuerunt / Et predicta et infrascripta vniuersa et singula grata / firma & Rata habentes / ac tenentes / nec contra facere Seu venire per nos uel per alium quacunque racione / uel causa seu ingenio de iure uel de facto promittimus pro nobis / . . heredibus & Successoribus nostris sub obligacione omnium bonorum nostrorum presencium / et etiam futurorum – Quodque ipsa / auctoritate sua possessionem eorundem locorum & Rerum possit apprehendere corporalem / quam possessionem volumus & expresse concedimus / quod ipsa . . Consors nostra post obitum nostrum / quandocunque voluerit auctoritate sua propria apprehendat / Et quod dictas Res & loca / eidem nostre . . Consorti garentizabimus / auctorisabimus & perpetuo defendemus / Considerantes que preterea matura deliberatione Super hiis habita predicta omnia & singula / iuste Rite ac legitime facta esse / auctoritate Regia decreuimus / statuimus et etiam declaramus / non obstantibus iure / vsu seu consuetudine quibuscunque in contrarium facientibus / quod quem / et quam in quantum contra predicta uel eorum aliquod facerent / irritamus & omnino tollimus / nec locum habere volumus / eadem omnia & singula supradicta firma & illibata esse / & habere debere perpetuam roboris firmitatem / Et quod contra ea uel aliqua de premissis / a quocunque in Iudicio vel extra nichil possit obici seu / oppponi': AN, JJ 53, fol. 47r, no. 106 (Guerout, no. 394) (March 1317; with the rubric 'littere de assignacione dotalicij domine Iohanne Regine franc. & nauarre'); also in Besançon, AD du Doubs, B 24. Cf. AN, JJ 53, fols 148v–49r, no. 352 (Guerout, no. 649) (October 1317), 'super hoc habita plena deliberacione Racione sincere dilectionis affectus / quem ad nos gerit Carissima Consors nostra / Iohanna dictorum Regnorum Regina . . Necnon alijs quamplurimis / Racionibus efficacibus / et causis [. . .] volentes / et eciam statuentes / auctoritateque nostra Regia / & ex certa sciencia decernentes / ut non obstante quocunque Iure / vsu / consuetudine quod quem / et quam auctoritate nostra Regia predicta / quo ad hec irritamus / ac omnino tollimus & cassamus'. Note also, in an undated act, issued at Vincennes, perhaps in December 1316, 'prouida deliberacione pensentes [*sic*] magne dilectionis affectum quem ad nos gerit Iohanna

gress [*societas*]' and the devotion by which 'his most beloved wife' was bound to him, as well her constant efforts to please him.[50] In January 1320, he mentioned her free and considerate services, honours, and courtesies, and the most faithful union she had carefully observed with him.[51] In his preamble

Regina franc. et Nauarr. carissima c[o]nsors nostra et exhibita per ea nobis obsequia dignum decreuimus ut ex munificencia Regia sui status exhigenciis quantum commode possumus nunc & inposterum consulamus ea propter nos pro nobis & successoribus nostris dedimus tradidimus & donauimus [. . .] volentes statuentes & auctoritate Regia decernentes ut non obstante quocumque iure vsu seu consuetudine incontrarium facientibus quod quem & quam omnino predicta auctoritate Regia quantum ad hoc irritamus tollimus & cassamus presens donatio & omnia suprascripta valeant & plenissimam firmitatem habeant vim que legis obtineat donacio Regia supradicta': AN, JJ 54B, fol. 37r, no. 58 (Guerout, no. 1425).

[50] 'pensata & considerata fideli & naturali societate ac deuocione quibus predilectissima consors nostra Iohanna eadem gratia franc. & nauarre Regina comitissa burgundie palatina nobis afficitur se que incessabili exhibicione gratam in omnibus Reddere consueuit nos mutua in nimirum affectione cumpunti eam prosequi fauore debite cupientes prouida deliberacione [. . .] volentes nichilominus ac eciam statuentes expresse nostraque auctoritate regia inuiolabiliter decernentes vt non obstantibus quibuscunque Iuribus vsu consuetudinibus in contrarium facientibus que quem & quas auctoritate Regia predicta quo ad hec adnullamus Irritamus & omnino tollimus reuocamus / & cessamus [sic]': AN, JJ 53, fol. 48r, no. 107 (Guerout, no. 395) (February 1317; with the rubric, 'quomodo dominus Rex dedit domine Iohanne franc. & nauarre Regine Manerium de cantiluppo cum his descriptis aliis bonis . . necnon et quingentas librarum terre'). Cf. AN JJ 56, fol. 196r, no. 464 (Guerout, no. 2092) (July 1318), 'pensata & considerata fideli ac naturali Societate / et deuocione quibus predilectissima consors nostra. Iohanna / eadem gratia franc. & Nauarre Regina / Comitissa Burgundie Palatina nobis afficitur seque incessabili exhibicione gratam in omnibus reddere consueuit / Nos mutua nimirum affectione compuncti ipsam prosequj fauore debito Cupientes / prouida deliberacione habita' (without any extraordinary validation formula); the rubric reads, 'donacio tocius Iuris quod dominus Rex poterat Reclamare in Rebus et locis hic descriptis facta domine Iohanne franc. et nauarre Regine', and a contemporary note beside this reads 'donum'. And also AN, JJ 56, fol. 258r, no. 590 (Guerout, no. 2220) (April 1319), 'pensata & considerata fideli & naturali societate / ac deuocione quibus predilectissima consors nostra . . Iohanna eadem gratia dictorum Regnorum Regina nobis afficitur / Seque nobis incessabili exhibitione / gratam in omnibus Reddere consueuit / Nos mutua nimirum affectione compuncti / eam prosequi fauore debito cupientes prouida deliberacione super hoc habita [. . .] Volentes Nichilominus / et eciam statuentes expresse / nostraque auctoritate Regia inuiolabiliter decernentes / ut non obstantibus quibuscumque / Iuribus / vsu / consuetudinibus / que / quem / & quas / auctoritate Regia predicta / in quantum contra premissa facerent adnullamus / Reuocamus / irritamus / et omnino tollimus & Cassamus / presens donatio / cessio / concessio/ ac omnia / & singula suprascripta valeant / & plenissimam firmitatem habeant vimque legis obtineat huiusmodj facte per nos / donatio / cessio / & concessio de predictis'. The rubric introducing this act reads 'donacio domus de nigella / facta domine Regine', and before the act appear contemporary notations, 'donum', and 'pro Regina'. Cf. as well the terms of the gift Philip bestowed on her in January 1320, quoted in the next act from AN, JJ 60, fol. 129r, no. 206 (Guerout, no. 3577).

[51] 'gratis consideratis seruiciis honoribus & curialitatibus / per Carissimam consortem nostram Iohannam Reginam francorum & Nauarre nobis exhibitis societate que fidelissima / quam erga nos studuit obseruare / Tanto eam maiori affectione prosequimur / quanto sinceriori puro que corde semper in omnibus voluit condescendere votis nostris. Hiis Ita que pensatis / & pluribus alijs que ad hoc nos Inducunt / Eidem consorti nostre pro se suis que

to the testament his wife completed on 27 August 1319, Philip himself declared that 'nous amons de tout nostre Cuer & desierrons la salu de lame de le'.[52] This is touching, but the statement can be read to mean not that Philip loved his wife with all his heart and desired her soul's salvation, but rather that with all his heart he loved her soul and desired its salvation. These statements, in short, have no real bearing on the question of whether Jeanne was indeed guilty of adultery, and whether her husband took her back because she was countess of Burgundy and he feared to lose the county if he abandoned her.[53] This seems to me unlikely – although it is not impossible. Philip may have loved his wife deeply, or feared her, or been bewitched by her – for whatever reason, he showered her with gifts, whose extravagance is exceptional and impressive.[54]

heredibus & successoribus': AN, JJ 60, fol. 129r, no. 206 (Guerout, no. 3577) (January 1320); with the rubric 'donacio castri et castellanie de chailliaco facta domine Regine franc. & Nauarre'.

[52] The act continues, 'a la fin que quant plus abundeusement donra & fera de biens en heneur de ihesuchrist nous & elle puissons plus legierement auoir & obtenir sa grant misericorde & que elle ait plus largement de quoi elle puisse plus plenierement faire & establir a heneur de dieu euures piteus & de charite . & donner au poures de iheuschrist et gueredonner a ses seruiteurs': AN, J 404A, no. 23; see also no. 23 bis, a copy of the will made on 26 February 1529.

[53] Paul Lehugeur cites as evidence the *Normanniae Nova Chronica* and a chronicle continued at Rouen to 1343 (which he calls 'témoignages contemporains'), but in the end he declares it unlikely that Philip of Poitiers would have 'sacrificed his honor' simply to retain possession of the county of Burgundy, which came to him from Jeanne: *Histoire de Philippe le Long, roi de France (1316–1322)*, 2 vols (Paris: Hachette and Recueil Sirey, 1897–1931), I, 16–18, esp. his statements on p. 18 ('D'un autre côté pourquoi admettre sans aucune preuve que Philippe le Long ait sacrifié son honneur à la possession d'une province, et qu'en songeant à son frère, il se soit contenté de dire comme Sagnarelle: *En tout cas ce qui peut m'ôter ma fâcherie, C'est que je ne suis pas seul de ma confrérie*. Quelle ne serait pas l'indignation des mêmes auteurs [who suggested that Philip kept Jeanne because of her lands], s'il avait répudié la femme et renoncé à la province! Il eût comme ils le disent précisément de Louis VII, qui l'a fait, "sacrifié les plus chers intérêts de la France" '.) Robert Fawtier does not note that Jeanne was by all accounts cleared of the charges of adultery in judicial proceedings. In commenting that she had brought the county of Burgundy to her husband, he implies that her lands may have won her release: *Les Capétiens et la France* (Paris: Presses universitaires de France, 1942; trans. [by Lionel Butler and R. J. Adam] as *The Capetian Kings of France: Monarchy and Nation (987–1328)* [London: Macmillan, 1960]), p. 55 (Eng. trans. p. 53); for similar opinions see Joseph Petit, *Charles de Valois (1270–1325)* (Paris: Alphonse Picard, 1900), p. 142; and Marcellin Boudet, 'Les derniers Mercoeur. Béraud VII de Mercoeur, connétable de Champagne, 1272–1321', *Revue d'Auvergne*, 21 (1904), 1–20, 93–127, 241–66, 373–96, 453–60 (p. 266); the article is concluded in ibid., 22 (1904), 47–63, 97–123, 161–92, 244–72, 333–46, 373–89.

[54] See the incisive comments and analysis of Robert-Henri Bautier, 'Critique diplomatique, commandement des actes et psycologie des souverains du Moyen Age', *Académie des Inscriptions et Belles Lettres. Comptes rendus des séances de l'année 1978, janvier–mars*, 8–26 (p. 19).

Philip's generosity to his wife began, modestly enough, during Louis X's reign, in June 1315, when he was count of Poitiers. Yet in assigning her dower of 6000 l.t. a year on property he had inherited from his mother in Champagne, he showed distinct concern about the durability of his act. Specifying his wish for the assignment to hold despite contrary law or custom, he nonetheless provided that 'if law or custom went against her', the dower would be assigned on any of his other lands she selected. Philip thus admitted that what he most wanted might not be possible to accomplish. He revealed his desire to be able to do as he wished, without regard for law or tradition, but also his awareness that he could not himself disregard or abrogate them. He evidently believed his brother, the king, could do so. Hence he asked Louis 'notwithstanding any law or custom that could be contrary', to exercise 'the power of his royal right, and of his certain knowledge' to consent to, confirm, and ratify the act, and join to it his decree and assent, and see that it was exactly executed. In January 1316, Louis X issued the confirmation, although the terms were not precisely what Philip had requested. Rather, Louis confirmed the act by his royal authority, with the interposition of the royal decree, and with certain knowledge. He did not abrogate law or custom.[55] Philip's wishes, which reflected his grandiose conception of the extensive power kings could exercise, were thwarted momentarily, even though he evidently enjoyed Louis's favour. In August 1315 his brother had awarded him a peerage[56] and had formally revoked the exclusion of females from succeeding to Philip's county of Poitiers which Philip the Fair, with Louis's and Philip's approval, had mandated on his deathbed.[57] Louis acknowledged that both

---

[55] 'Nous desirrans que se elle nous seuruist / que bonne pais / et bon acort / soit entre luy / et nos hoirs nourrie / et toute matire de discorde ostee . . . les dites sis Mile liurees de Rente assignons et asseons a nostre dite compaigne pour son douaire / a penre es terres que nous auons en champaigne / et en brie qui nous sont auenues de la Succession de bonne memoire / nostre tres chiere dame / et mere / Madame Iehanne iadis Roygne [*sic*] de france et de Nauarre et Contesse de Champaigne / et de Brie [. . .] Et se il auenoit que nostre hoir meissent empeschement [. . .] Si volons nous que ladite assiete teigne non contrastant droit ou coustume qui contre nostre volunte pourriont [*sic*] venir / en empeschant les dite choses / Et ou cas que droit ou coustume feroit contre nostre dite compaigne / si volons nous / que elle praigne son dit douaire de Sis Mile liurees de terre / ou de Rente / en nostre autre terre / en quecunque lieu elle voudra eslire / Car nous volons / que toute matire de descort / soit ostee / entre nostre dite compaigne et nos hoirs': Besançon, AD du Doubs, B 24 (January 1316, act of Louis X). Philip asked his brother Louis that 'non contrastant quelcomque [*sic*] droit ou coustume qui pourroient estre contraire / sus choses dessus dites / il vueille de la puissance de son droit Royal / et de sa certaine science / consentir confermer & ratefier / et y mettre son decret / et son assentement'. Louis confirmed the donation 'auctoritate nostra Regis / cum decreti nostrj interpositione / ex certa scientia', saving his and others' rights.

[56] Ed. in Guérin, *Archives historiques du Poitou*, 11 (1881), 115–16; see Guerout, no. 280. For background and context, see André Artonne, *Le mouvement de 1314 et les chartes provinciales de 1315*, Bibliothèque de la Faculté des Lettres, Université de Paris, 29 (Paris: Félix Alcan, 1912), pp. 41–2.

[57] Philip the Fair's act is ed. in Favier, *Enguerran*, p. 232, no. II; on its significance, see ibid.,

he and Philip had agreed to their father's restriction, but he took pains to justify and explain his decision to rescind it. He declared his act an inter–vivos gift, and said he was making it by special grace, and with certain advice and knowledge. He proclaimed null and void all letters, conditions, approvals, and renunciations (obviously including his own and his brother's) that might threaten the permanence and validity of his grant. Note, however: he did not mention law and custom (which his brother Philip believed that Louis, as king, could legitimately nullify). He ended by declaring that he was acting by his full power and authority and royal sovereignty, having received good advice from his council, with interposition and the authority of his decree.[58]

At the same time as he received the right to assign Jeanne's dower on the county of Champagne, Philip of Poitiers made another significant gift to her. Louis X doubtless knew of the grant, but Philip did not request and Louis did not give any formal confirmation. Decrying the arrangements that Philip the Fair had made with Othon of Burgundy, Philip granted Jeanne the county of Burgundy for her lifetime. The award was not quite as liberal as it might have been, nor was Philip's act as selfless as the indignation he expressed toward his father suggests it should have been. He carefully retained for himself the

---

pp. 97–8, and also Charles T. Wood, *The French Apanages and the Capetian Monarchy 1224–1338*, Harvard Historical Monographs, 59 (Cambridge, MA: Harvard University Press, 1966), pp. 48–64 (esp. 55–6 nn. 48–51). Philip the Fair's act was approved by his sons Louis and Philip, by his brothers Charles of Valois and Louis of Evreux, and by Guy de Châtillon, count of Saint-Pol, and the constable, Gaucher de Châtillon.

58 'Et a ce don / et a ceste condition Nous soiens autre fois consentis nous & nostre tres chier freres dessus diz . . Nous considerans et Regardans que Raisons & drois naturez donnent que en deffautes de hoirs males les fumelles [*sic*] doiuent aussi bien heritier et auoir successions es biens et es possessions des peres de cui elles ont este procrees & descendues en loyal mariage comme sont li malle / [Et, *expuncted*] a la Requeste & a la supplicacion dou dit nostre chier frere qui de ce nous a supplie & Requis humblement pour la grant amour et la grant affection que nous auons & deuons auoir a lui / par droit & par Raison / en acroissant le don & la prouision que nostre dit sires & pere li fist / li ottroions de grace especial et de certaine science que non contraictant ce que li dons [. . .] Et la condition dessus dite que si hoirs femelles ne heriteroient pas. La quele condition nous ostons et metons au noient / et rapellons du tout [. . .] et en ceste condition li donnons nous encor la dite Contee et ses appartenances pour lui & pour ses hoirs malles & femelles nez & a naistre de son corps en loyal mariage par la teneur de ces presentes lettres par don fait entre vis / sanz esperance de Rappel / de nostre grace especial / de certain auis et de certaine science. Et toutes lettres / toutes condicions / touz consentemenz / & toutes Renunciacions / faites / & donnees / au contraire de nostre tres chier seigneur & pere de nous / de nostre dit frere ou dautres / et toutes autres choses qui nostre present octroi / & don pourroient empeechier / Nous rappellons / ostons / cassons et metons du tout au noient / et voulons estre de nulle force / et de nulle valeur / en tant seulement / & non emplus comme elles pourroient estre contraires a nostre octroi / et a nostre don dessus diz. de nostre plain pouoir / de nostre auctorite / et de nostre seuurainete Royal / par bon auis eu sur ce par grant deliberacion de nostre conseil / auecques linterposicion / & lauctorite de nostre decret': Arras, AD du Pas-de-Calais, A 60, no. 27 (3013) (an exemplification of 17 April 1323, by Jehan Loncle, *garde* of the *prévôté* of Paris).

right to alienate any part of the county he chose, while limiting Jeanne's power to do so.[59]

Gifts continued when Philip became king. In December 1316, before he was crowned, he raised Jeanne's dower to 20,000 l.t., mentioning not only her affection for him, but also her right to a queenly endowment.[60] After February 1317, he took exceptional care in having her dower assigned on spe-

---

[59] Besançon, AD du Doubs, B 23 (Arras, August 1315), which has suffered severe damage. Philip issued the act as 'fils de Roy de France', count of Poitiers, count palatine of Burgundy, and lord of Salins, but in all other respects it appears virtually identical to the award Philip made to Jeanne on 6 February 1317 (AN, J 250 [Bourgogne IV], nos. 8–9 [no. 9 included in a vidimus by the *garde* of the *prévôté* of Paris, Jehan Loncle, dated 6 June 1322]; JJ 53, fol. 14r, no. 38 [Guerout, no. 323]; with the heading 'pro domina Regina' and the rubric 'littere donacionum factarum in matrimonio contrahendo inter dominum Regem. & dominam Reginam eius vxorem', and with the notation 'nichil' at the end). There (AN, J 250, no. 8) Philip remarked that 'ou Traitie / du dit Mariage / les deuant diz Conte & Contesse / Nous aient donne / et ottroie pour Raison de douaire & en Mariage / aueuques la dite Iehanne nostre compaigne / & a noz hoirs qui ystront de nous / & de la dite Iehanne / la Conte de Bourgoigne auec toutes les appartenances dicele / En tele Maniere que sil yauoit hoirs de Nous et de la dite Iehanne / Iasoit ce que elle Seuruesquist / la dite Conte / auec toutes les appartenances / seroit & demourroit / aus diz noz hoirs / Senz Iamais retourner au dit Conte & Contesse / ne a la dite Iehanne / Et aient voulu & accourde les diz Conte et Contesse / que se nous / & la dite Iehanne / de noz propres corps nauoiens hoirs / ou li hoir / de Nous cree en Mariage / mouroient sanz [sic] hoirs / de leur propre corps / que la dite conte / aueuc toutes les appartenances demourroit / a nostre treschier seigneur & Pere deuant dit & a ses hoiers [sic] . . Nous Attendanz quil seroit dure chose / que se nous Mouriens auant la dite Iehanne / nostre compaigne / que elle neust aucun proufit en la dite Conte qui nous est venue de son couste / & nous a este donnee / & a nos hoirs', granted her the county of Burgundy for her lifetime (with certain exceptions). This did not of course mean that Burgundy was lost to the realm. As a clerk noted on the folio of the register where the act was copied, 'Nota litteram per quam temporibus futuris posset comitatus burgondie Reuerti ad regnum francie'. Although the letter of donation included a clause in which Jeanne accepted her husband's gift, and stated that the letter was to be sealed by them both, in fact it was sealed only by Philip V (with the great seal, in green wax, on red and green silk laces). In January 1317, Philip had presented Jeanne with all the revenues of the county, for life, to cover the costs of her jewels and the clothing of her serving women: AN, JJ 54A, fol. 5v, no. 74 (Guerout, no. 735) (Paris, January 1317).

[60] 'nos attendentes sincere dilectionis affectum quem ad nos gerit Iohanna Regina franc. & Nauarr. carissima consors nostra / & quod ipsius condicione inspecta non decebat eam absque dotalicio Remanere causas pluresque rationes alias efficaces que nos ad assignandum Sibi dotalicium inducere debuerunt [. . .] considerantes que preterea matura deliberacione super hiis habita predicta omnia & singula iuste Rite ac legitime facta esse auctoritate Regia decernimus statuimus & eciam declaramus / ut quibuscumque iure consuetudine uel vsu in contrarium facientibus quod quam et quem in quantum contra predicta facerent irritamus et omnino tollimus nec locum habere volumus predicta omnia & singula firma & illibata esse & habere debere perpetuam Roboris firmitatem / & quod contra ea uel aliqua de eisdem a quocumque in Iudicio uel extra nichil possit obici uel opponi': AN, JJ 54B, fols 36v–37r, no. 57 (Guerout, no. 1424). In March 1317 he increased the dower by 1000 l.t.: Besançon, AD du Doubs, B 24; Guerout, no. 394. The dower of Clementia of Hungary, Louis X's second wife, produced 25,000 l.t. a year. Cf. the terms of Philip V's gift of the revenues of the county of Burgundy in January 1317, 'pensantes onera expensarum non modica & maiora solita que

cific sources of income.[61] He granted her additional lands and property: the manor (*manerium*) of Chanteloup and an annuity to support it;[62] the palace of Nesle in Paris;[63] the newly established bastide of Montgeard;[64] the château

dilecta consors nostra. Iohanna Regina franc. sustinet & habet necessario sustinere. pro conseruacione status Regis dignitatis': AN, JJ 54A, fol. 5v, no. 74 (Guerout, no. 735).

61 AN, JJ 53, fol. 41r, no. 91 (Guerout, no. 378) (February 1317); JJ 53, fols 148v–49r, no. 352 (Guerout, no. 649) (October 1317); Besançon, AD du Doubs, B 24 (24 December 1317; 16 March 1319; and 21 March 1319, for which see Jules Gauthier, 'Note sur un sceau inédit des exécuteurs testamentaires de Philippe le Bel, 1319, 21 mars', *Revue des sociétés savantes des départements*, 6th ser., 4 [1876], 280–2); AN, K 40, no. 28bis (through which slits have been cut, and from which the seals attached to the different membranes and the seal at the end have been detached; warranted 'per dominum Regem', and recorded by 'Gyem'); JJ 60, fols 37r–47v, no. 69 (Guerout, no. 3439), with the rubric 'Assignacio vinginti vnius milium librarum terre / pro dotalicio domine Iohanne Regine franc.', and lacking any indication that the act was later cancelled; J 408, no. 27 (from which the seals attached to the different membranes and the seal at the bottom of the act have been detached; a vidimus of the act of January 1320 of Charles of Valois, Charles of La Marche, and Louis of Evreux, which exemplifies Philip V's act of July 1319, the vidimus issued by Gilles Haquin, *garde* of the *prévôté* of Paris, on 26 November 1321); Besançon, AD du Doubs, B 24 (July 1319); I am grateful to François Maillard for providing me with a copy of his transcription of the act of July 1319, from AN, JJ 60.

62 AN, JJ 54B, fol. 37r, no. 58 (Guerout, no. 1425) (20 December 1316, with the notation 'non est signata'); JJ 53, fol. 48r, no. 107 (Guerout, no. 395) (February 1317); JJ 53, fol. 89r, no. 212 (Guerout, no. 503) (March 1317). Chanteloup is in Seine-et-Oise, ar. Corbeil-Essonnes, between Montlhéry and Arpajon, approx. 30 km. south of Paris.

63 AN, JJ 54A, fol. 41v, no. 545 (Guerout, no. 1209) (7 March 1317, for her lifetime); JJ 56, fol. 258r, no. 590 (Guerout, no. 2220) (April 1319, hereditarily).

64 'Omnes Redditus prouentus & Exitus. Iura deuera / obuentiones / Reddibencias et Emolumenta / seu Marchas quascumque / ac etiam Tallias Bastide noue de Monte Guiardo / in Senescallia Tholosana existentis / ac eciam nobis competentis seu competere valentis. occasione associationis seu Pariagij Bastide predicte / inter nos ex parte vna / et dilectum & fidelem nostrum. Hugonem Pictauinj domicellum facti / nuperrime & initi ex altera': AN, JJ 56, fol. 196r, no. 464 (Guerout, no. 2092) (July 1318); see also n. 50 above. Montgeard is located in Haute-Garonne, ar. Toulouse, c. Nailloux, 34 km. SE of Toulouse. The bastide was established as the result of an agreement made in Toulouse on 21 June 1317 by Guiard Guy, seneschal of Toulouse, and Hugues Peitavy, lord of Nailloux, who was to hold the bastide in pariage with the king. In the agreement, which the king confirmed in July 1318 in Paris, it was promised 'quod dominus noster Rex / seu eius Successores partem suam sibi in premissis ex dicto Pariagio pertinentem / non ponat extra manum suam. Nisi in Manu illius qui erit dominus Tholose': AN, JJ 56, fols 192r–93r (fol. 192v), no. 460 (Guerout, no. 2088), with the rubric 'approbacio paragij Rerum et Iuridicionum hic descriptarum facti domino Regi . . ab hugone pictauini domicello . . domino de alnahosio', and warranted 'per. dominum de lauro .M. de Essartis & Giraudum guete', and recorded by 'Iustic[e]'; see Claude Devic [de Vic] et Joseph Vaissete, *Histoire générale de Languedoc avec des notes et les pièces justificatives*, ed. Auguste Molinier et al., 15 vols (Toulouse: Édouard Privat, 1872–92), X, 570–1 no. 198 I. In the same month (and doubtless at the same time), Philip awarded a charter to the bastide, in accordance with the terms of the pariage (which did not, however, mention attachment to the king's hand); like the king's confirmation of the pariage, this act was warranted 'per dominum de lauro. M. de essartis & giraudi guete' and recorded by 'Iustic[e]': AN, JJ 59, fols 108v–110r, no. 231 (Guerout, no. 2952), ed. in Jean Ramière de Fortanier,

and village (*castrum et villa*) of Chilly.[65] He gave her money for jewels and her household;[66] 30,000 l.t. for her testamentary bequests;[67] the property of the Jews of Burgundy;[68] a debt of 80,000 l.t. that Mahaut of Artois, her mother, owed the crown.[69] Far more important than these gifts was the full and

Chartes de franchises du Lauragais, Thèse pour le doctorat en lettres, Faculté des lettres, Université de Toulouse (Toul: Imprimerie Touloise, 1939), pp. 510–17, no. 144; cf. as well AN, JJ 59, fols 81r–82r, no. 182 (Guerout, no. 2902), an act of July 1319, issued in Paris warranted in the same fashion, uniting Montgeard and Nailloux and granting the consolidated bastide a range of privileges, the majority of which reproduce those granted a year earlier to Montgeard, ed. in Ramière de Fortanier, *Chartes de franchises*, pp. 525–9, no. 154 (see also ibid., p. 518, no. 144 *bis*). The king's award to his wife was included in a list of royal gifts made in the seneschalsy of Toulouse in 1319, together with 1250 l. 'pro intragiis dicte bastide': BNF, fr. 32510, fol. 116v.

65 AN, JJ 60, fol. 129r, no. 206 (Guerout, no. 357) (January 1320), specifying that the grant was made 'pure simpliciter & irreuocabiliter / ac imperpetuum donacione facta inter viuos'; the king stated that he was giving it to Jeanne in addition to the *dos* he had assigned to her, and declared that he made the gift 'Nichil in eis Retinentes / nisi dumtaxat superioritatem homagium & Resortum / Nolentes quod propter huiusmodi donacionem / de donationibus al[iis] per Nos eidem alias factis uel de Rebus sibi traditis & assignatis in dotem / uel ex causa dotis / aliquid detrahatur sed donaciones & assignationes ipsas vna cum presenti donacione Tenere volumus sine diminuacione uel Impedimento quibuslibet & habere perpetuam Roboris firmitatem'. Chilly[-Mazarin] is in Seine-et-Oise, ar. Corbeil-Essonnes, c. Longjumeau, 20 km. NW of Corbeil-Essonnes, just SW of Orly. Philip the Fair acquired Chilly from the count of La Marche. He then granted it to Béraud de Mercœur, from whom Enguerran de Marigny purchased it in June 1312. See *Cartulaire et actes d'Enguerran de Marigny*, ed. Jean Favier, Collection de documents inédits sur l'histoire de France, ser. in-8º, 2 (Paris: Bibliothèque nationale, 1965). On 19 April 1315, after Marigny's fall, the property was (like Marigny's other holdings) united 'fisci nostri juribus [. . .] ut proprium nostrum domanium explectandos': AN, P 2290, p. 205 (an eighteenth-century copy of an act in Memorial A of the Chambre des comptes). Like most of Marigny's property, Chilly was soon granted out, in this case to Louis of Clermont: Guerout, no. 269 (July 1315, Crécy-en-Brie). Before 15 September 1317, Louis sold it to Pierre de La Vie, nephew of Pope John XXII: Guerout, no. 1314. In November 1319, Philip V obtained Chilly from Pierre in exchange for the barony of Villemur-sur-Tarn: Guerout, no. 2845.

66 AN, JJ 54A, fol. 5v, no. 75 (Guerout, no. 736) (January 1317).

67 AN, JJ 58, fol. 17r, no. 286 (Guerout, no. 2540) (3 December 1518). Jeanne drew up her will, with royal approval, on 27 August 1319: AN, J 404A, no. 23. Philip the Fair had authorised his wife Jeanne of Navarre to dispose of 40,000 l.p. and all her movables, as well as the income of her counties of Champagne and Brie for three years: AN, J 403, no. 14 (1 April 1304), and no. 16 (25 March 1305; ed. in César-Égasse Du Boulay, *Historia Vniversitatis Parisiensis* [. . .], 6 vols [Paris: François Noël, 1665–73], IV, 74–80).

68 Elizabeth A. R. Brown, 'Philip V, Charles IV, and the Jews of France: The Alleged Expulsion of 1322', *Speculum*, 66 (1991), 294–329 (p. 316).

69 AN, JJ 56, fol. 176r, no. 406 (Guerout, no. 2303). When, later, Charles IV attempted to collect debts that Othon of Burgundy owed to the crown, Mahaut of Artois asserted that Philip V had assigned them to Jeanne: BNF, Bourgogne 109, fol. 146r–v (a copy made in the eighteenth century by Dom Aubrée, from a copy in the Chambre des comptes at Dijon). ('La ditte Contesse respont que Li Roys Phelippe ses Sires qui darrainement trespassa cui Dex absoille donna par ses Lettres cete dete à la Royne Iehanne sa femme fille de la ditte Contesse qui les veult auoir de li'.) The act was prepared after Charles's marriage to Blanche

hereditary possession of the county of Burgundy that he bestowed on her in September 1318.[70]

was nullified on 19 May 1322, since Mahaut demanded, among other things, the return of the 200,000 l.t. she had paid in connection with the marriage on the grounds that 'Li mariage ait esté prononciez pour nul': see the comments of Chevanne, 'Charles IV le Bel', p. 345. The counterclaims that Mahaut made against Charles totaled some 700,000 l. Charles T. Wood edits Aubrée's copy in, 'Where is John the Posthumous? *or* Mahaut of Artois Settles her Royal Debts', in *Documenting the Past* (see n. 47 above), pp. 99–117 (pp. 111–12).

[70] AN, J 250 (Bourgogne IV), no. 10 (original act, elegantly executed, sealed with the great seal in green wax on red and green silk laces, with the notation on the fold-up, 'par le Roy . . P. Barr[iere]. doublee'); BNF, Mélanges de Colbert 350, no. 128 (original act, sealed in white wax on red and green silk laces, with the notation on the fold-up, '. . par le Roy . . . P. Barr[iere]. doublee'; endorsed in fourteenth-century script, 'Quitacio comitatus Burgund. per Regem tunc francie facta . . . ['Othoni comiti burg.', *cancelled*], 'Registrata est & collatio facta', 'Reddatur'; and in a later fourteenth-century hand, 'Declaration du roy Philippe que la conte de bourgogne a appartenu au conte othe & appartendra de la en auant a ['sa femme', *cancelled*] la fille dud. conte royne de france a la quelle led. roy quitte a la royne le droit que il auoit aud. [*sic*] conte'); BNF, Mélanges de Colbert 350, no. 129 (sealed exemplification and approval of Philip's act by Charles of Valois, Louis of Évreux, and Charles of La Marche, dated at Paris, 30 September 1318, endorsed 'Remissio & quittacio Comitatus Burgundie'); for Philip V's act, see also AN, J 250 (Bourgogne IV), no. 9 (a vidimus by Jehans Loncle, *garde* of the *prévôté* of Paris, dated 6 June 1322, Trinity Sunday). The preamble to this act (here cited from AN, J 250, no. 10) is especially elaborate: 'comme chascuns soit tenuz de garder droiture & de cognoistre bonne foi / en touz ses faiz / et de en exclurre toute maniere et toute cause de decepcion / Et par plus fort raison / nous qui de tant comme dieux nous a mis en plus grant estat / de tant sommes plus tenu et oblige a chascun de faire droiture / & de bonne foi recognoistre en touz faiz doster toute ochoison de maufaire / et de rendre a chascun son droit / Et si a ces choses acomplir / nous sommes tenu a chascune personne / par plus de causes sommes nous tenu a ce / a celles personnes / es quelles nous auons especial affection. Et pour ce nous Considerans les conuencions / iadis eues / entre nostre treschier Seigneur & pere . . Philippe. iadiz Roi des diz Roiaulmes dune part / et haut homme Othe lors Conte de Bourgoingne / dautre / ou traicte du mariage / dun des fils nostre dit seigneur et pere / & de Iehanne fille du dit Conte nostre treschiere compaigne / et sus la Contee de Bourgo-ingne / Es quelles conuencions len dit / quil a eu aucunes conuenances / es quelles li diz Contes auoit fait proumesses & ottroiances / sus la dite Contee grandement damageuses a li / et a ses hoirs en certains cas. Et nous attendens que droiz ne raisons ne sacorderoient / que pour telles couuenances nostre dite Compaigne / ne ses enfans que elle auroit euz de nous deussient souffrir aucun domage. Et apres ce nous considerans / que par cause de la dite Contee / a nulle personne / nous ne ferions houmage / et encore plusieurs autres causes / les quelles nous taisons apresent / qui nous ont du esmouoir droiturierement & loialment / es choses qui sensuient. Et oultre tout ce / attendue la grant affection que nous auons a nostre dite compaige / pour moult de aggreables seruices que elle nous a faiz / ou temps passe / et fait touz les iours. Eu aueques tout ce diligent traittie et loial conseil aueques nos Amez et feaulx / Charle de Valois & Loys de Eureux Contes nos treschiers Oncles / & Charle Conte de la Marche nostre treschier frere / et oueques [*sic*] plusieurs autres de nostre conseil / et tiex qui plus plenierement sauoient les choses dessus dites. Tant sus les dites choses comme sus celles qui sensuient / o nostre grant et ordene conseil / a perpetuel memoire & a prouision de nostre dite compaigne / et de nos diz enfanz / & a li faire remuneracion des aggreables seruices / que elle nous a faiz / si deuotement & si humblement. De nostre auctorite Roial par nous & par nos Successeurs a perpetuite / establissons / ordenons / decernons & declairons la

144

It seems clear that the death of their only son in February 1317 was the chief reason for Philip V's munificence to his wife. Had their son lived, Philip would naturally have assumed that if he died, his wife, a person of considerable stature and importance in France, would be regent. But after their son's death there was every reason to think that, as Philip V put it in March 1317, 'apres nostre deces li reaumes escheist et venist a nostre frere'.[71] Philip had good reason to be apprehensive about this eventuality. After his brother Louis died in June 1316, his widow Clementia had had some difficulty obtaining the full 25,000 l.t. due to her as her dower, which was not finally assigned to her until September 1318.[72] Philip indeed bore much responsibility for Clementia's problems, although he clearly realised – and perhaps sympathised with – her plight. In confirming, as regent, gifts that his brother had made to Clementia beyond her dower, Philip emphasised not only her affection for Louis, but also that she had come to France 'de lointainnes parties' and had suffered great grief at her husband's death.[73] Jeanne's circumstances were different from Clementia's, but there was still reason to foresee difficul-

---

dite Contee de Bourgoingne oueques touz ses droiz / honneurs et appartenances / fiez & houmages / et touz les autres droiz quieux que il soient auoir este iadis dudiz Othe pere de nostre dite compaigne. Et desores en auant / deuoir appartenir a nostre dite compaigne seule et par le tout entierement / & de plain droit'. In this grant Philip reserved his own rights for his lifetime (as he had in 1315). He stipulated that the county should pass to his and Jeanne's eldest son (if they had one), and that if their heirs died without heirs of their body, the county should return to the king. Perhaps because homage was owed to the emperor for the county, Philip became less convinced that his eldest son (who would succeed him as king) should become count. When Jeanne drew up her will in late August 1319, she stipulated that the county should pass to their second son unless the eldest desired it, in which case he would indemnify the secondborn with lands in France: AN, J 404A, no. 23.

71 AN, JJ 53, fol. 53r, no. 118 (Guerout, no. 406; ed. in Guérin, *Archives historiques du Poitou*, 13 [1883], 45; a grant to Charles of La Marche).

72 Brown, 'Double Funeral', pp. 233–4, 257–8; Guerout, no. 2050.

73 'consideranz aussi ce que elle estoit venue de lointainnes parties & le deuil que elle a eu du trespassement de nostre dit chier Seigneur & freres & pluseurs autres causes': AN, JJ 54B, fols 4v–5v (fol. 5r–v), no. 10 (Guerout, no. 1375) (August 1316); with the notation 'par monsieur le Regent en la presence monsieur diureus monsieur de Sauoie. le dalfin de Sauoie [*sic*]. le s. de Seuli a vostre relacion Molin'. The gifts were made in November and December 1315, and in making them Louis X had carefully abrogated all contrary custom. In the first letter (ibid., fol. 5r), he stipulated 'Et se par auenture estoit aucun droit ou aucune coustume de lieu ou de pais qui fussent contraire a nostre don ci dessus expresse en aucune chose. Nous de certene science de nostre auctorite Real & de nostre plain pouoir. les ostons cassons & annullons et volons estre de nulle force & de nule value encontre ces presentes lettres'; in the second (ibid.), he stated, 'Et se par auenture il estoit aucun droit loy ou coustume de lieu ou de pais qui fut contraire a nostre dite donacion en quelque maniere que ce soit. Nous de certene science de nostre auctorite Real & de nostre plain pouoir les anullons cassons & volons estre de nule value encontre les lettres & le don cy dessus expresse'. Philip's original validation, phrased simply, was altered (ibid., fol. 5v) by the addition of the phrases 'de certaine science & de nostre plain pouoir', and 'sauf nostre droit en autres choses & le droit dautrui en toutes'.

ties if her husband died and Charles of La Marche became king. Apart from any other considerations, having been betrayed by Jeanne's sister Blanche, Charles had little reason to feel affection for or to trust in Jeanne.[74]

How could Philip protect her? He would have been less than naive had he failed to recognize how difficult it was for a king to bind his successor. He himself had participated in and profited from acts that contravened his father's wishes. In August 1315, he had gained from his brother revocation of the restriction to male heirs that his father had solemnly imposed on his own county of Poitiers.[75] Further, Philip himself had played an important role in formalising the agreement that Louis X made with Philip the Fair's executors to modify Philip's last will and codicil because of the problems they posed for the finances of the kingdom.[76] Philip also knew that Philip the Fair's testament had not been executed in even this modified form. At Louis X's death, seeing to its fulfilment became Philip's responsibility, but the will Philip drew on 26 August 1321, five months before his death, shows that he had failed to implement not only his father's but also his brother's will.[77] This did not keep him from increasing his own bequests in a codicil he added to his will on 2 January 1322, just hours before he died.[78]

Philip seems to have believed that adding exceptional clauses and using extraordinary diplomatic procedures would protect his donations to his wife. Why this was so is unclear, although there is no question that he was mightily impressed with the nature of the powers kings could wield. As king, he insisted on and expanded the limits of the authority inherent in the royal office. The formulae used in his acts testify to a belief that the king of France could regulate the future by fiat. In grants made to Jeanne in the months following his accession, he announced 'by royal authority' that he was abrogating and annulling contrary *ius*, *usus*, or *consuetudo* (all concepts, note, that he had invoked in June 1315). He decreed, further, that his donation should have the fullest strength and stability, and should be accorded the force of law

---

[74] Divorce proceedings between Charles and Blanche began soon after Charles succeeded to the throne and were terminated on 19 May 1322. For contemporary use of the term *divortium* in connection with the trial, see AN, J 682, no. 2, and JJ 1[8], fol. 70v.

[75] See n. 57 above.

[76] Elizabeth A. R. Brown, 'Royal Salvation and Needs of State in Early-Fourteenth-Century France', in eadem, *Monarchy*, no. IV, esp. pp. 52–6 (an ed. of the act, dated December 1314 at Vincennes, AN, K 39, no. 2). Philip swore in Louis' name that he would observe the agreement. He also solemnly promised to do so himself, as did Charles of La Marche, Gaucher de Châtillon, constable of France, Mile, lord of Noyers, Guillaume de Harecourt, and Mahy de Trie, chamberlain of France. This essay modifies and corrects conclusions I presented in an earlier study, 'Royal Salvation and Needs of State in Late Capetian France', in *Order and Innovation in the Medieval West: Essays in Honor of Joseph R. Strayer*, ed. William C. Jordan, Bruce McNab and Teofilo F. Ruiz (Princeton: Princeton University Press, 1976), pp. 365–83, 541–61.

[77] Brown, 'Royal Salvation', pp. 45–7; eadem, 'Double Funeral', pp. 232–3.

[78] Brown, 'Funeral of Philip V', pp. 274–6.

(*vim legis*).[79] On 27 September 1318, assigning Jeanne her mother's debt to the crown of 80,000 l.t., Philip declared that the gift should hold despite 'ordonnances, statutes, customs, privileges, and written or unwritten law'. Interposing his decree, by his royal authority, exercising his full power, with certain knowledge and after full deliberation, he declared that if any such impediments existed, he broke, annulled, voided, eradicated, and declared them null and void with regard to the present act, which he confirmed.[80] On 16 March 1319, authorising Jeanne to select the lands on which his heir and successor would settle any unassigned portion of her dower, he waxed even more eloquent and expansive. With sure knowledge and by his royal authority, Philip said, he was establishing and instituting the act as a law or pragmatic sanction, and was interposing his sentence and decree, notwithstanding

[79] See Philip's acts of January, February, March, and 1 October 1317, and April 1319, in AN, JJ 54A, fols 5v–6r, nos. 74–6 (Guerout, nos. 735–37); JJ 53, fol. 48r, no. 107, and fols 148v–49r, no. 352 (Guerout, nos. 395, 649); JJ 56, fol. 258r, no. 590 (Guerout, no. 2290). The king did not use these formulae in the act of 20 December 1316 in which he increased Jeanne's dower (AN, JJ 54B, fols 36v–37r, no. 57 [Guerout, no. 1424], for which see n. 60 above), but they appear in the undated grant of Chanteloup to Jeanne, which immediately follows this act (AN, JJ 54B, fol. 37r, no. 58 [Guerout, no. 1425], for which see nn. 49 and 62 above).

[80] 'attendanz & consideranz les agreables seruices les biens. les honeurs & les courtoysies / la bonne & la loyal compaignie [*over* courtoisie, *cancelled*] que nostre tres chiere & amee compeigne [*sic*] Iehanne par la grace dieu. Royne de france & de Nauarre. Nous a fait & tenuz ou temps passe. & encores fait & tient touz. Iourz. senz cesser. en aucune remuneracion & recompensacion. des choses dessus dites. auons donne Baille & otroye. & encore donons Baillons & otroyons. pour nous & pour noz hoirs & pour noz successeurs. purement franchement Simplement irreuocablement & perpetuelment. Senz Riens retenir a nous ne a noz diz hoirs ou successeurs. par donacion faite entre vis de nostre droit propre a nostre dite compaigne [*sic*] present & stipulant. pour soy & pour ses hoirs. & pour ses successeurs. Et cestes donacion / cession / transport & toutes les choses dessus contenues / Nous volons estre fermes & estables perpetuelment / non obstant / ordenances / statuz coustumes priuileges / ou droit escript / ou non escript qui porroient estre contraires aus choses dessus dites / ou aucunes dicelles / en tout / ou en partie / les quelles ordenances / statuz / coustumes / priuileges / & droiz de nostre autorite Roial de nostre plain poair / de certaine science & plaine deliberation eue sus ce / Nous Cassons / anullons / irritons / aniantons & declairons estre nulles & de nulle value / en tant comme elles / ou aucunes de elles / sont ou peuent estre contraires aus choses dessus dites ou a aucunes delles en tout / ou en partie Et en toutes ces choses & chascunes dicelles nous mettons nostre decret Et enquores de nostre autorite Royal / de nostre plain poair & de certaine science les approuons loons & confermons & promettons non venir encontre par nous ne par autre / & a ce astreignons nous & noz hers & noz successeurs': AN, JJ 56, fol. 176r–v (fol. 176r), no. 406 (Guerout, no. 2033); the rubric preceding the act reads 'donacio cuiusdam debiti octoginta milium librarum facta domine Iohanne Regine / franc. in quo quidem debito domina Mathildes comitissa de attrabatesio tenebatur domino Regi'; the act is preceded by the contemporary notation, 'donum'. The second section of the text that I quote was transcribed by a scribe different from the one who copied the first section. It is noteworthy that the king forbade his wife to dispose of the money before his death, in case Mahaut should make some demand of him which might necessitate using the debt to repay her.

147

laws, customs, ordonnances, decrees, statutes, customs, usages, graces, or privileges that could nullify, impede, or invalidate the act – all of which he was breaking and voiding.[81] This act represented a pinnacle of royal assertiveness. It had been foreshadowed and even, arguably, surpassed by a clause in Philip's donation of Burgundy to Jeanne in September 1318. There, he said, he was making of the matters contained in the pronouncement 'loy et droit escrit', and was voiding contrary 'agreements, promises, covenants, statutes, ordonnances, privileges, customs and laws, reasons, conditions, objections, by our royal authority, exercising our full power, with certain knowledge, and having deliberated fully with our council, especially assembled for this purpose'.[82]

These clauses are remarkable for their elaborateness. As concerns their substance, they are not unprecedented. Philip V's father, Philip the Fair, had

---

[81] 'Nos eidem Consorti nostre in posterum prouidere volentes / ad maiorem cautelam & securitatem plenissimam prefate Consortis nostre voluimus statuimus / decernimus / et ex certa sciencia ordinamus [. . .]. Et ad omnia & singula premissa facienda / adimplenda / perficienda / tenenda & obseruanda / nos heredes et Successores nostros / & specialiter dicta bona in casu in quo / ad nos uel successores nostros reuerterentur & alia que ipsa in posterum eligeret firmiter & efficaciter obligamus / et esse volumus specialiter obligatos / premissa quidem omnia & singula / prout in presentibus & aliis super assignacione alia / & al[ias] per nos facta [factas, *in JJ* 56]/ confectis litteris sunt expressa / valere teneri & seruari volumus & precipimus tamquam legem / & de ipsis omnibus & singulis / in hac presenti scriptura contentis / ex certa scientia & auctoritate nostra Regia / legem condimus & facimus / seu pragmaticam Sancionem [*sic*; sanctionem *in JJ* 56] / Et in eis omnibus & singulis sentenciam nostram interponimus & decretum / non obstantibus legibus consuetudinibus ordinacionibus / decretis / statutis / consuetudinibus / vsibus / gracijs / & priuilegiis quibuscunque / per quas quos seu que / predicta omnia seu aliqua de eisdem / cassari seu impediri possent / quomodolibet uel infringi / quas leges / constituciones / ordinaciones / decreta / statuta / consuetudines / vsus / gracias & priuilegia / in quantum premissis uel alteri premissorum contrariari possent / auctoritate nostra Regia / & ex certa sciencia / cassamus adnullamus irritamus infringimus ac viribus penitus carere volumus / ac omnino nullius esse decernimus firmitatis': Besançon, AD du Doubs, B 24; AN, JJ 56, fols 245v–46r, no. 562 (Guerout, no. 2191), with the rubric 'quomodo dominus Rev vvlt quod si domina Regina franc. / in aliquibus locis pro docalicio suo assignatis Impediatur . . possit pro illo Impedimento Eligere alia loca', and the notation, 'Pro Regina'.

[82] 'Et voulons / ordenons / establissons et decernons de certainne science & de nostre auctorite Roial / faisons des choses dessus dites toutes et chascune delles / loy & droit escript. Et voulons & commandons que elles soient tenues de touz nos Subgiez / et de nos successeurs Rois de france / receues et gardees ausi comme loy & comme droit escrip [*sic*] / et fait par auctorite Royal / Et que elles aient fermete et establete & durablete en la fourme & en la maniere que elles sont dessus contenues. Non obstans conuencions / promesses / conuenances / statuz / ordenances / priuileges / coustumes / droiz / raisons / cauteles / ou cauillacions / qui porroient estre contraires / as choses dessus dites / ou a aucunes delles / les queles conuentions / promesses / conuenances / statuz ordenances / priuileges / coustumes / droiz / raisons / cauteles et cauillacions / de nostre auctorite Roial / de nostre plain pouoir / de certainne science / eue plainne deliberacion oueques nostre conseil assemble pour ce especialment / Nous cassons / anullons / irritons & anientons / entant comme elles porroient estre contraires as choses dessus dites / ou aucunes delles': AN, J 250 (Bourgogne IV), no. 10.

often abolished or nullified contrary custom, and between 1312 and 1314 (the last year of his reign) various acts concerning the transfer of property contained statements ordering their execution because, for good reason, the king was interposing his royal decree.[83] The most elaborate of these formulae appears in an act of May 1314, in which Philip the Fair confirmed an act of Charles of Valois dividing his property among his heirs. There, at his brother's request, the king said that he approved the arrangements 'with certain knowledge and for legitimate reasons, by royal authority and the plenitude of royal power, notwithstanding contrary customs, usages, and rights'. He refused, however, to declare (as his brother wished him to do) that he was confirming the act as if the matter had been formally judged before him and his court.[84]

Louis X rarely used the elaborate formulae his father employed.[85] When he confirmed another of Charles of Valois' property divisions in July 1315, the terms he used were far simpler than his father's, and like his father he refused to endorse the act as if he and his court had formally judged it.[86] Thus it is

---

83 Fawtier, index, s.v., 'Abolition', and 'Interpositions du décret royal'; see esp. nos. 2151, 2176, 2242, 2243, 2274 (AN, JJ 45, fols 100v–102v, 118r; JJ 50, fols 43v–44r, 57r). Jacques Krynen gives essential background, in ' "De nostre certaine science [. . .]". Remarques sur l'absolutisme législatif de la monarchie médiévale française', in *Renaissance du pouvoir légis-latif et genèse de l'État*, ed. André Gouron and Albert Rigaudière, Publications de la Société d'histoire du droit et des institutions des anciens pays de droit écrit, 3 (Montpellier: n.pub., 1988), pp. 131–44 (focusing on the triad 'de nostre certaine science', 'pleine puis-sance', and 'auctorité royale', as they appear in acts that Jourdain, Decrusy, and Isambert included in their *Recueil général* [see n. 4 above]; see also Krynen, *L'empire du roi*, pp. 395–402.

84 In the act, Charles and his sons requested Philip the Fair 'quil vueille / louer et approuuer / et de sauctorite Real confermer / toutes les choses / dons / conuenances / et ordenances deuant dites / en samble et chascunne [sic] par soy et de son plain pouer Royal par son decret discerner toutes les Coustumes vsaiges & drois / qui pourroient aider et valoir a faire et venir contre les dites choses ou aucunnes dicelles / non valoir / casser irriter et anuller du tout / et que il soient quant a ces conuenances / dons / et ordenances de nulle fermete / Et que il nous contraigne / ou ceus qui iroient / ou feroient encontre / a tenir / garder / et acomplir toutes les dites choses de plain comme de chose iugiee deuant luj et en sa Court'. The king accordingly approved the act 'ex certa sciencia / et ex causis legitimis [. . .] auctoritate regia & regie potestatis plenitudine [. . .]. Non obstantibus consuetudinibus / vsagiis / et iuribus contrariis quibuscumque / quas et que consuetudines vsagia et quecumque Iura / premissis contraria quantum ad premissa huiusmodi dumtaxat / de plenitudine Regie potestatis / et ex presentis interposicione decreti / cassamus / irritamus / ac etiam anullamus': AN, P 1364[1], no. 1311 (Charles's act is dated at Maubuisson on 20 May 1314, the king's confirmation, issued after Mahaut of Châtillon (or Saint-Pol) appeared before him to approve the act, is dated at Paris, in May 1314); for other copies of the act, see P 1364[1], no. 1315; P 1372[2], no. 2123; P 1365[2], nos. 1431 and 1433; JJ 50, fols 42v–44r.

85 Note, however, for interposition of the royal decree, Guerout, nos. 56 and 1375 (prop-erty arrangements involving Robert, count of Clermont [3 March 1315, Bois de Vincennes], and Clementia of Hungary [August 1316, Bois de Vincennes]).

86 The request that Charles and his sons presented to Louis on 6 July 1315 at Bois de Vin-

particularly noteworthy that the strategies used by Philip V are at least fore-shadowed in letters which Louis issued for him and at his explicit request. Although not as expansive as Philip requested when he assigned dower lands to Jeanne in June 1315, relatively dramatic declarations appeared in Louis X's confirmation of the act seven months later, and in his abolition of the female exclusion clause for the county of Poitiers in August 1315.[87]

In two instances Philip V took additional, extraordinary steps to protect his endowment of his wife. In attempting to bind close relatives who might contest his actions he was, consciously or unconsciously, reviving the custom of *laudatio parentum*.[88] His first such venture was prompted, unsurprisingly, by his hereditary grant of the county of Burgundy to Jeanne in September 1318. On 30 September he secured from his uncles Charles of Valois and Louis of Évreux, and from his brother and putative successor, Charles of La Marche, a solemn, sealed commitment stating that they approved the act, would uphold it, and would to the best of their abilities frustrate any attempt to hinder its fulfillment.[89] Philip adopted the same strategy in trying to ensure Jeanne's enjoyment of the dower lands whose assignment had just been completed. In the final assignment itself, completed in July 1319, the king stated that in granting Jeanne her dower, he had taken counsel with his late brother Louis and his two uncles. Still, for greater security he annulled all rights (*iura*), stat-utes, and customs contrary to the act.[90] Despite these measures, the thought

cennes was virtually identical to the one they made to Philip the Fair in May 1314. Louis agreed to confirm the award, but, in contrast with Philip the Fair, he simply did so 'de nostre auctorite Real / et i Mettons nostre decret Real': AN, J 164B, no. 31 (the royal confirmation was issued at Paris and dated July 1315).

87 See nn. 55 and 57 above.

88 For background, see Stephen D. White, *Custom, Kinship, and Gifts to Saints: The 'Laud-atio Parentum' in Western France, 1050–1150*, Studies in Legal History (Chapel Hill: University of North Carolina Press, 1988).

89 BNF, Mélanges de Colbert 350, no. 129 (original, sealed with three seals). The letter, issued by Charles of Valois, Louis of Evreux, and Charles of La Marche, 'Contes / filz de Rois de France', contains a vidimus of Philip V's letter of September, followed by the counts' approval ('Et Nous les choses contenues es dites leittres [*sic*] / en tant comme il nous touche ou chascun de nous / ou pourra toucher / ou temps aauenir / par quelque cause / que ce soit / voulons / approuons / Ratifions & consentons / Et prometons en bonne foi / pour Nous & pour noz successeurs / les choses contenues es dites leittres / et chascunes de elles / tenir / garder & acopmplir / et encontre non venir / pour nulle cause / ne consentir a persone qui en contre voudroit venir / mes contrester / & empescher de nostre pooir').

90 'nos tunc in Minoribus constituti / ante dictorum Regnorum suscepta Regimina / Caris-sime Consorti nostre . . Iohanne eadem gratia dictorum Regnorum Regine pensatis tunc nostrarum uiribus facultatum. Sexcies [*sic*] Mille libratas terre ad Turonenses / nomine dotalicij seu donacionis propter nuptias / dedimus / constituimus / et de hijs et nomine dicti dotalicij duximus prouidendum / Susceptis vero postmodum Regnorum Regiminibus pre-dictorum / que nobis Iure hereditario competebant / equm [*sic*] Reputauimus & iustum / quod sicut prefata Consors nostra Ratione vinculi coniugalis nos Invicem auctore domino viuentis Regie celsitudinis prefulget honore / sic amplioris dotalicij / seu donationis propter nuptias / ceterarumque largicionum Regalium prerogatiua debebat / et debet marito subli-

of the future continued to trouble him. A year and a half later, in January
1321, he obtained from Charles of Valois, Charles of La Marche, and Philip,
the eldest son of Louis of Evreux (who had died in May 1319), their solemn
approbation, their pledge on behalf of their heirs and successors, and oaths

mari / Quibus Regie celsitudinis statum / ad quem disponente domino est assumpta / ad suum
[sic] & Regni franc. gloriam & honorem feliciter supportet & conseruet. Nos igitur hijs / &
quamplurimum alijs Rationibus / & causis efficacibus ad hoc plurimum inductiuis pensatis
habitaque super hoc deliberacione matura / et specialiter de consilio & assensu inclite Rec-
ordacionis Carissimi Germani nostri . . Ludouici quondam dictorum Regnorum Regis illus-
tris / a [sic] Carissimorum auunculorum nostrorum Caroli valesij et . . Ludouici. Ebroicensis
Comitum Eidem consorti nostre priorem donationem & constitutionem dicti dotalicij sibi
per nos constituti prosequendo / & ei inherendo / secundum modum & formam inferius dec-
larat. / preter & vltra / sex Mille libratas terre predictas / sibi pro dotalicio al[ias] ut premitti-
tur datas & constitutas / Quindecim Mille libratas terre ad turonenses dedimus /
concessimus et constituendas duximus / ac ex habundanti damus / concedimus / & de presenti constituimus nomine & causa dotalicij / seu donationis propter nuptias / seu in dotalicij / aut donacionis propter nuptias augmentum / uel al[ias] prout melius & firmius possimus /
tenendas a dicta consorte nostra / & habendas nomine & causa predictis / vna cum dictis sex
Mille libratis terre [. . .]. Quas viginti vnam Mille libratas terre ad turonenses estimari / taxari
/ assideri / & assinari ac corporaliter ex nunc tradi volumus ordinamus constituimus / & nos
voluisse ordinasse & constituisse Recolimus [. . .] Ita quod nichil in predictis uel aliquo predictorum sic a nobis eidem consorti nostre concessis & contitutis aut in pertinencijs eorum-
dem nichil omnino Retinuimus nec Retinemus pro nobis aut nostris successoribus franc.
Regibus / aut alijs / sed quicquid nos / aut fiscus Regius in predictis & singulis predictorum
habebat / aut habere poterat Iuris commodi / & honoris / In ipsam Consortem nostram
nomine & causa predictis transtulimus & transferimus de presenti. Excepto tantummodo
nudo Ressorto / quod in predictis nostris successoribus duximus Resseruandum [. . .]. Concessimus insuper nostro & successorum nostrorum nomine & concedimus / promisimus &
de presenti promittimus / eidem Consorti nostre [. . .] quod nos non veniemus nec successores nostri venient contra donaciones / costituciones [sic] / & assignationes dicti dotalicij /
aut contra estimationes / taxaciones / & assignationes / ac traditiones / locorum / Rerum /
exituum prouentuum & emolumentorum predictorum / Eidem Consorti nostre / ex causa
predicta assignatorum & traditorum / ymo donationem [. . .] tenebimus firmiter / et Inuiolabiliter obseruabimus / dictique nostri Successores / tenebunt firmiter / & Inuiolabiliter obse-
ruabunt. Promittentes insuper pro nobis et successoribus nostris / quod nos predicta omnia /
& singula / deffendemus [. . .] et ipsi Successores nostri deffendent [. . .] Renunciantes quo ad
h[oc] nostro & successorum nostrorum nomine / omnibus Iuribus / & statutis / consuetudinibus / ac vsibus quibuscunque in Regno francie [sic] generaliter / uel in aliquibus ipsius Regni
partibus specialiter promulgatis / Editis / aut etiam obseruatis [. . .] que allegata proposita / uel
obiecta / & per quoscunque alleganda / proponenda / & obicienda / Cassamus / irritamus &
ex certa sciencia / cum nostri Regij Interpositione decreti / de plenitudine nostre Regie
potestatis adnullamus / Et quibuscunque allegantibus proponentibus & obicientibus /aliqua
de Iure uel de facto / contra predicta [. . .] omnem in Iudicio & extra / exnunc audienciam
denegamus / et volumus imposterum audienciam denegari. Eis perpetuum silencium super
hijs imponendo. Volumus preterea et nostra auctoritate Regia / statuimus / et statuendo
decernimus & precipimus / quod presentes littere pro veris & auctenticis habeantur [. . .]
Omnes autem & singulas alias litteras / que in & super premissis / aut aliquo premissorum
Reperirentur confecte / In quantum effectum presencium possent in toto uel in parte elidere
/ uel contenta in presentibus / seu aliquod earundem anullare / uel destruere / quaassantes
[sic] & adnullantes omnino / eos que / in quantum effectui & intentioni presencium / & con-

sworn on the gospels never to oppose the act. Ten months later, on 26 November 1321, when he lay dying at Longchamp, Philip secured an exemplification of the act.[91] Three months before this he had included an unusual provision in the will he drew up on 26 August 1321, in which he formally expressed his wish that all the gifts he had made to his wife should be respected, and explicitly admonished his successor, his executors, and all others not to obstruct his desires, and to permit his wife to enjoy the gifts in peace.[92] His reference to his successor and his executors suggests that he had forgotten the fate neither of his father's will and deathbed acts, nor of the dower his brother had assigned to Clementia of Hungary.

3. Philip V and his Ministers: The Case of Henri de Sully

Before examining the effectiveness of the various means Philip V employed on his wife's behalf, I should like to consider another strategy he used for similar ends, to protect the rights and property he had bestowed on his chief

tentis in eisdem concordant uel accedunt / tenore presencium approbamus / Innouamus / ac eciam confirmamus': AN, K 40, no. 28 bis, using François Maillard's transcription from the royal register JJ 60, for which I again thank him. For various surviving copies of this act, see n. 61 above.

91 'sponte ac liberaliter approbamus / laudamus & gratifficamus / ac ex certa sciencia supradictis omnibus & singulis consentimus specialiter & expresse. Promittentes nos & nostrum quilibet insolidum pro nobis / heredibus & successoribus nostris bona fide / Iuramus que ad sancta dei euangelia quod nullo tempore nulla causa ue Ratione / contra predicta / uel contra eorum aliqua veniemus / ymo quantum in nobis / & nostrum quolibet est / ac esse poterit infuturum / Nos & nostrum quilibet seruabimus / & complebimus omnia & singula in litteris supradictis contenta. Et prefatam dominam nostram . . Iohannam in assecutione predictorum ac defensione pro posse nostro Iurabimus / eique super hiis / auxilium fauorem et consilium prestabimus ac Iuuamen': AN, J 408, no. 27 (an exemplification of the act of January 1321, which contains a copy of the act of July 1319); on the act, see n. 60 above.

92 'Item. Nous voulons & ordenons / que touz les dons / que nous auons faiz a nostre treschere compaingne . . Iehanne Royne de france & de Nauarre / tiengnent en la maniere que nous auons ordene / Et defendons expressement a nostre Successeur / et a noz Exequteurs / et a touz autres / que nul empeschement il ne metent en chose que nous li aiens donne / ainz len leissent ioir paisiblement': AN, J 404A, no. 26. In the testament (dated June 1316) which Louis X prepared shortly before his death on 5 June, he specified that Clementia of Hungary should without fail receive the full 25,000 l.t. of dower that he intended her to have. See AN, J 404A, no. 22: 'Item a grant prouision et a grant deliberation / A Clemence nostre treschiere compaigne / Nous otrion pour son douaire / vint et cinc Mil liures tur. A prendre dan en An / en lieus certainz / sicomme Il est contenu expressement es lettres qui sont suz ce faites / seelees de nostre grant seel sicomme il apert es dites lettres. Et a greigneur seurte pour li / En cest present testament / Nous voulon et ordenon / que pour son douaire / ele ait .xxv. mil liures tourn. / de rente / a prendre chascun an / es lieuz qui sont nommez expressement es dites lettres. Et de ce nous charion [*sic*; chargons, *in the copy of the testament, no. 22bis*] especialment noz executeurs'. See Brown, 'Double Funeral', pp. 233–4.

minister, Henri de Sully.[93] Sully profited handsomely from his association
with Philip V. He had as much – and perhaps more – reason as Queen Jeanne
to be concerned about the future. Enguerran de Marigny and Philip the Fair's
other fallen servants were reminders of fortune's wheel. However, Sully,
cousin of Mahaut of Artois, was no Marigny. Although, owing to his birth
and status, he had less reason than they to fear a change of regime, nevertheless he was exceedingly prudent. He was concerned by a grant he had
received from Philip V in October 1317, 'en la nouuiaute de nostre gouuernement', as Philip expressed it. At that time, in exchange for property Philip
had earlier bestowed on Sully, the minister received valuable lands, castles,
revenues, and rights, as well as the privilege of holding his property as a
barony. The king promised never to put outside his hand the homage Sully
owed or the sovereignty that he, as king, was retaining. These, he pledged,
would remain perpetually with the king and royal crown. To safeguard the
grant, the king acknowledged that what he was giving Sully exceeded in
value the property he was recovering. This, he said, was his intention. These
guarantees were impressive. Nonetheless, even when the exchange took
place, the king must have thought the warranties insufficient. He further
decreed that his act should be treated as a 'contraut de donacion ou permutacion fait entre personnes priuees'. Stating that he and his council had studied
the matter carefully, he therefore declared ('with certain knowledge, full
power, employing our royal authority and decree') the perpetual validity of
the act, 'comme de chose Iugiee en la court de france'.[94]

---

[93] For Sully, see Langlois, 'Registres perdus', pp. 109–10 (Sully's publication in the
Chambre des comptes of the reforming ordonnance of Vivier-en-Brie of 1316), 143–6;
Brown, 'Double Funeral', pp. 242–4; eadem, 'Funeral of Philip V', p. 277; eadem, 'Alleged
Expulsion', p. 316 n. 67; and eadem, 'Royal Necessity and Noble Service and Subsidy in
Early Fourteenth-Century France: The Assembly of Bourges of November 1318', originally
pub. in *Paradosis: Studies in Memory of Edwin A. Quain*, ed. H. G. Fletcher III and M. B.
Schulte (New York: Fordham University Press, 1976), pp. 135–68, reprinted in Brown, *Poli-
tics*, no. VII.

[94] 'Sauoir faisons a touz presenz & auenir / Que comme nous aions donne a nostre chier &
feal cheualier . Henri Seigneur de Seully Bouteillier de france / Pour les bons & profitables
seruices quil a fait a noz predecesseurs / et a nous / non Sanz grant mises / trauaus & despens
ou temps passe / et fait chascun Iour diligemment & loiaument [. . .] / pour ce que ou temps
auenir les choses dessus dites ne peussent estre dites / faites / ne contenir en elles autre effet /
que de contraut de denacion [sic] / ou permutacion faites entre personnes priuees a plus grant
fermete dicelles / a grant congnoissance de cause / et par Informacion faite sur ce Raportee &
diligemment veue par nous & nostre conseil en toutes les choses dessus dites & chascune
dicelles de certaine science & de nostre plain pouoir Royal / mettons nostre auctorite Royal
& nostre decre . Et voulons que elles soient perpetuelment tenues & gardees sanz venir
encontre / comme de chose Iugie en la court de france': BNF, lat. 5414A, fol. 33r. Sully's cartulary (BNF, fr. 15642, fol. 148r–v [two copies]; partial seventeenth-century copy, from the
Séguier-Coislin collection) contains a special letter dealing with this problem (issued at
Lorris in November 1317), which also contains a clause of perpetual validation ('Nous
decernons valoir & tenir perpetuellement a tousiours et de nostre plain pouuoir & auctorité

Either Sully or the king must, with the passage of time, have been bothered by the clauses of validation. Perhaps the statement that the act was to be treated as a contract between private persons rankled. After all, the king could not rid himself by fiat of his public persona. The phrase 'comme de chose Iugiee en la court de france' may have posed problems. As has been seen, there were precedents for its use – or at least for subjects to request its presence in a royal act. But Philip the Fair and Louis X seem carefully to have

roial les confermons'). The first version of Philip's grant is also found in AN, JJ 53, fol. 157r–v, no. 363 (Guerout, no. 660), dated at Paris, in December 1317, with the rubric 'littere castrorum et castellaniarum chaliz chalebreul chasluces courbefin et de bexis. donatorum in Recompensacionem domino .H. de sueilli'; the copy in BNF, lat. 5414A (a collection of separate acts, bound together, which belonged to Baluze), fols 32v–33r (Guerout, no. 1653, esp. n. 3), was originally in AN, JJ 56, but was detached from the register, where the acts pass from no. 31 (on fol. 10v) to no. 34 (on fol. 11r). See ibid., fol. [A], the table, where no. 32 is listed as 'Littera donacionis castrorum castellaniarum de chalis / chebrol & aliarum hic descriptarum facte domino .h. de soulliaco .. pro castellania de lunel', and no. 33, as 'Littere donacionis castrorum & castellaniarum in litteris precedentibus contentarum [sic] / facte dicto domino henrico de souilliaco'. The detached quire begins (BNF, lat. 5414A, fols 32v–33r) with the copy of the letter, ending, 'Per dominum Regem presentibus dominis Ebroicensis Borbonesij / et Comite Sabbaudie / Laudunensis & Mimatensis Episcopis / ac domino Rynelli . . . P. Barriere . . . duplicata'; a note indicates that Sully was to receive three copies with the same formula of validation, and two more with the validation 'per dominum Regem. I. de templo / et ponitur in eis duplicata in gallico'. Another note states that two other Latin letters, extracted from the French, preserving the substance of the award, and beginning 'cum nos donauerimus donacione facta inter viuos' ended 'Duplicata in latino . et per dominum Regem .I. de templo'; see the seventeenth-century copy of Sully's cartulary, BNF, lat. 15642, fols 146v–47r ('Item Lettre de leschange de la Terre de Limel [sic] et de la terre de Maumont en latin'), where the Latin version is followed (ibid., fol. 147r–v) by a French translation ('Scauoir faisons que comme nous eussions donné par donation faicte entre viuans'). The detached quire also contains a letter (in Latin) issued by Philip at Lorris-en-Gâtinais on 19 November 1317, testifying that Sully had relinquished to him the letters relating to the original award, which he had had cancelled. The day before, 18 November, the king had exempted land he had recently given Sully from attachment by his creditors, and it is hardly surprising that he issued this privilege, 'decernentes auctoritate Regia. & ex nostre plenitudine potestatis. statuentes quantum ad ipsum super hoc. nostram legem. Regiam promulgantes': AN, JJ 56, fol. 10r, no. 29 (Guerout, no. 1650; see also AN, JJ 56, fol. 10r, no. 30, a charter *Ad perpetuam Rei Memoriam*, dated at Lorris in November 1317, making the lands the king had given him a barony, and guaranteeing that neither he nor his successors could place the lands 'extra ipsum immediatum ressortum dicte Corone Francie'; a copy of the letter, in Latin, followed by a French translation is found in the partial seventeenth-century copy of Sully's cartulary, BNF, fr. 15642, fol. 155r–v; the previous July, the king had issued letters [in both French and Latin] designed to protect Sully's property from his creditors [AN, JJ 59, fol. 37r–v, nos. 96–97; Guerout, nos. 2816–17]); these two acts and the following one, also issued in favour of Sully, to protect his wife's interests should he predecease her (AN, JJ 59, fol. 38r, no. 98 [Guerout, no. 2818]), were issued by the king in his council 'ad Relationem vestram', were recorded by Pierre Barrière, and were duplicated. The king confirmed the privileges issued in favour of Sully's wife, 'ex certa sciencia / & vt Robur firmum obtineant super eis auctoritatem nostram interposuimus & decretum'.

avoided it, perhaps because the formula called into question their commitment to fair and equitable rule, and to rendering 'to all their due'.[95] For whatever reason, Philip V decided that the whole validation should be altered, and the letter redrafted and transformed into a solemn charter. At the beginning of the revised act he laid far heavier stress than before on Sully's merits and his own duty to reward his servants. As to the validation, Philip removed what were apparently offending phrases. In the new version he asserted his knowledge and judgment that the award was 'just and valid' – although he also invoked 'the plenitude of his royal power'.[96]

[95] See Fredric L. Cheyette, 'Suum cuique tribuere', *French Historical Studies*, 6 (1970), 288–99, and Geoffrey Koziol, *Begging Pardon and Favor: Ritual and Political Order in Early Medieval France* (Ithaca and London: Cornell University Press, 1992), p. 214. Charles of Valois requested both Philip the Fair (on 20 May 1314) and Louis X (on 6 July 1315) to enforce property divisions he arranged, 'comme chose iugiee deuant lui et en sa court', but neither monarch did as he requested; see above, n. 84 and the accompanying text.

[96] 'Et se par liberalite Roial la main de nostre Munificence poursieut dune general regularite nos amez & foiaus soubgiez / toutes voies a ceuls sestent gracieusement par vne especiaute plus volentiers // Les quiels elle esprouue estre touziours continuelment necessaires & proufitables par clers experimenz & demonstremenz / a ses seruices / Car par ce que nous donnons & remunerons conuenablement a ceus qui bien le deseruent / par ce nous esmouuons les autres a nous seruir loiaument / Et ainsi sentons nous euidaument les proffiz de nostre Roiaume quant par digne retribucion nous les faisons estre diligens & ententis a nos profis [*sic*] & a nos honneurs. Et pour ce nous attendens la feaute / la pure deuocion et les aggreables seruiges [*sic*] que nostre ame & feal cheualier / henri seigneur de Seuly bouteillier de france a faiz loiaument ou temps passe a nous & a nos predecesseurs / & a nostre Roiaume non mie sanz grans despens / coustemens / peris / & labeurs / & fait encores continuelment sanz cesser / Piecza donnasmes a lui & a ses hoirs' ; '[. . .] la deuant dite donacion & ceste presente recompensacion / sachanz & Iugans [*sic*] estre iuste & vaillable / Et que il ne loise a nous ou a nos successeurs ou a autre qui que il soit / venir en nul temps en lencontre / par deliberacion de nostre grant conseil / de la plenitude de nostre Roial poissance icelle donacion & recompensacion decernons & Iugons de certeine science valoir & tenir perpetuelment': AN, JJ 60, fols 29r–30r (29r, 29v–30r), no. 63 (Guerout, no. 3433 (dated at Paris in October 1317), with the rubric 'donacio castrorum / castellaniarum / et Reddituum hic descriptorum . . facta a domino Rege . . domino H . . de sueilliaco buticulario franc.', whose beginning was altered to read 'Confirmacio donacionis [. . .]'; a copy of this letter is found in the seventeenth-century copy of Sully's cartulary, BNF, lat. 15642, fol. 146r–v, with a Latin version on fols 145r–v, 146v–47r, 148v–49r. This act was inserted in the solemn charter issued by Philip V in Paris and dated simply February 1321: AN, JJ 60, fols 29r–30v, no. 63 (Guerout, no. 3433). The seventeenth-century copy of Sully's cartulary contains a letter of Charles IV, wrongly dated at Paris in March 1327 (*sic* [i.e., old style; Charles IV died on 1 February 1328), in which the king indicates that his brother's award contained the following, inappropriate provisions: 'faisans mencion entre les autres choses que, ou cas ou les successeurs dudit nostre chier seigneur et frere empescheroient audit [henry] les terres et chasteaux dessus diz, il les condempnoit en certaine somme d'argent a li paier une fois, et certaine rente [&] a assoir, demorant le don et permutacion en leur vertu, et quittoit audit [henry] le fié et l'omage, et que il [le] peust reprendre a temps ou a toujours de quelque personne qu'il vousist, de eglise ou seculiers, et fu[s]t ore dehors de nostre royaume'. See Langlois' ed. of the letter from the seventeenth-century copy, BNF, fr. 15642, fol. 156r–v, in 'Registres perdus', p. 145, and note esp. his comments, 146 n. 1; corrections in brackets are

Even this redrafted version did not completely alleviate Sully's apprehensions. Before February 1321 the king and he decided that he should voluntarily submit to the judgment of the king and his chief counsellors. A solemn meeting, carefully planned, was convoked in Paris on 5 February 1321.[97] The king summoned his counsellors to discuss the reformation of the kingdom in general, and in particular the revocation of undue alienations.[98] The distinguished attendance included Charles of Valois, Charles of La Marche, Louis of Clermont, Robert of Artois, Gaucher de Châtillon, Mile de Noyers, and Anseau de Joinville. Sully appeared and asked them to determine whether the lands and rights that Philip had bestowed on him in October 1317 should be taken from him wholly or in part. As he doubtless hoped (and expected), his holdings were confirmed. The king seized the occasion (which had obviously been meticulously orchestrated) to make a ringing declaration regarding royal responsibility,[99] and to proclaim the precise conditions under which he believed alienation just and proper. The munificence of royal liberality

taken from BNF, fr. 15642, fol. 156v. In the table of contents in BNF, fr. 15642, fol. 144r, the letter is described as 'du Roy Charles en coue double et en cire Iaulne daucunes Lettres baillees aud. Roy charles sur les dons et confirmacions de la terre de Limozin faict en francois', which precedes the lettre, on fol. 156r (with slightly different spelling). In 1357 and 1358, Charles, acting as lieutenant for his father Jean II, made declarations proclaiming the appropriateness of rewarding royal servants that are similar to these: *Ordonnances*, IV, 140, 162–4, 176–7, 225.

[97] The act concerning Sully is dated simply February 1321. There seems no question, however, that it was issued on the same day and in the same place as the solemn act, dated at Paris on 5 February 1321, in which Philip formally relieved Sully of the necessity of accounting for two sums (amounting to more than 30,000 l.t.) which the king had entrusted to him in 1317 and 1319. As he did in the case of the other act, Philip signed the act himself and wrote that he had ordered its issuance, and sealed it with his signet. See AN, JJ 60, fols 30v–31r, no. 64 (Guerout, no. 3435) ('Seignee dou petit seignet le Roy / au Griffon /. Et Subscripte de la main le Roy . . philippe . . Cest passe par nostre commandement'). Cf. the detailed releases the king issued to Sully on 11 April 1317 and 6 July 1319, ed. in Michel de Marolles, *Inventaire des titres de Nevers de l'abbé de Marolles* [. . .], ed. le Comte de Soultrait, Publication de la Société nivernaise (Nevers: Paulin Fay, 1873), pp. 617–27.

[98] 'sus la reformacion de nostre Royaume en plus granz besoignes Et entre les autres choses sus la reuocacion & attrempement de ramener a estat deu pluseurs [sic] choses indeuement alienees dou demaine de nostre Royaume & appliquees par moins pouruuz & non conseilliez dons aus vsages de ceus qui ne lauoient pas deserui / des quiels dons aucuns ont este faiz plus par limportunite des requerenz que par deue deliberacion ne resgart / Quar par leur non vergondeuse poursuite & enbatement / & leur fardees paroles controuuees & pourpensees a ce / Nous & nos predecesseurs auons otroie souuent moult de choses qui iustement feissent a deuter': AN, JJ 60, fol. 29r, no. 63 (Guerout, no. 3433).

[99] 'A la pourueance de la Roial maieste conuient / au gouuernement a lui bailliee de dieu ainsi esueilliement entendre / et la chose publique a lui commise par tele dispensacion ordener / que le bien de son auctorite soit cogneu en transquillite des soubgiez / et que touz iours [sic] par honneur & proffit & deue Reuerence sesclarcisse / la quele chose sanz doutance y ert ass[ou]uie / se les merites de chascun par balance de droit Iugement sunt [sic] pesees / si q[ue]s [sic] a chascun soit Remunere pour la qualite de ses merites / Et ainsi la fealte des deuoz seruiteurs a mieulz seruir sera touziours encouragiee / & la malice des autres en

156

should rightly be opened, he proclaimed, to those who exposed their persons and their property for king and kingdom. Indeed, what is conferred on those who render good and loyal service is not alienation of the wealth (*biens*) of the realm, he announced, since it gives to all subjects heart, will, and encouragement to maintain and increase the realm's honour.[100] These are persuasive

remaindra confuse / Adecertes comme nous naguieres traitans & entendens': AN, JJ 60, fol. 29r.

100 'Pensans par deliberacion de droit Iugement / quil nous conuient ouurir la munificence de la liberalite Royal a ceus qui leurs personnes & leurs biens mettre & abandonner franchement pour nous & nostre roiaume ne doutent / et que ceus qui ainsi de leur bon gre se souzmettent aus necessitez voluntaires de nos seruices / soient recompense dignement par nos Roiaus prouisions / Si que par lexemple de euls / les cuers des autres soient atraiz a faire teles & semblables oeuures / Et pour ce Nous dun commun & accordant conseil a nous donne de touz nos feaus conseilliers dessus diz et de chascun diceuls pleinement acertenez sus toutes ces choses / disons & affermons en bonne verite / que pensez les seruices dessus diz & pluseurs autres qui seroient trop lons a raconter / et des quiels il [sic] estoient tuit certein / Considerans aueques ce / que en faisant la dite reformacion / tout aussi comme nous deuons entendre / que li guerredon qui bien iustement ont este fait et a ceuls qui bien les ont deseruiz leur demeurent comme cil qui ont este fait indeuement soient rappele / Quar ce qui est donne a ceuls qui bien & loiaument lont deserui nest mie alienacion des biens dou Roiaume / aincois est donner cuer & volente & exemples a touz autres dacroistre & maintenir lonneur dou Roiaume loiaument & diligeaument / les dites donnacions [sic] recompensacion [sic] & eschanges / estoient petites & que a greigneurs li estions bien tenuz comme a celui qui bien les auoit deseruies / Icelles donacions recompensacions & eschanges toutes ensemble & toutes autres choses contenues en nos lettres dessus dites. disons pronuncons & de certeine science decernons iustement deument & raisonablement estre faites / et confessons estre astrains au dit nostre cousin a greigneurs choses & meilleurs / pour les seruices & les causes dessus diz aggreables & fructueus / que par experience cognoissons mieulx que autres & plainement sunt demousterez par lobscurte des temps passez & par lestat & la clarte du temps present. Et dabundant les dites donacions recompensacions & eschanges / par le conseil dessus dit & de certeine science / approuuons / loons / rateffions / & innouons et de la grandeur & puissance Roial / et par nostre decret perpetuel roborons & confermons pour les causes & les raisons dessus dites / aueques pluseurs autres certeines & secretes / les queles nous ne voulons mie a present desclairier pour certeine cause. Et enioignons a nostre sucesseur ou a nos successeurs Roys de france que seur la Reuerence & lonneur que il seront tenuz de porter a leurs deuanciers & a leurs faiz / que contre aucunes des choses dessus dites ne viengnent ne seuffrent a venir en quelque maniere que ce soit / Ne que li diz henri si hoir ou si successeur soient moleste perturbe ou inquiete par quelconques [sic] cause / es choses dessus dites ou en aucune dicelles Et se il auenoit que aucun vousist dire ou propouser aucune chose contre les choses dessus dites ou aucunes dicelles la quele chose deuroit tourner a grant indignacion a nos successeurs. Si voulons nous & a ce obligons nous & nos successeurs Roys de france a Garantir au dit Henri a ses hoirs ou a ses successeurs toutes les choses dessus dites et chascune dicelles a nos propres cousz [sic] & despens / en Iugement & hors / touteffoiz que mestier sera / et a iceuls maintenir paisiblement es choses dessus dites sanz nulle moleste & sanz nulle inquietacion. Et que ce soit ferme & estable perpetuelment a touziours / Nous auons fait mettre nostre seel en ces presentes lettres': AN, JJ 60, fol. 30r–v, no. 63. The sixteenth-century historian and jurist Guy Coquille (1523–1603) expressed a similar view in his *Institution au droict des Francois*. There he stated, 'selon mon aduis', that 'les gens du Roy ont esté trop exacts obseruateurs en ce point de Domaine non alienable', and proposed that only 'le droict

sentiments, eloquently expressed. But the king and his minister must have doubted that they would be sufficient to protect Sully in the future, as the rhetorical flourishes with which the king confirmed his council's decision show. The king declared that he was acting by royal grandeur and power after taking counsel; he interposed his perpetual decree; he enjoined his successors, by the reverence and honour they were bound to feel for their predecessors' persons and deeds, never to contravene the decision. Finally, he sealed the act with his own signet, and wrote on it in his own hand, 'Philip. This is passed by our command'.

Sully retained the property and rights Philip V had given him. However, he suffered long and severely before being, as Langlois put it, 'relégué avec de grandes charges dans les provinces du Midi'.[101] Why Charles IV allowed him to retain the property Philip V had bestowed on him is unclear. Charles may have been affected by the fact that he himself had attended the meeting of the royal council which explicitly approved Philip's award in 1321. Further, Sully's status, lineage, connections, and accomplishments were impressive. However, Charles was not comfortable with the extravagant terms his brother had used to confirm Sully's rights. Sully was doubtless informed of the king's displeasure – why else would he have acted as he did, surrendering Philip V's letter, and renouncing the guarantees it contained?[102]

Charles IV challenged another of Philip V's gifts to Sully, in this case the town of Dun-le-Roi, whose inhabitants the king said had complained to him. On this occasion Charles explicitly invoked his brother's own principles, referring as he did to 'an ordonnance on gifts and exchanges made in the time of our lord and brother Philip regarding revocation to the domain of gifts and exchanges wrongly made in the time of our father and brother'.[103] But no more in this case than in that of the extensive privilege in whose confirmation he had participated did Charles wrest from Sully what Philip V had

---

de souueraineté, qui represente la Maiesté Royale, & est le vray droict de la Couronne, est non alienable'. As to the rest, the king should be able to use lands to reward his subjects' services, rather than money. 'Car les deniers', he continued, 'ne se leuent sans l'oppression du peuple & n'estanchent iamais la soif d'vn auaricieux, & le benefice n'apparoist pas à la veuë de tous, pour semondre tous gentils cœurs à faire seruice à leur Roy'. See *Les Œuvres de Me Gvy Coqville Sr de Romenay* [. . .], rev. edn (Paris: Anthoine de Cay, 1646), pp. 4–5 of the separately paginated treatise.

[101] Langlois, 'Registres perdus', p. 146.

[102] 'lesquelles lettres ledit Sully, doubtant qu'il ne fussent trop apres, pour ce que en aucune chose ne nous peust desplaire, de son bon gré et volonté, sans contraincte ne demande que on li feist, nous apporta et bailla, retenant a soy toutes voies que aus autres lettres faictes et accordées a luy sus le transport desdites choses ne lui soit faict nul prejudice, disant que de celles lettres a nous baillées ne se voloit aidier ne n'en voloit user, lesquelles nous receusmes ensuite et preismes de li': Langlois, 'Registres perdus', pp. 145–6.

[103] AN, JJ 62, fol. 20r, no. 40; for Philip's grant to Sully in November 1317, see AN, JJ 56, fol. 10r, no. 30 (Guerout, no. 1651).

granted to him.[104] This seems a testimony not only to Sully's prudence and authority, but also to simple good fortune.

4. Jeanne of Burgundy and Charles IV

Queen Jeanne was not as lucky as Sully in dealing with Charles IV. True, she succeeded in keeping much of what Philip V had bestowed on her, most notably the county of Burgundy and her mother's debt of 80,000 l.t.[105] Charles would have been ill-advised to try to dislodge her from the county of Burgundy, where she was exceedingly popular. In any case, the county's status posed problems for the king, since homage for it was owed to the emperor. As to the debt of Mahaut of Artois, Charles IV attempted to claim it, as did his successor Philip VI of Valois – although, in the end, Mahaut's extravagant (but not entirely unfounded) counter-claims discouraged both kings from pressing their claims.[106]

As his pursuit of this debt suggests, Charles was not prepared to permit Jeanne to have all her husband had given her. Only two months after Philip V's death, Charles declared that he had 'many good reasons' for refusing Jeanne's request for the property on which her dower had been assigned, which he himself had approved. In the face of his opposition, Jeanne retreated, stating that 'she did not want to enter into pleading with the king but rather wished to remain always in his good graces'. She agreed to accept property worth 16,000 l.t. (5000 l.t. less than Philip had pledged).[107] Charles also denied

---

[104] *Les Journaux du Trésor de Charles IV le Bel*, ed. Jules-Édouard-Marie Viard (Paris: Imprimerie nationale, 1914), no. 6875 (Charles IV's restoration of Dun-le-Roi to Sully before 31 January 1325).

[105] Jeanne was also able to keep Chanteloup, south of Paris, although Charles IV apparently denied her the revenue Philip V had provided for the manor's support. Charles IV may possibly have had designs on the county of Burgundy. On 6 June 1322 Jehans Loncle, *garde* of the *prévôté* of Paris, exemplified Philip V's acts of 6 February 1317 and September 1318 transferring rights over Burgundy to Jeanne: AN, J 250 (Bourgogne IV), no. 9.

[106] Wood, 'Where is John?', pp. 109–10, 113–17, and n. 69 above.

[107] 'Et nous li eussiens fait respondre / que nous auiens pluseurs bones causes pour les quelles / nous ne deuiens mie faire sa Requeste. A la parfin nostre dite suer vint par deuers nous / & en disant quele ne voloit mie plaidier auecques nous / et quele voloit touz Iours demourer en nostre bone grace / de son dit doaire / & de tout son droit que elle y pooit auoir et demander / elle sen mist de haut & de bas a toute nostre volente / et voult & acorda de son bon gre / & de sa pure volente / que nous en ordenessiens & feissiens ce quil nous plairoit / et les dites lettres que ele se disoit auoir sus le dit doaire. Nous Rendi & bailla': AN, J 408, no. 31 (dated March 1322, at Bois de Vincennes; with the notations, 'Par le Roy a la Relation de vous et de Maistre I. Cercemont'; 'Tesson'; 'Collation est faite des commencemens & fins des dites peaus de parchemin'; 'donne pour copie'; sealed in white wax on a single strip of parchment); see also no. 32, with the same date, in which Jeanne accepted the agreement. Jeanne was to collect 8000 l.t. a year in cash, on the fee-farms of Normandy, and 8000 l.t. were to be assigned in land at Vernon, Les Andelys, Poissy, Pontoise, Beaumont-sur-Oise, the forest of Carnelle,

Jeanne the 30,000 l.t. that Philip V had promised her for her testamentary bequests. She had enough resources, it was argued, to cover her legacies, which in any case, the king's counsel maintained, were excessively lavish.[108] In May 1325, Jeanne indeed drew up a codicil restricting the bequests in her

and Asnières-sur-Oise: AN, J 408, no. 31; Petit *et al.*, *Essai de restitution*, p. 120, no. 716. Jeanne thus lost property in many of but not all the places on which her dower had been assigned. On 29 March 1322, at Bois de Vincennes, Charles IV commissioned Ami d'Orléans and Fremin de Cocquerel to effect the assignment: AN, J 408, no. 30 (sealed on a single strip of parchment in white wax, with the notations, 'par le Roy / a la Relation de vous et de Maistre Iehan de Cercemont'; 'Tesson'; 'doublee'; 'per Copiam'). In September 1318, Philip V had ordered Ami and Fremin to assign Clementia of Hungary her dower lands, for which see AN, JJ 56, fol. 183r–v, no. 423 (Guerout, no. 2050). A year earlier, on 27 August 1317, Philip had commissioned Ami to copy a number of documents relating to his marriage contract with Jeanne. Ami and other notaries duly transcribed the acts, which apparently comprised eight letters and a public instrument, relinquished to Philip's squire Garin d'Esarnes, at Montereau-Faut-Yonne: Besançon, AD du Doubs, B 20. The surviving exemplifications, which contain Philip's mandate to Ami, are dated 29 August 1317: AN, J 250 (Bourgogne IV), nos. 3–4 (see n. 35 above); J 408, nos. 5, 9.

[108] Dijon, AD de la Côte-d'Or, B 308 (a memorandum on parchment, copied in a bastard curial script, giving Philip VI's replies to requests presented to him by Jeanne's heirs c.1330): 'Li Roys Charles a grant deliberacion de son conseil fit respondre aus genz la Reyne Iehanne de Bourgoigne qui poursuyoient & demandoient XXXM liures [pour poier son, *canceled*] que le Roy phelippe le long son seigneur ly auoit promises & donnees pour aide de poier son testament / que la dite Reyne estoit assez riche pour son testament poier & pour ce que le testament le quel elle auoit fait de la volente de son dit Seigneur estoit / grant si que de ses meubles Il ne peust auoir este poiez / elle fit vn codicille & retrancha moult les lais que elle auoit faiz en son dit testament & aucuns en rappela du tout / pour ce que elle vit bien que elle ne si executeur nauroient riens des dites XXX^M. liures & par ensi li hoir nen sont de riens chargie / ne nen peuent riens demander ce semble. Item de la bastie de monguiart que li hoir de la dite Reyne demandent pour ce que li Roys phelippe la donna en perpetuel heritage / Il ne la doyuent demander ne le Roy ne leur peut bailler / car des la fondacion de la bastie auant le dit don / cil de la dite bastie ont priuilege en cire vert & en laz de saye [*sic*] que len ne les peut metre pour nulle cause hors du patremoyne de la corone de france. Item quant a cinc cenz liures de Rente pour le manoir de chantelou / onques mais au temps du Roy phelippe qui fit le don ne au temps du Roy charle / riens nen fu demande. Item quant a chailli / il est verite que par eschange de villemur en tholosain qui estoit patremoyne du Royaume & anciene-ment fu baronie & de la value a present de deux tanz que ne vaut chailli / [il vint, *canceled*] Messire pierre de la vie le bailla au Roy phelippe le lonc li quels le donna a la dite Reyne / mas li Roys charles eu grant deliberacion le retourna au patremoyne du Royaume / & a plusieurs requestes que la dite Reyne li en fit fere & sur plusieurs raysons baillies par escript a fin que il ly deust rendre / Il fu respondi que remiz ny estoit / [mas, *canceled*] pour ce que cestoit patre-moyne du Royaume qui ne deuoit estre alienez senz Iuste cause & [fut, *canceled*] apres ce de grace especial si comme aucuns dient le dit Roy charles le donna a la dite Reyne a sa vie tant seulement la bastie de monguiart & chailly & doyuent estre les lettres du dit don en la cham-bre des Comptes ou deuers le Receueur de paris qui pour le temps estoit mais cis qui ce vous enuoie nest pas auisiez se ce fu fait par maniere de deliurance / ou dons [dons, *inserted*] de grace especial & pour ce sen rapporte es lettres'.

will of 1319, which had included heritable annuities worth 2915 l., lifetime annuities totalling 1200 l., and individual legacies amounting to 28,480 l.[109]

In the case of two pieces of property that Philip V had given to Jeanne, Charles IV voided the grants but seems graciously to have permitted her to keep them for her lifetime. The grounds on which Charles annulled the gifts reveal the emergence of more clearly developed ideas about the domains of the crown, although they also show how sorely fuller definition and clarification were needed.

Charles contested the validity of his brother's award of the bastide of Montgeard to Jeanne in July 1318 because of a pledge that Philip V had made in the same month he made the gift. In an agreement of pariage regarding the new bastide the king had promised never to place it outside his – i.e., the king's – hand. The only exception which the king envisaged was the possibility that the bastide might be given to the lord who held Toulouse. Nothing was said about the queen. Nor did Philip present any special justification of the grant when he bestowed Montgeard on Jeanne. He might have argued, as Henry III of England did in 1247, that there was no surer proof of the king's intention to retain property in the royal hand, attached perpetually to the crown, than to assign it to the queen.[110] However, like Philip V's defence of his favours to Sully, such arguments would have seemed contrived and indeed ridiculous to those whose rights were threatened. They would hardly have been accepted in France, where the Parlement of Paris voided at least three of Philip V's assignments of dower property to Clementia of Hungary (two of them in July 1317) because the property was perpetually attached to the royal hand or crown.[111]

---

[109] AN, J 404A, no. 30 (the codicil, dated at Asnières-sur-Oise); the sums are taken from BNF, fr. 13085, fols 18r–21r, a contemporary itemised analysis of Jeanne's will.

[110] In 1243 Henry III granted the county of Chester to Queen Eleanor of Provence. Four years later, announcing his intention of retaining the county and its appurtenances 'in manu nostra ut semper spectantia ad coronam nostram', he said that he had awarded it to Eleanor, 'vt manifestum vobis sit signum quod eundem Comitatum sine ulla aliquo tempore separatione. ipsi corone nostre retinere uelimus annexum'. See London, Public Record Office, C 66/58 (Patent Roll 31 Henry III, 10 May 1247; *Calendar of Patent Rolls, 1232–1247*, 501). For background, consult Ranald Stewart Brown, 'The End of the Norman Earldom of Chester', *English Historical Review*, 35 (1920), 26–54 (p. 52); and Geoffrey Barraclough, 'The Earldom and County Platine of Chester' (read on 19 May 1951), *Transactions of the Historic Society of Lancashire and Cheshire for the Year 1951*, 103 (1952), 23–57 (p. 39).

[111] Edgard Boutaric, *Actes du Parlement de Paris, Première série – de l'an 1254 à l'an 1328*, 2 vols, Ministère de la Maison de l'Empereur et des Beaux-Arts, Archives de l'Empire; Inventaires et documents (Paris: Henri Plon, 1863–67), II, 189, nos. 4920–21 (4 July 1317, involving the guard of the abbey of Saint-Benoit-sur-Loire and rights over the castle of Moulinet which the king held jointly with the abbey; cf. Guerout, no. 1754, an act of December 1317 regarding Moulinet). The third nullification occurred in May 1326 (AN, JJ 64, fol. 79r, no. 139).

In annulling his brother's grant of Montgeard to Jeanne, Charles stated that Philip had promised not to place the bastide 'outside the patrimony of the crown of France'. The concept of the crown's patrimony is more abstract than that of the royal hand, which Philip had in fact invoked – or the notion of the royal crown, which he cited in making his award to Sully. The other donation that Charles contested in principle but permitted in practice was Philip's grant of Chilly. Because Chilly had been exchanged for land that had been 'patremoyne du Royaume' and a former barony, Charles had decided to return it 'au patremoyne du Royaume'. Jeanne protested, but the king remained adamant: this was 'patrimony of the kingdom which should not be alienated without just cause'. He nonetheless permitted Jeanne to have Chilly as long as she lived.[112]

The phrases 'patremone du Royaume' and 'patremoyne de la corone de france' were attributed to Charles IV by ministers of Philip of Valois some-time around 1330. They recall the key formula in the ordonnance of Moulins of 1566, 'le Domaine & patrimoine roial de notre Couronne'. Charles may indeed have used the words that appear in the memorandum of 1330. Letters of attachment to the crown that he granted contain the phrases 'corone nostre franc. patrimonio et domanio', 'corone francie patrimonio', and 'sub dominio et patrimonio'.[113] These terms recall the expressions 'patrimony of the church' and 'patrimony of God', entities which Roman and Canon law – and Bracton – declared absolutely inalienable. The terms' appearance in Charles IV's acts might suggest that Charles was particularly sensitive to the welfare of kingdom and crown, and that he consequently opposed alienation of the realm's lands and revenues. This was not the case. Once set in motion, the dialectic of royal successional proprietary antagonism asserted itself repetitively and irrepressibly. Like Philip V, Charles IV employed the princi-ple of inalienability when it suited him. Alienation without just cause was, to be sure, wrong, and should be undone. This, however, did not foreclose the possibility of alienation for good reason.[114]

Charles's acts with regard to Jeanne of Burgundy demonstrated that 'le vif saisit le mort'.[115] As he showed, a living king could easily annul the acts of his

---

[112] See the text in n. 108 above. In granting Chilly to Jeanne, Philip V and his advisers seem to have had no special concern that it would be challenged, for the act was relatively simple and lacked any elaborate clause of validation: see n. 65 above.

[113] The first phrase appears in a letter of attachment to the crown, issued in July 1326 (AN, JJ 62, fols 214v–15r, no. 392). The second is found in a letter affirming the status of a Bene-dictine house, dated 6 May 1326 (AN, JJ 64, fol. 79r, no. 139). The third is used in a letter of attachment to the crown dated November 1322 (AN, JJ 61, fols 124v–25v, no. 280). In May 1323 Charles confirmed a letter of attachment issued by Philip V in July 1318 which em-ployed the phrase 'dominium proprium corone franc.' (AN, JJ 61, fol. 96r–v, no. 200).

[114] *Ordonnances*, I, 762–8, and especially the extract from register *Noster* of the Chambre des comptes, fol. 58, ed. in ibid., n. (a).

[115] For background concerning the maxim, see Krynen, *L'empire du roi*, pp. 135–51.

predecessor, however much respect he owed his royal predecessors and ancestors. The failure of Philip V's rhetorical tactics demonstrated that words alone could not enable the dead to control the living, particularly when the property the dead person hoped to bequeath was – or could be – considered part of the endowment of the kingdom and the kingdom's living ruler, who replaced his predecessor as the realm's spouse. This did not discourage later kings from imitating Philip V's strategies, and devising new tactics. Thus, in assigning his wife's dower, Philip VI of Valois not only included provisions to ensure her immediate, peaceful access to it after his death, but also had the names of the fifteen witnesses recorded under the document's fold-up, to protect them from alteration or obliteration.[116]

5. Conclusion

Neither Philip V nor his successors succeeded in resolving the problems inherent in the dialectic of royal successional proprietary antagonism.[117] Given the particular evolution of notions of the crown's patrimony in France, these problems were essentially unresolvable.[118] Philip V's attempts to protect the grants he made to his wife and his ministers did result in elevating the monarchy's authority, even if the king was unable to achieve his own immediate, personal goals. Philip's repeated assertions of the king's power to abrogate custom and law provided his successors with rhetorical strategies, and challenged them to implement the maxim. By the sixteenth century, kings were thought able to abolish custom if they wished, although this prerogative was limited to royal contracts and did not extend to the king's subjects, 'to take away their right'. As the practical-minded theorist Jean du

[116] AN, J 357A (Reines II), nos. 4–4 bis (March 1332), 7–7ter (October 1332); J 537B (Reines II), no. 8 (October 1332) (where the witnesses' names are written in the gutter of the fold-up), and no. 15 (December 1347).

[117] See Saenger's analysis of the policies of Louis XI, in 'Burgundy and the Inalienability of Appanages', pp. 25–6 ('Louis XI, like his predecessors, continued to alienate the royal domain, [but he did so] only when it was politically expedient and did not unnecessarily jeopardize the essential defenses of the kingdom').

[118] Thus, citing a number of Roman law texts, the author of the tract *Miranda de laudibus Francie et de ipsius regimine regni* declares, 'Rex potest donare & alienare', but cautions 'donacio vero facta per regem contra publicam vtilitatem sui regnj manifeste presumitur subreptitia': BNF, lat. 6020, fols 1r–12v (fol. 10v). As the preamble to the work declares (ibid., fol. 1r), it was written for Charles VII, the Dauphin Louis, and the three estates of France, and finished on 1 January 1450, 'the jubilee year of Pope Nicholas V'; see fol. 12r–v, for the Epilogue, dated 1 January 1465 (possibly 1466, new style dating). The work was surely written by the legist and ecclesiastic Bernard de Rosier (Bernardus de Rosegerio), with other works of whose it is copied in BNF, lat. 6020. See Saenger, 'Burgundy and the Inalienability of Appanages', p. 6 n. 21; and Patrick Arabeyre, 'Un prélat languedocien au milieu du XVe siècle: Bernard de Rosier, archevêque de Toulouse (1400–1475)', *Journal des savants*, (1900), 291–326, esp. p. 305.

Tillet saw it, 'customs are accorded by the king's subjects, not ordained by kings', and hence rulers could not tamper with customs that protected subjects.[119] On the other hand, Du Tillet viewed with approval Philip VI's demonstration of his authority to abrogate custom in his two testaments[120] and in

119 'Les Roys abolissent les coustumes s'ilz veulent, quant a leurs contractz, Non quant a ceulx de leurs subiectz, pour tollir leur droict: *Car les coustumes sont accordees par lesdits subiets, non ordonnees par lesdits Roys.* Ainsi fut Iugé par arrest, en la cause de Sibile de Garencieres, Le seizeiesme Iuillet, mil trois cens cinquante vng: La Raison est La Reigle susdicte. Le Roy Philippes de Valoys en ses deux testamens *faicts mil trois cens quarante sept, & trois cens cinquante,* pour la validite d'iceulx, derogea a tout droict escript, disant ny estre subiect, quant a son temporel [*à la temporalité*], et aux coustumes de son Royaulme, comme estant [*pour son regard*] pardessus Icelles. Luy mesmes par la donacion, qu'il feyt ala Royne sa femme *le 21. Nouembre, mil trois cens trente,* de tous ses Ioyaulx, bagues et meubles de son hostel, ou vsaige, qu'elle auroit lors de son deces, Sil mouroit le premier, pour la validité osta [*osta pour la validité*] toutes coustumes, loix, et vsaiges contraires: Qui suffira pour exemples de bien vser du pouuoir que les Roys ont pardessus les loix et coustumes. Aussi sont ceulx de france, pour n'auoir superiour, Iuges en leurs propres causes'. I base this ed. on one of the copies that Jean du Tillet offered to Henri II (Saint Petersburg, National Library of Russia, Fr. F. v.IV, no. 8/1, fol. 122r); additions made in the recension that Du Tillet presented to Charles IX in 1566 are in italics, and the phrase that Du Tillet suppressed is underlined; for the second recension I use Jean du Tillet, *Recveil des Roys de France, Levrs Couronne et Maison [. . .]* (Paris: Iaques du Puys, [1579]–1580), pp. 173–4. The chapter is entitled, 'Tiltres, grandeur et excellence des Roys & Royaulme de France'. On Jean du Tillet and his *Recueils,* see Elizabeth A. R. Brown and Myra Dickman Orth, 'Jean du Tillet et les illustrations du grand *Recueil des Roys', Revue de l'Art,* 115 (1997), 8–24, and also Elizabeth A. R. Brown, 'Jean du Tillet, François Ier, and the *Trésor des chartes',* in *Histoires d'archives: recueil d'articles offert à Lucie Favier par ses collègues et amis* (Paris: Société des amis des Archives de France, 1997), pp. 237–47; and eadem, 'Jean du Tillet et les Archives de France', *Histoire et Archives,* 2 (1997), 29–63. For the case of Sibylle de Garancières, see AN, X^{1A} 13, fols 144v–46r (16 July 1351); I am grateful to Marie-Claire Chavarot Dessert, who located the case for me. In the suit, Thomas, son of Sibylle's late husband, argued 'que le Roy ou preiudice du dit monsieur thomas ne pouoit adnuller ou abolir les dites coustumes ou vsages', whereas Sibylle maintained that 'suppose sans preiudice que les dites coustumes ou vsages feussent telles comme dit le dit monsieur thomas ce que la dite dame ne confesse mie / toutesfoiz les pouoit le Roy adnuller casser & abolir de sa puissance & auctorite Royal par la maniere quil est contenu es dites lettres / mesmement que aucun droit nestoit encores acquis audit monsieur thomas Inconmutablement viuant le dit monsieur pierre son pere et par especial pouoit le Roy faire les dites choses au traitie du dit Mariage et douaire'. The Parlement finally decided *per arrestum,* that 'dictas aboliciones de quibus in dictis litteris dicti dominj genitoris nostri et accordo suprascripto [one between Sibylle and Thomas] fit mencio non tenere nec valere'.

120 See the preceding note. In his will of 23 May 1346, the king declared that his provisions should be observed 'Non obstant quelcunque droit escript / au quel nous ne sommes en Riens subgiez quant a nostre temporel ne coustume de nostre Royaume / quele que elle soit / en successions de Duchees / Contees / et autres baronnies / soient en parries tenues de nous & de la couronne de france ou dautruy / Et touz vsages [&] obseruances de pays qui porroient estre contraires en aucune chose a noz ordenances dessus dites / les quelz / drois / coustumes / vsages & obseruances de quelque / pays que ce soit en tout nostre Royaume Nous de nostre auctorite & puissance Royal / et de nostre certaine science / par la deliberation de bon conseil & sanz erreur / ostons / Rappellons abolissons & mettons dutout au nient / quant ace quelles ne vaillent ne ne sen puissent aidier aucune personne en Iugement ou dehors en aucune Maniere encontre les choses dessus dites en tout ou en partie / Et quant ace de nostre

a grant of property to his wife.[121] Having described these acts, Du Tillet declared that they manifested 'the good use of the power that the kings [of France] possessed over laws and customs'.[122] In Du Tillet's eyes, the royal power to nullify custom provided convincing testimony of the 'grandeur and excellence of the kings and the kingdom of France'. For this, in some part, Philip V was responsible. His ingenuity and boldness in advancing claims to such authority, arguably the most enduring of his accomplishments as king, were prompted by his determination – in the end unrealised – to resolve the royal conundrum with which he struggled throughout his reign.

auctorite & puissance Royal / ordenons faisons & establissons / et de nostre certaine science / loy / laquele loy soit [nous voulons estre] valable tenue / & obseruee [& gardee] en Iugemens & dehors comme loy de nous faite / escripte & ordonee / Non obstant quelcunque autre loy ou droit escript / coustume vsage ou obseruance ace contraire / Et se par auenture es choses dessus dites ou aucune dicelles auoit aucuns deffaus en solennite de droit / de coustume vsage ou obseruance daucun pays de nostre Royaume quelque part que ce soit ne en quelcunques choses que ce soit [quelque part / ne en quelconque chose que ce soit]. Nous de nostre auc-torite / [&] plain pooir Royal et certaine science dessus dis / les suppleons en tout & par tout en touz les poins ou neccessaire et proffitable sera / a faire les choses dessus dites et chascune dicelles valables fermes & estables tout aussint [aussi] comme se toute solennite de droit de Coustume vsage & obseruance de pays ace necessaires [y] estoient entreuenues & gardees de point en point': AN, J 404B, no. 33 (also preserved in a contemporary copy, no. 33 bis). The corresponding section of Philip's testament of 2 July 1350 (AN, J 404B, no. 34) is virtually identical; significant changes are inserted in brackets above.

[121] Philip used the following clause of validation: 'et de certaine science de nostre auc-torite. & puissance royal nous quant au fait de ceste dite donnaison. et de tout ce qui en puet dependre. Nous ostons & anullons toutes coustumes & vsages se aucuns en ya / qui puissent estre contraires. ou preiudiciaus contre ceste dite donnaison': AN, JJ 66, fol. 338r. The orig-inal act (AN, J 357A, no. 3) is dated simply November 1330 and contains only minor differ-ences of spelling and punctuation; the seal is now missing, although the red and green silk laces by which it was appended survive.

[122] Du Tillet believed that because the kings of France could abolish custom, gifts between the kings and their wives were valid. He declared in his chapter 'De l'auctorité et preroga-tiues des Roynes de France', 'Combien que par le droict et coustumes les dons faictz entre mary & femme constant leur mariage soient nul, ceulx faictz par les Roys aux Roynes leurs femmes valent', and for explanation ('la Raison') he referred his readers 'ou chapitre prece-dent'. See Saint Petersburg, National Library of Russia, Fr. F. v. IV, no. 8/1, fol. 125r (the first recension), and Du Tillet, *Recueil des Roys* (1580 ed.), p. 178. More conservatively, the sixteenth-century jurist René Choppin limited the king's right to endow his wife to property 'quæ nondum Fiscali Patrimonio nexa sint nominatim, aut tacite confusa, redituum posses-sione decenni': *De Domanio Franciæ*, p. 386. Citing many sections from the Roman law, Choppin declared (ibid., p. 385) that in the case of king and queen, 'connubiale istud hono-rum dignitatisque consortium non inducit parem fortunarum inter Regios coniuges com-munionem: Nisi dotalibus Pactis nuncupatim mouentium & acquisitorum societatem coierint. Vix est enim, vt Rex curator Reipub. ac mysticus adeo ipsius coniunx, alteri acqui-rat, ex Fiscali præsertim Ærario: Nihilo magis, quam res Fisci administrans, ceu Antistes Templi, qui publico, sacrove ære fundum mercatus censetur Iure Ciuili. Atque ideo sic empta prædia quæruntur Templo, pupillo, vel Fisco'.

Dice-games and the Blasphemy of Prediction

RHIANNON PURDIE

DICE-GAMES were one of the most popular forms of entertainment in the Middle Ages, and also one of the most heavily criticised. The most common reasons for censure, cited in both secular and religious sources, were the crippling losses, endemic cheating, violence, and crime with which dicing was associated. That these were, and remain today, the main causes for concern over all forms of gambling is indisputable. Greed cannot have been the only or even the main motive to gamble, however, since it will not have escaped even the most ardent (or dim-witted) player's notice that the most likely outcome would be embarrassing loss: the tavern songs in the *Carmina Burana* collection, among many other examples, are full of drunken players losing the shirts off their backs.[1] This paper will concern itself with those other, secondary aspects of both the attraction of dice-games and the reasons behind their censure in the Middle Ages. The attractions of dice-games for their medieval adherents were in fact much the same as for modern players, but some aspects of the medieval condemnation of dicing are less readily comprehensible. The reliance on chance as a determining factor in human affairs, coupled with the ancient pagan use of dice in divination, led to the medieval association – unexpected for a modern audience – of dice-games with blasphemy.[2] This is rarely discussed directly by medieval commentators

---

I was helped in the writing of this paper by the great scholarship and generosity of the members of the 'medtextl' internet discussion group ('Medieval Texts – Philology Codicology and Technology': MEDTEXTL@postoffice.cso.uiuc.edu), who suggested many of the primary and secondary sources used here.

[1] *Carmina Burana*, ed. B. K. Vollmann (Frankfurt: Deutscher Klassiker Verlag, 1987), items 195–215.

[2] For some writers, the reliance on chance alone was enough to condemn dicing. John of Salisbury writes in book I, chap. 5 of the *Policraticus*: 'Do you not think the gamester foolish who by grace of dice lives, nay rather perishes, and makes each throw the arbiter of his fate? Does that pursuit conform to reason, in devotion to which one becomes less devout?' (trans. Joseph B. Pike, *Frivolities of Courtiers and Footprints of Philosophers* [Minneapolis: University of Minnesota Press, 1938], p. 26).

on the subject, although it is often represented by the emphasis placed on descriptions of the violent swearing of dice-players. The perceived blasphemy of the actual activity of dicing formed an important part of the disquiet felt about it by at least some of its medieval critics. The reasons behind, and consequences of, this perception will be explored in some detail later on.

Since the prospect of monetary gain evidently cannot be the only attraction of dice-games, we must look elsewhere for the source of their addictiveness. The gambling impulse is a fundamental part of human nature: every society has some form of gambling in its traditions and pastimes, whether or not that society actually condones it. The root of this impulse lies, quite simply, in the sheer perverse pleasure of trying to predict the outcome of an unpredictable event. People are obsessively curious about the future – 'future' here meaning *all* that lies beyond the present moment, not just the long-term view. We love to have the opportunity to guess, even when the matter is as inconsequential as whether a tossed coin will show heads or tails. George Eliot sums up this aspect of human nature astutely in a passage from *The Lifted Veil*:

> So absolute is our souls' need of something hidden and uncertain for the maintenance of that doubt and hope and effort which are the breath of its life, that if the whole future were laid bare to us beyond today, the interest of all mankind would be bent on the hours that lie between; we should pant after the uncertainties of our one morning and our one afternoon; we should rush fiercely to the Exchange for our last possibility of speculation, of success, of disappointment: we should have a glut of political prophets foretelling a crisis or a no-crisis within the only twenty-four hours left open to prophecy.[3]

This sheer love of prediction is especially relevant to dice-games. Medieval people gambled on chess and a variety of other board-games,[4] on cards (from the fourteenth century onwards), and on all kinds of sporting events,[5] but in dice-games the *sole* operative factor (barring cheating) is chance.[6] In the

---

[3] Quoted in Clemens J. France, 'The Gambling Impulse', in *The Psychology of Gambling*, ed. Jon Halliday and Peter Fuller (London: Allen Lane, 1974), pp. 115–56 (p. 130).

[4] See H. J. R. Murray, *A History of Board-Games Other Than Chess* (London: Oxford University Press, 1952), pp. 117–29.

[5] On cards, see David Parlett, *The Oxford Guide to Card Games* (Oxford: Oxford University Press, 1990), pp. 27–46. On all other forms of gambling, see John Ashton, *The History of Gambling in England* (New York: Burt Franklin, 1968); Teresa McLean, *The English at Play in the Middle Ages* (Windsor: The Kensal Press, 1983).

[6] The consequent use of dice as a convenient metaphor for the instability of the world was as common in the Middle Ages as it is now. Even John Gower – 'Moral Gower' – frequently employs dicing metaphors in his *Confessio Amantis*. See for example Prol., Latin verses no. V; 'Mundus in euentu versatur vt alea casu, / Quam celer in ludis iactat auara manus' ('The world is tossed and turned by chance, as dice / are quickly thrown by greedy hands at play.'); also I line 54; IV lines 1093–5 and lines 1778–9; V line 2437 in *The English Works of John Gower*, 2 vols, ed. G. C. Macaulay, Early English Text Society, e.s. 81 and 82 (1901–2); trans-

Middle Ages, this game of prediction was magnified by the faint but allur-
ingly sinful shadow of the earlier pagan use of dice in divination.[7] One of the
crucial elements in games of chance that draws gamblers back to them time
and time again is the way in which success at them appears to demonstrate
some sort of divine favour.[8] When a guess as to the outcome of a random
event is confirmed, it suggests to the gambler that he actually *knew* what the
result was going to be: in a small but instantly gratifying way, the gambler
feels he has demonstrated clairvoyance.[9] The stakes are really just to make
the answer more meaningful; the higher the stakes, the more definitive the
answer. Such an activity throws up all sorts of philosophical difficulties as
soon as one tries to place it in a Christian context, and forms part of the fine
web of associations between the playing of dice-games and blasphemy, most
often represented by its association with that more overt form of blasphemy,
cursing.

I will begin with a brief description of some of the dice-games in question,
since their rules and regulations are now foreign to most of us.[10] Dice-games
could be played with one, two or three dice, but three seems to have been the
most common number in the Middle Ages, and is the one most often encountered in literature and visual art. The fact that Middle English texts sometimes refer to a 'pair' of dice has, understandably, led some modern historians
using English sources to assume that two dice were normally in use,[11] but
'pair' evidently could refer to a collection of things, as when fifteenth-century
players spoke of a 'payre' of cards,[12] or in John Skelton's *The Bowge of Courte*,

---

lation from Latin kindly provided by Siân Echard. In art, William L. Tronzo discusses a
twelfth-century mosaic in San Savino, Piacenza, which addresses the theme of fortune and
virtue by contrasting illustrations of chess, representing order and reason, on the right-hand
side of the central panel, with illustrations of dicing, representing disorder, on the left:
'Moral Hieroglyphs: Chess and Dice at San Savino in Piacenza', *Gesta*, 16:2 (1977), 15–26.

[7] For a history of the use of dice and astragali in pagan divination, see F. N. David, *Games,
Gods and Gambling* (London: Griffin, 1962); see especially Chapters 1 and 2. On Roman use
of dice for divination as well as gambling, see the note by Genevra Kornbluth, 'Late Roman
Gemstone Dice: Tools for Divination', *American Journal of Archaeology*, 100 (1996), 349.

[8] Cf. France, p. 142: 'Ultimately, it is the belief that Luck, or Fortune, or God or a sympath-
etic saint – *some* kind of external supernatural force – controls what is apparently a chance
event, that has attracted gamblers through the history of humanity.'

[9] For a report on a study of the scientific basis of the gambler's sense of foresight, see Philip
Cohen, 'Gut reaction is your best guide', *New Scientist*, 2072 (8 March 1997), p. 17.

[10] For comprehensive works on the subject of medieval dice-games, see: Franz Semrau,
Würfel und Würfelspiel im alten Frankreich (Halle: Beihefte zur Zeitschrift f. Rom. Phil. 23,
1910); Jean-Michel Mehl, *Les jeux au royaume de France: du XIIIe au début du XVIe siècle*
(Paris: Fayard, 1990); Walter Tauber, *Das Würfelspiel im Mittelalter und in der frühen Neuzeit:
eine kultur- und sprachgeschichtliche Darstellung* (Frankfurt and New York: Lang, 1987).

[11] McLean, p. 103, thinks *hazard* was played with two dice, and has led other scholars to
perpetuate the assumption: see for example Roger Munting, *An Economic and Social History
of Gambling in Britain and the USA* (Manchester: Manchester University Press, 1996), p. 8.

[12] Parlett, p. 27.

where the character Ryotte uses a *payre of bones* to gain the triple score *quater treye dews*, 'four, three, two'.[13]

One very common game was known as 'highest points' – *plus points* – and is just that: the player who throws the highest score wins. The most popular game, however, was undoubtedly 'hazard'. Although the word became syn-onymous with dicing, and is often now translated simply as 'dicing', this was a distinct form of dice-game. Roger Munting, in his history of English and American gambling, notes that it later became the most popular game in eighteenth- and nineteenth-century gaming houses, but it was already wildly popular in the Middle Ages.[14] Its modern descendant, the American game of 'craps', is apparently still the highest-earning game for the Las Vegas casinos.[15] The name is thought by some to date from the first crusade at the end of the eleventh century, when soldiers besieging the Syrian or Palestinian fortress of 'El Azar' were supposed to have whiled away the days playing a dice-game they named after the fortress. Others have suggested that the name derives from the Arabic name for the die, *al-zhar*, *azzar*, though the *OED* notes that early evidence for this sense is wanting. The medieval rules for at least one version of the game were set out by King Alfonso X 'el Sabio' of Spain in his treatise the *Libro del ajedrez, de los dados y de las tablas*, 'The Book of Chess, Dice and Tables'.[16] Written around 1283, this guide testifies to the irrepressible popularity of these games at all social levels. Although chess is the game Alfonso admires, he carefully sets out the rules for more accessible games such as *azar*, 'hazard'. 'Hazard' is in fact the name given to the sudden-death scores in this game: these lie between either fifteen and eighteen, or three and six (in some versions, seven and fourteen are also included). The existence of upper and lower 'hazard' ranges is related to the distribution of points on a die. The most common arrangement from Roman times onward (it still holds today) is to have opposite sides always total seven: six is oppo-site one, five is opposite two, and four is opposite three. Thus, when a 'hazard' score from one range is shown on the uppermost faces, the undersides will show the corresponding score from the other range. The point of the 'hazard' scores is that they are less likely to come up than intermediate scores: playing with three dice, there is only one way to score three, four, seventeen or eight-een, but there are six ways, for example, to score ten.

The game itself is a contest between two players, or at least two sides. They might begin by rolling the dice for highest points to see who will go first.[17]

---

13 *John Skelton: The Complete English Poems*, ed. John Scattergood (Harmondsworth: Penguin, 1983), lines 346–7.

14 Munting, p. 8.

15 Robert D. Herman, *Gamblers and Gambling: Motives, Institutions, and Controls* (Lexing-ton: Lexington, 1976), p. 22.

16 The relevant sections are translated in C. A. Knudson, 'Hasard et les autres jeux de dés dans le *Jeu de Saint Nicholas*', *Romania*, 63 (1937), 248–53 (pp. 251–2).

17 Cf. Scene II in the *Jeu de Saint Nicholas*, discussed below.

The first player then throws, and if he scores 'hazard' on this first throw, he wins. If it is another number, this becomes the opponent's 'chance', or lucky number. The same player rolls again. If he scores 'hazard' this time, he loses outright, but if it is another ordinary number, this becomes his own 'chance'. He then keeps throwing the dice, and whoever has their 'chance' reappear first wins the game. In some versions of the game, the person throwing the dice could also lose if a 'hazard' score reappears, but this does not seem to have been the usual manner of play, and it would certainly have been less attractive to play a game with such unequal odds.[18]

Alfonso unfortunately gives no information on how the betting operated in such games, but there is evidence to suggest that the hazard was particularly associated with high stakes, heavy losses and presumably the inevitable violence that accompanied them. (Perhaps this is why 'hazardour' came to be used as a general derogatory term for dice-players.) In the early thirteenth-century Old French fabliau *St Pierre et le Jongleur*, the saint descends into Hell to engage a damned minstrel in a dice-game in order to win the souls in his charge.[19] There is no discussion as to which game they should play, although several choices were open to them and indeed they agree to switch to *plus poinz* later, but they launch into what is clearly a game of hazard. Kitty MacGillavry speculates that the saint's suggestion that there is a lot of money to be won – 'Tu puez bien a moi gaaignier / Bons esterlins priveement' (lines 136–7) – is the signal that he is proposing a game of hazard.[20]

We move now to the kinds of objections raised against dicing. The evils described most frequently are the collection of socially disruptive ills sometimes labelled the 'tavern sins': drinking, the irresponsible loss of money (perhaps beggaring a player's family), physical violence, endemic cheating, and violent swearing.[21] This last problem is something of a special case, as noted earlier, and I shall return to it later. The losses associated with dice-games were often symbolised in literature by the loss of the gambler's clothing. In the tavern songs of the *Carmina Burana* collection mentioned earlier, the regularity with which dice-players gamble themselves naked is as constant a source of amusement as their drunkenness. In the Middle English fifteenth-century *Tale of Beryn*, the hero is presented as a medieval teenaged tearaway, his pawned clothes constantly replaced by over-indulgent parents:

[18] F. Lecoy, note on article by W. Noomen ('Encore une fois la partie de "Hasard" dans le *Jeu de saint Nicholas*', *Neophilologus*, 43 (1959), 109–13) in *Romania*, 81 (1960), 139–41 (p. 140).
[19] 'St Pierre et le Jongleur', in *Fabliaux*, ed. R. C. Johnston and D. D. R. Owen (Oxford: Blackwell, 1965), pp. 67–77.
[20] Kitty MacGillavry, 'Le jeu de dés dans le fabliau de Saint Pierre', *Marche Romane*, 28 (1978), 175–9 (p. 177).
[21] See R. F. Yeager, 'Aspects of Gluttony in Chaucer and Gower', *Studies in Philology*, 81 (1984), 42–55; Frederick Tupper, 'The Pardoner's Tavern', *Journal of English and Germanic Philology*, 13 (1918), 553–65; G. R. Owst, *Literature and Pulpit in Medieval England* (Oxford: Blackwell, 1961), pp. 425–49.

Berinus ferthermore loved wele the dise
And for to pley at hazard, and held therof grete pryse,
And al other games that losery [i.e. risk] was in,
And evermore he lost and never myghte wyn.
Berinus atte hazard many a nyghte he waked,
And offt tyme it fill so that he cam home al naked.

(lines 923–8)[22]

This particular passage does not allude to brawling, though this was another much-criticised aspect of dice-games, and dice-players are often depicted as being on the verge of, if not in the middle of, a fight.[23] One widespread source of illustrations of gambling is the crucifixion scene, which often included the soldiers who are described in the Gospels as gambling for Christ's robe.[24] The soldiers are nearly always shown playing dice, and snarling faces and drawn daggers are standard.[25] The fighting and general destructiveness occasioned by dice-games in art and literature were clearly an accurate reflection of the reality of dicing, as is demonstrated by a series of gaming laws drawn up on behalf of the same Alfonso X of Spain who was responsible for the *Book of Chess, Dice and Tables*. These were designed to regulate those gaming parlours of thirteenth-century Castile that enjoyed royal sanction. Whatever Alfonso's private attitude to dice-games may have been, he took the pragmatic approach of controlling and profiting from gaming rather than trying to eliminate it. The regulations, fascinatingly detailed, were collected in a work known as the *Ordenamiento de las tafurerías*, 'Ordinances of the gaming parlours', and they deal with such matters as the punishments for blasphemy, fighting, and damage to the premises; cheating; pawning; the financial management of gaming houses; payment of debts; fraud, and the prohibition of unauthorised gaming houses.[26] The feverish nature of play is best illustrated by the more lenient regulations: in Law 5, a distressed player who either grinds the dice to bits with his teeth or actually swallows them is exempt from punishment, and likewise in Law 7, no further punishment is imposed on the enraged player who manages to break the gaming table with his head.[27]

[22] 'The Canterbury Interlude and the Merchant's Tale of Beryn', in *The Canterbury Tales: Fifteenth-Century Continuations and Additions*, ed. John H. Bowers (Kalamazoo: Medieval Institute Publications, 1992), pp. 55–196.

[23] See for example the illustration on fol. 70v of the manuscript of Alfonso X's 'Book of Chess, Dice and Tables', reproduced in facsimile in *Das Spanische Schachzabelbuch des Königs Alfons des Weisen vom 1283* (Leipzig: 1913), plate CXL, and also printed in Tronzo, figure 11, p. 24.

[24] See Mark 15. 24; Luke 23. 34; John 19. 23–4.

[25] For some fine examples, see Ruth Mellinkoff, *Outcasts: Signs of Otherness in Northern European Art of the Late Middle Ages*, 2 vols (Berkeley: University of California Press, 1993). Soldier-gamblers are discussed in vol. I, pp. 131–2.

[26] Dwayne Carpenter, 'Fickle Fortune: Gambling in Medieval Spain', *Studies in Philology*, 85 (1988), 267–78.

[27] Carpenter, 'Fickle Fortune', pp. 272–3.

The usual spark for a brawl was the accusation of cheating. Cheating was as rife as it was inevitable. In games of chance, there is no other way to employ any skill, and it has the added attraction that one might thereby persuade others that one simply enjoys divine favour. Since dice-games were usually played indoors, poor light gave ample opportunity for trying to claim a more attractive score before the others had seen the dice. Jolting the table at crucial moments was another common trick. For the more dedicated cheat, loaded dice were in common circulation, the usual method being to weight one of the sides with lead or silver. These were known in French as *dés pipés*, and Villon specifically lists *pipeurs* along with *hasardeurs de dés* in a rogues' gallery which also includes robbers, traitors and counterfeiters in his 'Ballade de Bonne Doctrine a ceux de mauvaise vie'.[28] Jean-Michel Mehl, in his study of cheating at dice in medieval France, notes that the *Livre des Métiers* of Etienne Boileau, written c.1260, forbids the manufacture of loaded dice and goes into some detail describing the various methods of tampering with the dice, as does a 1297 Statute of Dicemakers from Toulouse.[29] (It should be noted, however, that the profession of dicemaking seems to have been an honourable one apart from these transgressions; condemnation of dicing was not universal, despite the best efforts of the moralists.) As well as carrying extra weight, or being partially hollowed in order to alter its centre of gravity, a die could be shaved so one side was slightly convex; or be made slightly oblong so as to not roll true; or be misnumbered. Such dice formed the basic equipment of the career cheat: the idea was to secrete the false dice on one's person and introduce them into the game only periodically, so as not to awaken suspicion in the other players. And despite multiple prohibitions against the manufacture of such dice, they seem to have been widely available, as is suggested by the thirteenth-century *Dit d'un mercier*, where a haberdasher says: 'J'ai dez du plus, j'ai dez du moins, / De Paris, de Chartres, de Rains' ('I have high dice, I have low dice, from Paris, Chartres and Rheims').[30]

If a container of some kind were not used to shake and throw the dice, the player also had the option of controlling their fall by hand, usually by performing what is now known as the 'slide-shot', a technique referred to in Old French as *assoeir les dés*, or to 'plant' the dice. It consisted of manipulating the dice in the hand so that the desired score is uppermost, then throwing the dice so that they merely skid rather than roll. This technique is frequently alluded to in literary descriptions of dicing. It is obviously harder to convey visually, but Michel Dillange has noted that this particular practice must lie behind the scores occasionally shown on the dice in the scene of the soldier-

[28] François Villon, *Oeuvres*, ed. André Mary (Paris: Garnier, 1962), pp. 104–5, lines 2–6.
[29] Jean-Michel Mehl, 'Tricheurs et tricheries dans la France médiévale: l'exemple du jeu de dés', *Reflexions historiques*, 8 (1981), 3–25 (pp. 13–15).
[30] Quoted in Mehl, 'Tricheurs', p. 15.

gamblers at the Crucifixion.[31] He noticed that an early medieval sculpture in a church in Civray, a fifteenth-century mural in Thann, and a sixteenth-century tapestry in the Château d'Angers all showed dice displaying the score '6, 5, 3'. The consistency could not be coincidental, and he realised that this score is what lies on the opposite sides of the dice from the best possible score of '4, 2, 1' in one popular game named after this score. For the practised cheat, it would be an easy matter to flip over such dice in the act of scooping them up, and then 'plant' them in the manner described above to win. These artists evidently expected their audiences to recognise the situation and know what the one gambler is accusing the other of planning. This lends added significance to the scene, since not only are these tormentors of Christ engaged in the generally disreputable pastime of dicing, but they are clearly cheating as well.

The knowledge of methods of cheating, and even of this precise manoeuvre, is also required of the readers of one particular scene in Wace's twelfth-century *Roman de Brut*, an Old French rendering of Geoffrey of Monmouth's Latin *History of the Kings of Britain*. Dicing is often depicted as a disreputable, lower-class occupation, but this is more symbolic of its moral status than of the social realities of dice-playing. Several household accounts of nobles include payments made specifically for dicing: the register of John of Gaunt, to take a famous example, solemnly records a withdrawal of £45 10s. 8d. in 1375 'to play at dice and for our other privy expenses and necessary occasions',[32] while Chrétien de Troyes describes, quite without censure in this case, knights who amuse themselves playing *a hazart* in the courtly romance *Erec et Enide*.[33] When Wace comes to translate the description of a great feast at Arthur's court, he expands it with the addition of vignettes of gaming and dicing:

> A la foiee gietent quinnes,
> A la foiee gietent sinnes;
> Sis, cinc, troi, quatre, dui et as
> Ont a plusors toluz lor dras.
> Bon espoir a qui les dez tient;
> Quant ses conpainz les a, se crient.
> Asez sovant noisent et crient;
> Li un as autres sovant dient:
> 'Vos me boisiez, defors gitez,
> Crozlez la main, hociez les dez!

---

[31] Michel Dillange, 'A propos du jeu de dés au moyen age', *Bulletin Monumental*, 151 (1993), 137–8.

[32] John of Gaunt's register, II, 315, quoted in *Chaucer's World*, compiled by Edith Rickert, ed. Clair C. Olson (London and New York: Oxford and Columbia University Presses, 1948, repr. 1949), pp. 231–2.

[33] *Erec et Enide*, ed. Mario Roques (Paris: Champion, 1981), lines 355–7.

Je l'anvi avant vostre get!
Querez deniers, metez, g'i met!'
Teus s'i puet aseoir vestuz
Qui au partir s'an lieve nuz.   (lines 2027–40)[34]

(Sometimes they throw fives, sometimes they throw sixes; six, five, three; four, two and one: these have stripped several of their clothes. He who holds the dice has high hopes; when his companion holds them he fears. So often they shout and cry out, the one to the other often saying, 'You're cheating me – throw openly! Shake your hand, toss the dice! I'll raise the stakes before your throw! Get out your deniers, bet; I'm betting!' Some may sit down clothed that on departure get up naked.)

In this scene we see not only the commonplace of gamblers desperately staking their clothes once the money runs out, but that same sleight of hand to produce the '4, 2, 1' score which we encountered in the Crucifixion scenes, and which the other player, with his shouts to throw properly and shake the dice first, has evidently spotted. Not all of the manuscripts retain this section.[35] Since this is unlikely to have been through ignorance of the games involved on the part of scribes, dicing being the widespread practice that it was, it may suggest scribal disapproval of the material. What is clear is that Wace felt he could rely on a thorough knowledge of these dicing tricks in his courtly audience.[36]

Many critics of dicing contented themselves with discussing the problems outlined above. For some, these were their only concerns, but in other cases they may simply have been the easiest things to concentrate on, although other less obvious aspects were equally worrying. San Bernardino of Siena preached one series of sermons against gambling in Florence over Lent, 1424–25, in which he focused on the misuse of money it entails, but at other times he elaborates on the full blasphemous import of dicing. In the Play of the Talents in the late Middle English *Towneley Plays*, the three tormentors of Christ, having just enacted the familiar scene of the three men gambling for Christ's robe, turn to the audience and inveigh against dicing. Owst notes that the whole scene follows the pattern of the preachers' regular attacks on gambling.[37] The evils they list are, once again, the needless waste of goods and money, and the violence:

---

[34] Wace, *La Partie Arthurienne du Roman de Brut*, ed. I. D. O. Arnold and M. M. Pelan (Paris: Librairie Klincksieck, 1962).

[35] See *Le Roman de Brut*, ed. Judith Weiss (London: Dent, 1997), p. 63.

[36] The fifteenth-century poet Charles D'Orleans also expects his audience to catch his reference to the technique of 'planting' the dice – 'J'asserray les dez sans faillir; / Par quoy puisse, sans plus languir, / Gaagnier le jeu entierement' ('I will plant the dice without fail, / So that I may, without further delay, / Win the game entirely'): Ballade XLVI in *Poésies*, ed. P. Champion, vol. I (Paris: Champion, 1923), pp. 68–9; cited in Mehl, 'Tricheurs', p. 16.

[37] Owst, p. 511.

2nd Tortor. By hir meanes she [i.e. Fortune] makys / dysers to sell,
As thay sytt and lakys / thare corne and thare catell;
Then cry thay and crakkys / bowne vnto batell. . . .

3rd Tortor. what commys of dysyng / I pray you hark after,
But los of good in lakyng / and oft tymes mens slaghter!
Thus sorow is at partyng / at metyng if ther be laghter;
I red leyf sich vayn thyng / and serue god herafter.

(lines 386–98)[38]

The one evil not actually listed by the torturers – perhaps because their identity made it unnecessary – is blasphemy. The blasphemous swearing of players (rather than the blasphemy of using dice at all) is in fact the most common criticism to be levelled against dicing. Literary depictions almost always include a player who swears violently by God, Mary or the saints, and who heaps bitter insults upon them when he loses. Occasionally this would take a more graphic form: the Sienese chronicler Paolo de Montale records that a man who had lost at hazard flung a stone at a fresco of the Annunciation, 'as if the Virgin Mary had been the cause of his defeat'.[39] Alfonso X's *Ordinances of the Gaming Parlours*, discussed earlier, actually begins with the fines for various levels of blasphemy, which range from simply having to reaffirm one's faith, to having two finger-widths of one's tongue chopped off.[40] Elsewhere, in nine of the poems from his collection of *Cantigas de Santa María*, Alfonso describes violent, blaspheming dice-players getting their just deserts. Dwayne Carpenter notes that 'Mary's patience is neither infinite nor all-embracing' when it comes to these gamblers, although this is generally her role in such miracle-stories.[41] The dice-players in Eustache Deschamps' 'Le dit du gieu des déz' swear by and at God, the Virgin, and assorted saints:

> Un coup commença a couchier
> Qu'il perdit. Si ne l'en plut mie,
> Si parle a la vierge Marie;
> Chetive gloute l'appella,
> Elle et son filz moult diffama;
> Mains sains villena, maintes saintes,
> La furent chandelles estaintes,
> Et tous les dez ruez ou feu,
> Et tousjours en maugreant Dieu.   (lines 300–08)[42]

---

[38] *The Towneley Plays*, ed. G. England and A. W. Pollard, EETS, e.s. 71 (1897, repr. 1973), pp. 291–2. See also Rosemary Woolf, *The English Mystery Plays* (London: Routledge and Kegan Paul, 1972), p. 267.
[39] Iris Origo, *The World of San Bernardino* (London: Cape, 1963), p. 149.
[40] Carpenter, 'Fickle Fortune', p. 270.
[41] Dwayne Carpenter, ' "Alea jacta est": at the gaming table with Alfonso the learned', *Journal of Medieval History*, 24 (1998), 333–45 (p. 341).
[42] Eustache Deschamps, *Oeuvres Complètes*, ed. the Marquis de Queux de Saint-Hilaire, vol. IV (Paris: Firmin Didot, 1884), p. 263.

(He began a throw, which he lost. It didn't please him at all, and he spoke to the Virgin Mary; 'despicable crook [lit. "glutton"]' he called her, he slandered her and her son greatly; he slandered many saints, male and female; there candles were extinguished and all the dice thrown into the fire, all the while he was cursing God.)

With the violent cursing, the suggestive extinguishing of the candles, and the hurling of the dice into the fire, Deschamps has painted a scene that suggests a connection between dicing and blasphemy far more profound than swearing alone can account for. The swearing of dicers, depicted by such writers, and commented on by critics of dicing, seems to represent a less fully articulated sense that dicing itself is a sinister form of blasphemy. This sense is more apparent in the objections of the Sienese friars, who often allegorised dicing as a form of satanic ritual. Bernadette Paton sums up the substance of their comments:

> Because the gambler inverted the sacred by calling on holy names to condone and even bear witness to his sins, a process diametrically opposed to the true function of prayer which was to induce grace and the disposition to good works in the petitioner, Observant preachers suggested that the whole business of gambling inverted sacred ritual and ran directly counter to Divine Will. . . . Bernardino brings a direct charge of idolatry against gamblers, claiming that they obey the will of the dice above that of God.[43]

The idea of dicing as a direct inversion of sacred ritual is elaborated upon in the parodic Gambler's Mass contained within the *Carmina Burana* collection, in which the 'congregation', instead of rejoicing in the Lord, lament in Decius the god of Dice. Parts of the real mass are cleverly parodied:

> Gaudeamus omnes in Domino, diem festum celebrantes sub honore sanctorum omnium, de quorum solemnitate gaudent angeli.

> (Let us all rejoice in the Lord, celebrating a festival day in honour of all the saints: at whose solemnity the angels rejoice.)

becomes:

> Lugeamvs Omnes in Decio, diem mestum deplorantes pro dolore omnium lusorum: de quorum nuditate gaudent Decii.

> (Let us all lament in Decius, bewailing a mournful day for the sorrow of all gamblers: at whose nakedness the dice rejoice.)[44]

---

43 Bernadette Paton, *Preaching Friars and the Civic Ethos: Siena, 1380–1480* (London: Centre for Medieval Studies, Queen Mary and Westfield College, 1992), pp. 315–16.
44 Vollmann, item 215, p. 668.

The similarity between Deus and Decius was evidently no mere convenient coincidence for this satirist: the inverse of the worship of God is not now simply satanic worship, but specifically the worship of Decius, god of dice. San Bernardino made use of such parody masses, which must have been reasonably well known, to convey the similarity he likewise perceived between dicing and inverted religious worship.[45] He followed such sermons with a call for people to renounce gambling and to bring him their game-boards, cards and dice to be burnt: the fact that people apparently did so in every city in which he preached demonstrates how readily people must have sensed this link. The fourteenth-century English prior John Mirk also depicts dicing as satanic ritual in this extract from his *Manuale Sacerdotum*:

> What shall we say of the priest who, while flinging the dice upon the gaming-table, at the same time flings his soul to the Devil! He makes of the gaming-table an altar for himself, upon which he offers up the goods of the Church to the Devil and even the goods of others too. With false oaths and other crafts of deception he toils to win profit.[46]

In Chaucer's *Pardoner's Tale*, the Pardoner incorporates a small sermon on the evils of drinking, hazardry and blasphemy into his tale of three 'hasardours' who seek death and find it via a pile of gold florins. Criticism usually concentrates on the Pardoner's stated theme of avarice – 'radix malorum est cupiditas' – and the appropriateness of this tale to this most distastefully avaricious and deceitful of the pilgrims. But there is an added significance in the fact that his tale specifies, and roundly criticises, dice-players: the blasphemy of dice-playing is the parallel to the Pardoner's own sacrilege in selling false relics.

Sometimes the dice themselves were allegorised. The Dominican preacher Gabriel de Barletta (of whom Boccaccio commented: 'he who does not know Barletta, does not know preaching')[47] observed that 'Just as God invented the twenty-one letters of the alphabet, so the Devil invented the dice, on which he placed twenty-one points.'[48] An anonymous French poem called 'Du Jeu de Déz', probably from the fourteenth century, expands this idea into a complete allegory. The Devil persuades a Roman senator in his power to invent the dice, and then explains to him the meaning of the pips on each face: one in despite of God; two for spite of God and the Virgin Mary; three for the Trinity; four for the evangelists; five for the wounds of Christ; and six for the six days of Creation.[49] The die is thus transformed into a symbol of the Fall.

---

[45] Martha Bayless, *Parody in the Middle Ages: The Latin Tradition* (Ann Arbor: University of Michigan Press, 1996), pp. 126–7.

[46] Owst, pp. 275–6.

[47] Owst, p. 150.

[48] Christian Morin, *La roue de la fortune* (Paris: Perrin, 1991), p. 57.

[49] *Nouveau Recueil de Contes, Dits, Fabliaux et autres pièces inédites des XIIIe, XIVe et XVe*

This kind of thinking is what ultimately lies behind the scenes of the gamblers at the foot of the Cross, and why even in the fifteenth and sixteenth centuries, the artists usually continue to show them gambling with dice rather than the equally popular cards. The painter Jörg Ratgeb draws on the connection between dice and the betrayal of God in his *c.*1519 painting of the Last Supper, part of the Herrenberg altar. Ruth Mellinkoff draws attention to the yellow of Judas's robes, a colour often used to denote villains, but the unusual feature is in the detail. Judas's obviously erect penis beneath the codpiece denotes his lustful nature, but right above it the artist has painted cards and dice tumbling from his pocket:[50] the accoutrements of gambling do not merely indicate a rogue, but carry here the full weight of the association of games of chance with the betrayal of God.[51]

It is clear, then, that dicing *was* held to be a form of blasphemy in itself, but we have yet to address the question of *why* this should be so. The answer lies in the fact that it is a descendant of both pagan divination and biblical lot. The first association is made clear by the fourteenth-century writer Master Robert Rypon of Durham:

> For the game of Dice or knuckle-bones was a theatre-game of the Ribalds in Rome, who believed in false gods, one of which gods or goddesses was the god or goddess of Fortune, to whose gift and grace they imputed any good piece of luck that befell them.[52]

The connection with biblical lot is rarely spelt out by medieval commentators, but it is even more fundamentally concerned with blasphemy. In the Bible, the use of lot, or an activity whose outcome is governed by chance, was a means of learning God's will. Thus any activity of which the outcome relies entirely on chance is a form of lot, and this includes dicing. The acceptable use of lot was demonstrated to the medieval audience in, for example, the

---

siècles, ed. Achille Jubinal (Paris: Challamel, 1842), pp. 229–34; see also Mehl, 'Tricheurs', p. 22.

[50] Mellinkoff, II, fig. VI.55 for illustration, and I, pp. 51 and 206 for commentary.

[51] There is some evidence of a more general medieval association of Jews with dicing. The owners of the Sienese gambling booths condemned by San Bernardino were often depicted in art with the conical cap also worn by Jews and usurers (Origo, p. 147). Jacques de Vitry's *Exempla ex Sermonibus Vulgaribus* contains two examples of dice-players, and both are associated with Jews: in CCXVIII, a gamester appals his Jewish opponent with his blaspheming, while in CCXCVI a destitute gamester saves himself by refusing to concede to a Jewish moneylender's request to deny the Virgin: *The Exempla or Illustrative Stories from the Sermones Vulgares of Jacques de Vitry*, ed. Thomas F. Crane (London: Nutt, 1890), pp. 91, 124–5. In 'Der Würfelzoll und andere antijüdische Schikanen in Mittelalter und früher Neuzeit', *Zeitschrift für Historische Forschung*, 22 (1995), 1–48, Gerd Mentgen discusses the curious custom of extorting dice from Jews passing toll stations in later medieval Germany: he suggests that the connection between Jews and dice might derive from the gambling soldiers in the Passion.

[52] Quoted in Owst, p. 182.

conversion of St Augustine. In Book Eight of his *Confessions* he describes the deciding moment of his conversion, in which he imagined a voice exhorting him to read: he opened the book of Paul's Epistles at random and read the first passage his eyes fell upon, which exhorted him to 'spend no more thought on nature and nature's appetites' (Rom. 13:13–14).[53] The connection of games of chance with biblical lot is more often made explicit by the sixteenth century. In 1593, James Balmford published 'A Short and Plaine Dialogue concerning the unlawfulnes of playing at Cards, or Tables, or any other Game consisting in Chance'. It is in the form of a dialogue between a professor and a preacher, and the latter is explaining to the former that games of chance are unlawful precisely because they depend on 'lot':

> First, that we reade not in the Scriptures that Lots were used, but only in serious matters, both by Jews and Gentiles. Secondly, that a Lot, in the nature thereof doth as necessarily suppose the special providence and determining presence of God, as an oth in the nature thereof doth suppose the testifying presence of God . . . Thirdly, that the proper end of a Lot, as of an oth, is to end a controversie . . . Whatsoever directly, or of itselfe, or in a speciall manner, tendeth to the advancing of the name of God, is to be used religiously, and not to be used in sport, as we are not to pray or sweare in sport . . . Againe, we are not to tempte the Almightie by a vaine desire of manifestation of his power and speciall providence . . . But God hath sanctified Lots to a proper end, namely to end controversies, therefore man is not to pervert them to a worse, namely to play, and, by playing, to get away another man's money, which, without controversie, is his owne.[54]

In contrast to St Augustine's exemplary use of lot, the dice-player calls upon God or the saint of his choice to help him acquire money, and, more importantly to the compulsive gambler, to demonstrate thereby that he is providentially favoured. This is the ultimate source of the blasphemy of dice-games.

Various kinds of texts illustrate the idea that gambling, almost always dicing, represents misdirected and misused prayer – misused in that the gambler hopes to win money that is not his, and misdirected in that it is neither God nor the saints to whom their prayers are really addressed in their attempts to alter the course of their futures; they are vying instead for the attentions of Fortune. The link between gambling and spiritual intercession seems to underlie Dante's choice of the opening lines for Canto VI of the *Pur-*

---

[53] *The Confessions of St Augustine*, trans. R. S. Pine-Coffin (Harmondsworth: Penguin, 1977) p. 178.

[54] Quoted Ashton, p. 30. Similar sentiments are expressed by his contemporary William Perkins in his *Discourse of Conscience* and *Cases of Conscience*: 'the vse of a lot is a solemne act of religion, it may not bee applied to sporting' (*The Works of . . . W. Perkins* (London: J. Legatt, 1616–1618), II, 141), quoted in Joachim K. Rühl, 'Religion and Amusements in Sixteenth- and Seventeenth-Century England: "Time might be better bestowed, and besides wee see sin acted" ', *British Journal of Sports History*, 1:2 (1984), 125–65.

gatorio: in this canto he begins to consider 'the real, operative force of inter-cession',[55] and his initial metaphor is of the close of a game of hazard in which the loser is left disconsolate while the winner is surrounded by others clam-ouring for help. The many tales in exemplary literature of saints gambling – and often cheating – for fallen men's souls are also related to this association of gambling and intercession. St Bernard splits a die in order to top his oppo-nent's score of eighteen and win the soul he has staked, a trick also employed by the Virgin Mary herself on occasion.[56]

The French play *Le Jeu de Saint Nicholas*, written by Jean Bodel of Arras around 1200, tackles the relationship between gambling and saintly interces-sion more subtly. The play is an enactment of one of the miracles of St Nicholas, but much of the action consists of the arguments and dice-games of three rogues in a tavern. Critics have disagreed widely over why this should be so, and whether indeed the play has any dramatic unity at all.[57] The story in brief is that the pagans, having wiped out an invading Christian army, come upon one lone Christian praying devoutly to the statue of St Nicholas. They bring both man and statue before their king, who wants to know what is so special about the statue. When the Christian explains that St Nicholas is a powerful protector and that anything he guards will be safe, the king decides to test this by leaving his treasure unlocked with only the statue to guard it, and having word of this proclaimed throughout the country. The Christian will be put to death if the treasure goes missing. Three thieves dicing in a tavern hear of this and decide to steal the treasure, though not before gam-bling on the strength of their future gains. They steal the treasure and return to their dice-games in the tavern (it is interesting to note that as soon as they have the treasure in hand, they change the game from 'plus points' to 'hazard'). Meanwhile the theft is discovered; the prisoner is threatened with death and prays fervently until reassured by an angel. St Nicholas himself appears to the gamblers and terrifies them into returning the treasure. The king is overjoyed at the return of his treasure and, inevitably, converts both himself and his vassals to Christianity.

---

[55] Dante Alighieri, *The Divine Comedy*, ed. and trans. John D. Sinclair, 3 vols (New York: Oxford University Press, 1961), II, *Purgatorio*, p. 91 (Canto VI, lines 1–12).

[56] On St Bernard, see Mehl, 'Tricheurs', pp. 14–15, where his source is the *Liber de moribus hominum et officiis nobilium sive super ludo scachorum* of Jacques de Cessoles (ed. F. Vetter, Bibliothek älterer Schriftwerke der Deutschen Schweiz, Erganzungsband 7 [Frauenfeld, 1892], III, 8, 268b). On Mary, see the version of this widespread story in Cantiga 214 of Alfonso X's *Cantigas de Santa María*, ed. Walter Mettmann, 3 vols (Madrid: Editorial Castalia, 1988), II, 270–2. On the possibility that St Pierre cheats in the aforementioned *St Pierre et le Jongleur*, see Mehl, 'Tricheurs', pp. 9, 24. His argument rests on the interpretation of *tremelé* in line 355 as 'cheated', though some editors gloss this simply as 'played dice' after the dice-game *tremerel*: see for example Johnston and Owen, *Fabliaux*, glossary-entry for *tremeler* and note on page 106.

[57] See the summary of critical opinion in the introduction to *Le jeu de Saint Nicholas*, ed. Albert Henry, 2nd edn (Bruxelles: Presses universitaires de Bruxelles, 1965).

This summary gives no sense of how much of the play's running time is actually taken up by the dicing scenes, which needless to say are entirely of the playwright's own invention. Although some critics have seen them as mere local colour and comic relief, there are good reasons why Bodel might have intended their dominance. It is partly a question of audience: St Nicholas is the patron saint of, among other things, merchants, and his particular talent is in setting injustices to rights, particularly where they involve money. The connection between merchants, who might be assumed to have formed a large part of the audience for this play, and gambling is underlined in these lines from Chaucer's *Canon's Yeoman's Tale*:

> Us moste putte oure good in aventure.
> A marchant, pardee, may nat ay endure,
> Trusteth me wel, in his prosperitee.
> Somtyme his good is drowned in the see,
> And somtyme comth it sauf unto the londe.   (lines 946–50)[58]

But the connection between dicing and divine intercession is more relevant here. The dicing rogues in the play enact the now-familiar scenes of arguing, threatening, and swearing upon and at various saints; at one point one of them even implores St Nicholas for help (Cliquet at l.1135). Shortly thereafter, St Nicholas duly appears, although this does not turn out to be to the gamester's advantage. The standard gambling scenario in which saints are wrongly called upon is juxtaposed with the proper prayers of a Christian for a saint's aid, and St Nicholas's response to this genuine prayer is in turn mirrored amusingly by his unwelcome response to the 'prayer' of the dice-player. True prayer is thus contrasted directly, and instructively, with blasphemy. This suggestion of prayer as the correct alternative to gambling is strengthened by the information given in the prologue that St Nicholas is such a good guardian of one's worldly goods that he will actually return with interest anything entrusted to him: in short, that he is a better bet than a dice-game, where the future outcome is uncertain.[59]

There is one category of dice-game that seems largely to have escaped censure. These are the fortune-telling games, some of which evidently used dice as their means of random selection. The genre is represented in Middle English by 'The Chaunse of the Dyse' and 'Ragman Roll', though only the former uses dice.[60] Their popularity is indicated by the fact that both exist in

[58] *The Riverside Chaucer*, ed. Larry D. Benson, 3rd edn (Oxford: Oxford University Press, 1988).

[59] 'Et s'est si bonne garde eslite / Que il monteploie et pourfite / Canque on li commande a garder' (lines 37–9).

[60] 'Ragman Roll' in *Early Popular Poetry*, ed. W. C. Hazlitt, vol. I (London, 1864), pp. 68–78; 'The Chance of the Dice', ed. E. P. Hammond, *Englische Studien*, 59 (1925), 1–16. See also W. L. Braekman, 'Fortune-Telling by the Casting of Dice: A Middle English Poem and Its Background', *Studia Neophilologica*, 52 (1980), 3–29.

more than one manuscript copy, and both are referred to in passing by Gower in the *Confessio Amantis*.[61] Similar texts survive in most European languages.[62] These texts normally consist of a series of short stanzas, one of which is selected randomly by each player: they deal with such matters as a very general prediction of good or ill fortune; elusive answers to such questions as whether or not one will obtain honour; a horoscope-like character description ('Ragman Roll'); advice on matters of love; or, in the case of a particularly riveting game devised by the tenth-century Bishop Wibold of Cambrai, a virtue on which one was to concentrate for a certain length of time.[63] This last case probably represents an attempt to offer some acceptable means of playing with the immensely popular dice, but it is hard to imagine many gamesters being tempted by it.

Given the associations we have just demonstrated between dice and blasphemy, why were such games not more criticised? It is true that they operate in the potentially dangerous arena of chance, and they involve a wish to pry into the future. However, the player of such games is not attempting to gain anything from them beyond hints as to future trends or the most general advice, and in many cases even this is clearly only meant to be light-hearted. The gamester, on the other hand, is not only employing a specialised form of lot, but is trying to alter his or her own future by staking money or other material goods on its outcome. The crucial difference lies in whether or not something *is* at stake. It would seem that blasphemy only becomes an issue when it is, and when divine aid is invoked in combination with chance (itself ultimately under God's control) in order to gain the desired end.

The place of dice-games in medieval society is a complex one. On the one hand they were almost universally condemned by the moralists, and frequently prohibited by both church decree and secular law. And on the other hand, their extreme popularity at all levels of society remained constant. Periodic royal and civic prohibitions occurred alongside state-sanctioned gambling parlours. The sense that gambling dice-games not only encouraged blasphemy but were themselves a sinister form of blasphemy is detectable in both direct comments on gaming, and in art and literature. San Bernardino was able to draw on the latent unease felt about games of chance when he so readily persuaded crowds to burn their dice, cards and tables, and yet all levels of society, from clerics to kings to commoners, continued to play them avidly. The irresistible appeal of dice-games lay in the very elements that gave the

---

61 On the 'Chance of the Dice', see book IV, lines 2792–3: 'Bot on the Dees to caste chaunce / Or axe of love som demaunde'. On 'Ragman Roll', see book VIII, lines 2377–9: 'Venus, which stant withoute lawe / In noncertein, bot as men drawe / Of Rageman upon the chance'. 'Ragman Roll' is equally reliant on chance, but it was played by attaching a coloured thread to each prophetic verse, rolling the manuscript up, twisting the threads all together, and inviting each participant to select one.
62 For a useful survey of such texts and their contents, see Braekman, pp. 4–11.
63 David, pp. 31–3.

moralists such cause for concern: the feverish pursuit of money; the spice of the illicit; and most of all, the desire to put one's future and fortune at the mercy of Chance. Prayer was an acceptable means of attempting to influence one's future; dicing, the inverted form of prayer, was not. That this message was understood by medieval people is shown by the prevalence of associations between dicing and blasphemy in art and literature. That the message remained largely unheeded is demonstrated by the continued popularity of dicing throughout the Middle Ages. The 'souls' need of something hidden and uncertain' described by George Eliot was an altogether more powerful force.

Index